Factory Women in Taiwan

.

Factory Women in Taiwan

by
Lydia Kung

COLUMBIA UNIVERSITY PRESS
NEW YORK

Columbia University Press Morningside Edition
Columbia University Press
New York   Chichester, West Sussex

Morningside Edition with new preface

Library of Congress Cataloging-in-Publication Data

Kung, Lydia.
    Factory women in Taiwan / Lydia Kung.—2nd ed.
      p. cm.
    Includes bibliographical references (p.   ) and index.
    ISBN 0-231-10010-8 — ISBN 0-231-10011-6 (pbk.)
    1. Women—Employment—Taiwan. I. Title.
HD6068.2.T28K86   1994
305.42—dc20   94-17873
                                    CIP

∞

Contents

Table of Contents

List of Tables

List of Tables

Acknowledgments

Fieldwork in Taiwan in 1974 was funded by a Graduate Fellowship from the National Science Foundation, and grants from the Yale Concilium on International and Area Studies and from Sigma Xi. A fellowship from the American Association of University Women allowed preliminary analysis of the data in the following year. I am grateful to these agencies for their support.

During my stay in Taiwan I was affiliated with the Institute of Ethnology, Academia Sinica (Nankang, Taipei) as a Visiting Scholar. I wish to thank the Institute for their assistance in obtaining a visa and for permitting me to use their facilities.

I owe a great debt to Dr. Lien-hua Chow, who was an invaluable source of advice and encouragement, and whose help in numerous areas made fieldwork proceed much more smoothly.

Data collected at Western Electronics (a pseudonym) form a significant part of this study, and I gratefully acknowledge the kindness of the management in allowing me to carry out research in their firm.

I am also indebted to the female workers and their families; their patience and receptiveness to our questions made this study possible. (All names have been altered.) Most of all I would like to thank my assistant, Miss Hsiou-yuan Liu, and her family for their friendship and hospitality. Miss Liu's social skills and her good cheer facilitated our informants' acceptance of us, and her own insights and resourcefulness were important contributions to fieldwork.

Lastly I wish to thank Professor Emily Martin Ahern of Johns Hopkins University, Professor Harold Scheffler of Yale University, and Linda Perry for their support, comments, and valuable suggestions.

Foreword to the Morningside Edition

by Janet W. Salaff
Department of Sociology
University of Toronto

The First Generation of Industrial Workers

Women workers in low-wage, labor intensive assembly jobs in large factories and small family-run workshops fueled the early stages of Taiwan's industrialization. This small island economy, set on the major sea routes, is plugged into the world's most advanced economies for historical reasons—Japan from the colonial era and the United States with political ties. Through these channels, Taiwan shipped out televisions, garments, shoes, and other light industrial consumer products, the foundation of the republic's export industry. Since then, industry's profile has shifted to medium range capital intensive goods. The recent goal is to compete with the most advanced products of the developed nations. The industrial labor force now differs greatly from the first generation of working daughters, the subject of Lydia Kung's classic study.

Working Daughters: The First Generation of Taiwan's Industrial Workers (1965 to 1973)

In 1974, Lydia Kung studied young factory workers in an electrical machinery plant an hour from Taipei ("Western Electronics"). She lived in a nearby market town and came to know parents of working daughters. Half of the company's 4,000 women workers were farm daughters from the south who lived in factory dormitories, and Kung talked with them as well.

We commonly refer to the industrial profile in the decade leading to the 1973 "oil shock" as Taiwan's labor intensive period of export industry. In these factories, young women worked for a bit more than their subsistence. However, that bit was very crucial. They turned over from one-third to three-quarters of their wages to their parents to support the family. Although many migrated to find work, their parents still controlled this central area of their lives and could count on this money (Huang, 1984). Net remittances came to one-eighth of the household income for poor farmers (in 1980) and narrowed the earnings gap between social classes (Wiltgen, 1990). That remitting money home gained the young women crucial permission to work, yet brought them only a small increase in control over their own lives, is Kung's central finding.

To the factory, the ideal labor force was short term and replaceable. The firm paid assemblists around $50 USD a month with little credit for seniority. Management pressured mature married women to quit (Diamond, 1979; Arrigo, 1984). Since labor was a chief factor of production, they preferred a naive work force with few visions of alternatives. In the 1975 recession, large firms let their young women workers go with little compensation. Workers felt betrayed. Although there was no collective protest, they refused to return to the same factories afterwards. Again, during the 1978–81 recession, only women were let go, while the male manufacturing labor force even increased (Wiltgen, 1990). This highlights women's role as a "flexible labor force" to which employers were not committed contractually or morally.

Beginning with their narrow age range (14 to 30 years), this first generation of industrial workers shared many features in common. They had primary level education, modest expectations, and poor family backgrounds. Youthful and healthy, they had never ventured far from home and looked forward to this first step. They had few demands and incurred little overhead (a dozen women shared one dormitory room). Quick turnover was the rule. Few expected to work past marriage. Unrealistic about their future married life, they did not bargain for higher wages that could bring some independence (Arrigo, 1984). Their employment experience was limited to low wage women's labor.

For this first generation of industrial women, commitment to wage labor followed that to family. Even if the firm had let them remain after marriage, family came first. Indeed, responsible for their home tasks, wage earning married women were mainly informal workers. Women who worked before marriage and then moved into their husband's home some distance away from their work place could rarely continue on. Instead, they could only work in the local labor market in either a family business without a formal contract or at home (Lu, nd; Lu, 1991).

The family ideal was to marry young; in 1981 the average marrying age was 28.8 for men and 22.8 for women. (It was younger when Kung did her study). Women bore children soon after getting married. Teenage daughters turned over their wages to the household until they in turn married and moved into their in-law's home. In contrast, a son brought his wife to live with his parents. He became the main support for the family and his wife took over the chores from the older folk. Older women, having no productive property of their own, could not survive without sons or daughters to care for them. In 1967, 55% of all households included a young couple and at least one parent.

Very few parents passed their golden years alone. A working daughter knew she was expected to work for her family before marriage and for her husband's family afterwards. In sum, the first generation of women workers with whom Kung and others spoke had similar reasons for working—they came from poor families and they were working for them (Salaff, 1981; Ong, 1987; Arrigo, 1984; Diamond, 1979; Wolf, 1992).

The Second Generation of Industrial Workers: from unmarried women to mothers: mid-1970s–late 1980s

Sociologists commonly compare successive "generations" of women workers, by which they mean mothers and daughters. These would be 20 years apart. Given the great industrial change Taiwan experienced since the 1960s, I prefer to use work structures as the basis of generations. I will thus speak of industrial generations instead of female generations. These appear to be a decade apart. Women that join the labor force ten years apart experience very different work settings, that has led to social change.

Kung documented the life of low wage workers at a turning point in this industrial platform of labor intensive work. By the mid-1970s, factories had mushroomed and competed for workers. Village girls no longer needed to leave the south to find industrial work. Young women still gave a substantial proportion of their earnings to their families (Wiltgen, 1990:177). But now, as sisters combined their wages over the years, family incomes rose. The youngest children could afford to remain in school, at least until junior high graduation. Then, they demanded more money and higher status jobs. As the decade progressed, fewer young women presented themselves for low wage labor. As the pool of female workers grew smaller in the early 1970s, married women who had finished bearing children joined the labor market (Liu, 1983). With the recession at the turn of the '80s, factories restructured, adding costly automated machinery; management changed their view of their primary labor force.

A decade after Kung's study of the first industrial labor force, I interviewed 40 workers and managers in a multibranch American capitalized electronics factory, similar to Western Electronics. This factory had been set up for 20 years. In this era, management no longer drew on unskilled young women as their primary labor force. Instead, they sought reliable and steady workers. Their labor force had long tenure. They no longer recruited new workers from outlying areas, and they had sold their dormitories. As society became more industrialized, the sources of factory labor varied. Married women from nearby neighborhoods were a main source of new labor to this firm.

This second industrial generation had more complex reasons for working. This complexity does not bespeak of individuality or liberation. Family was still central to their lives. Nevertheless, this second generation of industrial workers in the firm I studied came from a broader age group. They were older, averaged in their 30s, and included women in their 50s and near retirement. They received a wide range of schooling (many had more than a primary level education) and most had earned wages since youth. They expected steady employment and to work past marriage, even until they retired.

Their age, marriage status, and the number of years worked varied. A few of the women I met had escaped the marriage net entirely. While living at home, they formed close bonds with other women who had long work tenure in the firm and sought to enjoy with them the working woman's single life. Unmarried women, not too common in the mid-'80s, got both tenure and pension and found a sanctuary in the factory. (Today remaining unmarried has become more common; their middle class yuppy counterparts are called "single nobility".) In that decade, too, the ROC put into place improved pension and labor schemes. Women like these planned to work until they retired. With some help from their family, they could survive without sons or daughters of their own.

Others had years of wage labor experience before they married and remained in the labor force after marriage. As young parents, they first looked to their kinfolk for childcare and then many turned to babysitters or preschools which doubled in number between 1985 and 1991. A 1991 survey found only 57% of parents had cared for their children through age four (Yun, 1993). These married women continued working not to make ends meet but to satisfy the rising demand of their households for the consumer items they can now buy. In 1986 consumer spending accounted for 62% of the gross national product, up to 72% in 1992 (Tseng, 1993).

Then there were older women, fondly referred to as "obasan", a remnant Japanese term for grandmother. With less education than younger women, these older middle aged women were the last untapped low wage workers. Most lived near the factory. With little employment choice, they are committed to the firm. I met two main types of obasan factory labor. Some had successfully raised their children, who were now working. Even today, older folk rarely live alone (over two-thirds of elderly parents live with their children). Their children often take over household tasks and support (Weinstein, et al., 1990; Yuan, 1993; Hu and Ma, nd). Their sons and daughters had around two children. If the older women did not help with child care, they had the time to do factory labor. Their households no longer so needy, obasans were free to use their earnings for themselves. They organized outings for coworkers, played mahjong, sang karaoke, and parlayed their earnings with investment clubs. These women could legitimately meet their own private needs.

In contrast, other middle aged women were compelled to work because their families failed them. A wife of a nonearner (a drinker, gambler, ill or older man), a widow, or a divorcee turned to factory work to survive. They worked until retirement or until their children took on the wage earning burden. They felt lucky that factories gave them a small pension. Like other married women, they enjoyed workplace social contact. And for some that were divorced and stigmatized, factory work overcame social isolation (Hu and Ma, n.d.)

Post 1988—The Next Stage of Taiwan's Economic Transformation: A Third Generation of Industrial Workers

Taiwan shares with world economies a decline of manufacturing and increase in services. As living standards improve, people demand more services and the mature manufacturing industry also needs support services. And, Taiwan's production costs have increased due to higher labor costs, land shortage, belated environmental concerns, and the revalued NT dollar. Taiwan investors began to look offshore. In particular, they took advantage of Taiwan's location and their cultural ties to the mainland.

In the late 1980s, the first industries to move to China were labor intensive "sunset" export industries (toys, garments, shoes) that had outpriced their market. They moved rather than restructuring and upgrading. Once in China, many are expanding past export industries to sell to the huge domestic interior market. An estimated 15,000 Taiwan companies have set up production facilities in the mainland, investing more than US $10 billion (Tseng, 1994). This relocation means that not only are labor intensive factories and workshops in which semi-skilled Taiwan women toil not expanding but that they are slated to come to a dead end. These trends give rise to local political fears that manufacturing will disappear from the island and integrate Taiwan into "Greater China". Accounting for 40% of gross domestic output in 1986, manufacturing plummeted to 33% in 1992. The female labor force followed suit.

Since manufacturing was Taiwan's engine of growth, there is a concerted state-led effort to reverse trends. And so, despite continued investment in offshore manufacturing, Taiwan is now upgrading and diversifying its economy (Bowring, 1994; Liu, 1993a, 1993b). Some manufacturers are aiming for the high end of consumer products. While China manufactures Taiwan's running shoes, Taiwan makes the high fashion shoes that rival those from Italy. If Taiwanese toy factories in China make stuffed dolls, those in Taiwan build 3 foot long electronic cars for children. Holding central place in this strategy is Taiwan's information hardware industry, the seventh largest in the world, which is now investing in an integrated circuit industry in its support. Domestic production is also moving away from a reliance on export towards meeting popular needs. These production goals renew interest in technical training and labor force upgrading. The labor force of the '90s is changing again.

At the same time, better educated young women now move into the tertiary sector. Since 1982, more women hold white collar than blue collar jobs, and "women's jobs" have expanded in retail business, social work, civil service, insurance, and commerce. Some women do enter jobs that were seen as men's (eg. computer sciences, [Li:1985]).

Changes in Women's Work Experiences Over the Years Seen Through Statistics

As wage labor has become the norm, women work more evenly over the life cycle, they get more training, and their family roles have adapted to their work roles. Labor force statistics over the years since Kung's study show this clearly.

The proportion of women aged 15 to 64 that is employed has increased from 33% in 1966, to 42% in 1973, and again to 46% in 1986. Probably reflecting lengthened schooling, the proportion then dropped to 42% in 1991 (*Yearbook* . . . : Tables 7, 92). The expectation of working through their lifetime affects many other realms of women's experience, beginning with education. In 1978, women aged 15 and over had a fairly low educational level. Whereas 65% of women had primary school or less education in 1978, only 22% had at least senior high (senior high, vocational, junior college, college). By 1991, the proportions with no more than primary school had dropped to 35%, while 45% had senior high or more (*Yearbook* . . . : Table 5). Leaving school later, they start work later. Whereas in 1978, nearly half the young women aged 15 to 19 were wage workers, this dropped to one-third in 1987, and dipped further to one-quarter in 1991. But once they enter the labor force, women stay in longer. In 1991, the numbers of working women peaked at age 20–24, when nearly two-thirds worked for wages. Then there was a gradual decline in women workers, as they quit the labor force, most for good. Still, nearly half of the women aged 45–49 remained in the labor force. This was not the case in 1978, when only one-third aged 45–49 worked (*Yearbook* . . . : Table 10). The modal experience for employed Taiwan women today is continuous work. Over one-third of contemporary women did not stop working due to marriage or childbearing. The comparable proportion in 1979 was one-quarter (*Yearbook* . . . : Table 113). Thus, the overall proportions of working women describes an "n" shaped curve by age, although some new women enter and replace the older ones. This shows a committed and tenured labor force has emerged, that differs greatly from the first generation of industrial women Kung spoke with.

Women have put off marriage. Whereas in 1979, 41% of women aged 20–24 had married, only 23% in that age group in 1990 had married. For those women aged 25–29, the proportion in 1979 was 83% and in 1990, it was 68%. Nearly all married, however. The proportion of married women aged 35–39 was 98% in 1979 and 95% in 1990 (*Yearbook* . . . : Table 108). One reason women put off marriage is to get more education. Thus as women's education achievement rose so did their average age at first marriage. In 1979, women married at an average age of 21. The majority with primary school education married at 21, but those with more education put the event off. Women with vocational schooling married at age 23, junior college, 24, and those with college education at age 25. The trend was the same in 1990, but was later yet. That year, the average age all had married was 22; those with only primary education still married at age 21, those with vocational education at 23, junior college at age 25, and college educated women married at age 26 (*Yearbook* . . . : Table 109). The more schooling women have, the more likely they are to work, even as they grow older. In 1991, those with college educations were most likely to be employed. Thus, for women aged 40–44, four-fifths of those with a college education were working for a wage, but only half of those with a junior high school education. The difference was greater yet for those women aged 55 to 59, only one-quarter with a junior high education, but two-thirds of the older women with college education still earned wages (*Yearbook* . . . : Table 47).

Married women clearly have employment opportunities. In 1978, less than one-third of currently married women worked for a wage, but by 1991 more than two-fifths did (*Yearbook* . . . : Table 46). Women without partners can now work to support themselves. In the prime working ages, 20–54, single women were most likely to work, next came divorced, separated and widowed women. Of the three groups of women, currently married women living with partners were least likely to work (*Yearbook*. . . . : Table 46).

The likelihood that women will work throughout their lifetime, while not the same as men, has become more similar to men. In 1978, the female labor force aged 20–24 was 70 percent of the male labor force that age. By 1991, there was little difference between women and men in that age group. And while as women built families, they dropped out of the labor force (men did not), they dropped out much more slowly in 1991. In 1978, the ratio of women aged 30–34 who worked was 41% of their male colleagues; by 1991, this ratio increased to 55%. Women's retirement experience is moving closer to that of men's as well. Thus, in 1978, women workers aged 45–49 were 39% of their male colleagues; the gap narrowed to 49% by 1991 (*Yearbook* . . . : Table 7).

Women still work in manufacturing (they comprised two-fifths of the manufacturing labor force both in 1978 and in 1991). But the prominance of manufacturing is declining. In 1978, one-third of all workers were professional, administrative, clerical, sales and service workers, increasing to half by 1991. Women kept pace with the change. Although manufacturing is still a central experience for Taiwan women, it is becoming less so. The proportion of employed women in manufacturing first rose from 17% in 1966, to 38% in 1978, and up to 40% in 1986, and then fell to 34% in 1991 (*Yearbook* . . . : Tables 12, 95). Hardly any women work in agriculture, they were only 7% of the labor force in 1978, and 4% in 1991 (*Yearbook* . . . : Table 12).

These deep set economic changes had immense effects on women's family roles. Few now marry before their 20th birthday, and most wait until they are over 25. The birth rate has also dropped sharply as Taiwan turned the corner from an agrarian to an industrial republic. In 1979, women 15 years and older bore an average of 3.7 children. By 1990, the number fell to 2.7 children. Younger women bear fewer offspring yet. From these figures, we can see that no longer being responsible for sizable families, women can extend their labor years past childbearing (*Yearbook* . . . : Table 111).

These statistics help us understand the quality of women's lives. Concern for family remains central to most Taiwan women. But they now share the focus of their attention between family and the work place. They have a structural niche in the Taiwan labor force, not equal, but central.

References

Arrigo, Linda Gail. 1984. "Taiwan Electronics Workers". Pp. 121–145 in Mary Sheridan and Janet W. Salaff (eds). *Lives: Chinese Working Women*. Bloomington, Indiana: Indiana University Press.

Bowring, Philip. 1994. "Shared Prosperity At What Price?" *Free China Review*, 44.1 January: 37–39.

Diamond, Norma. 1979. "Women and Industry in Taiwan." *Modern China* 5.3 July: 317–340.

Directorate-General of Budget, Accounting and Statistics, Executive Yuan, Republic of China. May 1992, *Yearbook of Manpower Survey Statistics, Taiwan Area, Republic of China, 1991*, Taipei. (Henceforth, *"Yearbook . . ."*).

Hu Yow-Hwey and Ma Su-Jung, n.d. "Marital Status, Living Arrangement, and Social Connectedness of Chinese in Urban Taiwan." Institute of Public Health, National Yang-Ming Medical College, Taipei, typescript. Data collected in 1987.

Huang, Nora Chiang. 1984. "The Migration of Rural Women to Taipei." In *Women Migrants in Asian Cities: Migration and Urban Adaptation*. Fawcett, Khoo, and Smith (eds). Boulder Co: Westview Press.

Li Mei-chih. 1985. "Changes in the Role and Personality of Chinese Women in Taiwan." Pp. 449–470 in *Proceedings of the Conference on the Role of Women in the National Development Process in Taiwan*. Taipei: Population Studies Center, National Taiwan University (in Chinese).

Liu, Paul K.D. 1983. "Trend in Female Labor Force Participation in Taiwan," *Academic Economic Papers* 11.1 March: 292–323.

Liu, Philip. 1993b. "An Industry in the Chips," *Free China Review*, 43.12 December: 42–47.

Liu, Philip. 1993a. "Is Manufacturing on the Ropes", *Free China Review*, 43.10, October: 52–57.

Lu, Pau-ching. 1990. *Entering and Continuing Labor Force Participation: Taiwanese Women, Marriage, and Work*. Ann Arbor: University of Michigan, Department of Sociology, Ph.D.

Lu, Yu-hsia. n.d. "Married Women's Informal Employment in Taiwan." Typescript, Academia Sinica, Institute of Ethnology.

Lu, Yu-hsia. 1991. "Kin Networks and Women's Employment". Paper presented at the 1991 Symposium on Modern Life Adjustment and Mental Health, Kauhsiung, ROC, July. Typescript.

Ong, Aiwa. 1987. *Spirits of Resistance and Capitalist Discipline: Factory Women in Malaysia*. Albany, State University of New York Press.

Salaff, Janet W. 1981. *Working Daughters of Hong Kong: Female Filial Piety or Power in the Family?* Cambridge: Cambridge University Press.

Tseng, Osman. 1994. "Risky Business", *Free China Review*, 44.1 January: 34–35.

Tseng, Osman. 1993. "Every Rose Has Its Thorns", *Free China Review*, 43.5 May: 43–45.

Weinstein, Maxine; Sun, Te-Hsiung; Chang, Ming-Cheng; Freedman, Ronald. 1990. "Household Composition, Extended Kinship and Reproduction in Taiwan, 1965–1985." *Population Studies* 44.2 July: 217–239.

Wiltgen, Richard J. 1990. "The Family, Female Employment and the Distribution of Income in Taiwan." *Journal of Developing Societies*, V1:166–181.

Wolf, Diane Lauren. 1992. *Factory Daughters: Gender, Household Dynamics and Rural Industrialization in Java.* Berkeley: University of California Press.

Yuan, Yvonne. 1993. "Small is Still Big." *Free China Review,* 43.11 November: 5–13.

Yun, Eugenia. 1993. "Childcare Choices", *Free China Review,* 43.11 November: 20–25.

Introduction

The establishment and expansion of light industries in Taiwan over the last fifteen years have stimulated a proliferation of factories engaged in food processing, and in the manufacture of garments, textiles, plastic and electronic products. Ranging from firms that employ several thousands of workers to family-run businesses employing a handful of neighbors, these enterprises provide wage-earning opportunities for young women that were previously unavailable. The sight of young women waiting for company buses in the mornings and being dropped off in the early evenings in the villages and small towns of Taiwan has become commonplace by now, and it is an indication of the widespread acceptance of factory work as a respectable, if not prestigious, occupation for young women. Their work experiences and the effects of wage-earning on the lives of these women and their position at home are the subjects of this study.

My data are based on material collected in northern Taiwan in 1974. Fieldwork was first carried out in a market town, Sanhsia, and in its neighboring communities (primarily Ch'inan and Ch'ipei) among women who lived at home. In the second half of the year, this study was carried out in a factory that I shall call Western Electronics. The firm is located in Taoyuan city, situated west of Taipei (the capital city) and north of Sanhsia; Western Electronics employs over four thousand women workers, about half of whom live in dormitories provided by the company.

I chose Sanhsia because ethnographic information on the area is already available (Ahern 1973, M. Wolf 1972). Margery Wolf's *Women and the Family in Rural Taiwan,* in particular, contains data collected during an earlier period (between the late 1950s and late 1960s) that provide a backdrop against which to measure changes in the lives of young women today. A second reason is that there are factories of varying sizes in the Sanhsia vicinity, including subsidiaries of American and Japanese firms as well as Chinese-owned enterprises.

Sanhsia is located an hour's bus ride west of Taipei, and buses depart for Taipei from Sanhsia approximately every fifteen minutes. The convenience of public transportation allows residents of the area to commute to jobs in Taipei and in towns along the way. Sanhsia's main street is lined with shops and businesses catering to the needs of local residents; included are markets, clinics, two movie theaters, and temples. Ch'ipei is a smaller market center where people from the primarily agricultural village of Ch'inan and other surrounding communities can make small day-to-day purchases. The majority of residents in the area are descended from people who migrated to Taiwan from Anch'i county in Fukien province over two hundred years ago, and they speak Hokkien, a southern Fukien dialect. Today the communities continue to share ritual ties (Ahern 1973).

During my stay in Sanhsia I lived with a Taiwanese couple and their small child, and the families of both are long-time residents of Sanhsia. In the Sanhsia area, then, I had the opportunity to speak with women who commuted to work, with their families, and with the families (fewer in number) of factory women who lived away from home.

Western Electronics is engaged in the manufacture of television sets and solid-state components. Since Western Electronics is one of the largest factories on the island, it should not be regarded as nor do I claim that it represents a "typical" industrial organization in Taiwan. It should be remembered, nonetheless, that Western Electronics is one of a handful of well-known factories in which many women in Taiwan, at one time or another, have had the occasion to work. In terms of age, education, family background, previous work experience, and ethnic groups, there is a much broader spectrum of women at Western Electronics than is the case in Sanhsia.

At Western Electronics I was permitted to carry out informal interviews in the plants during work hours and to live in the dormitories. Conversations with women took place inside the factory, in dormitory rooms, and during after-work activities. I first gained familiarity with the operation of the factory in much the same fashion that newly hired women do, through orientation sessions designed for new workers. These sessions not only gave me the opportunity to observe the behavior of newly arrived women, but it became a simple matter to follow the adjustment of each worker. I was given desk space and also had access to the office staff and managers. During the time I was at Western Electronics, I maintained contact with informants in the Sanhsia area through weekly visits.

The female industrial labor force in Taiwan is young, and my informants range in age from fourteen to thirty years of age, with a small number of working mothers who are older. In both settings I presented myself as a student interested in Taiwan's industries and Taiwan's youth. (At Western Electronics I took care to convince women that I was not a salaried employee of the company.) Contacts in the Sanhsia area were initially established through my assistant, a twenty-three year old woman living in Ch'inan. At Western Electronics I met women through trainers, through orientation sessions, and through workers with whom I was already acquainted. In addition, I came to know groups of dormitory residents simply by asking the dormitory supervisors to introduce me.

A few comments about how I use the term Taiwanese are in order.[1] Taiwan was administered as a portion of Fukien province between 1863 and 1887, and then provincial status was conferred on Taiwan. After the Sino-Japanese War of 1894–95 Taiwan was ceded to Japan, and Japanese occupation lasted until 1945. The term Taiwanese refers to persons who or whose families were in Taiwan prior to retrocession (and for brevity I include Hakka-speakers in this group), and the term Mainlanders refers to persons from other provinces who or whose families came to Taiwan after 1945. In a population of 15,565,000 (Economic Planning Council 1974b:4), Mainlanders number approximately two million. In addition there is a small category of non-Chinese native to Taiwan who speak a Malayo-Polynesian language, and I use the term aborigines to designate these persons.

The four languages of Taiwanese, Mandarin, Hakka, and that of the aborigines are not mutually intelligible, but Mandarin is the official language and is used in schools. I studied Taiwanese after I arrived in Taiwan. Since all factory women had attended school, conversations were conducted in Mandarin and, where I could manage, in Taiwanese.[2] Notes were recorded as soon as possible after each conversation.

Writers interested in the effect of industrialization on Chinese family structure have suggested that as women enter the labor force, their standing both inside and outside the family is raised because their wage-labor contributes to household income (Fei 1939, Lamson 1931, Lang 1946, Levy 1968). The opportunity to earn income on a regular basis outside the home has also been cited as a major factor enabling young women to refuse undesirable marriage arrangements, to resist marriage entirely (Topley 1975), or to exercise greater authority at home. These propositions do indeed seem reasonable and logical: as women assume economically productive roles in the public domain, and as their families benefit from the rewards, their economic independence might well increase. This, in turn, might facilitate greater autonomy in other spheres, affording women more control over their futures.

The objectives of this study, then, are to describe this first generation of Taiwanese working women, and to record their perceptions of and their families' view of their employment. This book attempts to answer questions pertaining to the effects wage-earning has on the status and lives of women and on the parent-daughter relationship. In the process of analyzing data on the Taiwan case I hope to be able to refine concepts such as "improvement in status" and to add some precision to the meaning of "economic contribution."

The data from Taiwan do not conclusively support hypotheses that predict an improvement in the position of women resulting from wage-labor and from contributing to family income. I do not wish to deny the very real transformations that have occurred: working daughters enjoy greater mobility, peer contacts, and their participation in production has enhanced their economic value to their families. These conditions have not, however, substantially elevated the standing of women at home or in society, and the problem is one of explaining why changes have occurred in some areas of women's lives and accounting for the persistence of traditional patterns in other areas.[3]

My argument can be summed up this way. Working daughters have made a number of personal gains: most have a bit more spending money; they dress a little better; they take part in more recreational activities. The expansion of freedom is greatest for factory women living in dormitories; the simple fact of distance from home means that there is no one to supervise their activities or to control their leisure time. But with the exception of women who use their wages to go to school, the changes listed above are brought about by the fact of being outside, away from home, and not by wage-earning itself. At the same time, factory women's experiences beyond the home grant them no power to influence family decisions and do not necessarily better their future options. Greater freedom of movement and more time spent with friends are not changes that have long-lasting effects nor will they improve a woman's future prospects. I might add here that many female workers are ambivalent about their new-found independence, a state sometimes forced upon them by circumstances.

I will show that factory work for young women is merely a new opportunity to meet already existing role expectations, and that the values on which role definitions are based have not changed. The fact of wage-earning has not conferred upon women the right to control their incomes. Two questions arise at this point: how are parents able to retain control over their daughters, and why do women continue to meet familial obligations in the form of regular remittances home? The answers lie partly in the nature of the family system in which these women were socialized and in the lack of alternatives open to female workers. Their dependence on their families was demonstrated most vividly during the recession in 1974 when women who had lost their jobs had no choice but to return home. But it is not simply a matter of commitment to one's own family; the family, as an institution, looms large in the futures of these women, be it their own or their husbands'.

Factory work has not led to changes in all spheres of their lives, and the Taiwanese family is only one structure that has permitted many women to use their new wage-earning capacity to fulfill traditional values. This fact is central to my argument, and the way in which family structure shapes the responses of women to wage-employment bears closer examination.

Writing about the attitudes of Taiwanese villagers toward prostitutes, M. Wolf states that rather than scorning them, villagers recognize that these women have repaid their debt to their parents more fully than other young women (1972:208). Wolf goes on to recount the case of a family where one daughter had been sent to work as a prostitute. When her adopted sister was old enough, her parents tried to send her too: "she didn't want to go either, but when she refused the family was very angry and wouldn't talk to her" (1972:209). Although this might be a particularly callous presentation of relations between daughters and parents, this passage underlines two factors shaping the lives of Taiwanese daughters: the debt that is owed to one's parents and the relative lack of alternatives available to young unmarried women. That debt can now be repaid with wages from a factory job.

Much attention has been paid to the Chinese family as an economic unit in which income and consumption are pooled and redistributed by the household head. Seen in this light, factory women are simply an additional source of income. The fact that a daughter is able to make a regular and often substantial economic contribution to her natal family is new; the meaning of making such a contribution (as a child to one's family), however, has not been revised. The notion that parents have a rightful claim to the earnings of their sons has now merely been broadened to include the wages of daughters as well. Moreover, the fact that daughters, once they marry, are "lost" to their natal families, only gives further support to the belief that parents are entitled (perhaps even more so) to at least a portion of daughters' wages, since it repays the costs of bringing up a "useless" daughter.

Thus, one important notion integral to the Chinese family structure—the belief that daughters eventually and inevitably leave their natal families—has not been altered by paid employment for women. Combined with concepts about the debt a child owes her parents, these beliefs exert a strong influence on what daughters are permitted or not permitted to do.

The tenacity of such features of the Chinese family can be seen in certain practices in the People's Republic of China. Sidel, after visiting families in the city of Fengsheng, writes of one family in which the father earned 112 yuan a month and the eldest daughter earned thirty-three yuan a month: "the implication was clear that they combine these two salaries in order to provide for the family" (1974:18). A report in *Red Flag,* describing a brigade in Kansu province, revealed that just prior to the Cultural Revolution only three of the forty school-age children attending the brigade primary school were girls; during the Cultural Revolution when an investigation was undertaken to determine the reason for this, parents answered: "Our daughters will be members of other families sooner or later. What is the purpose of sending them to school?" (cited by Chan 1974:205–06). After their survey of rural small-scale industry in the People's Republic of China, one American delegation states that as women are drawn into these industries, they acquire new economic power and authority vis-à-vis their family of birth as well as family of marriage (American Rural Small-Scale Industry Delegation 1977:232). But so long as women in rural China leave their natal families at marriage, and sons are expected to care for their aged parents (cf. Parish 1975), we must view such a conclusion with caution.[4]

This line of reasoning is still deeply ingrained in rural Taiwanese. A number of factory women are keenly aware that they are disadvantaged with respect to education precisely because they are daughters and not sons. Women express their consciousness of the temporary quality of their stay with their natal families in other ways. Liu Su-fong, for instance, said that there was little point in continuing to argue with her sisters-in-law about the proper disciplining of her nieces and nephews since, in any case, she will leave someday: "It's just a matter of time, and when I return it will be as a guest, so I just try to remain on good terms with them; why make for poor relations later on?" The mother of one factory woman described to us how neglectful of her welfare her grown-up children were: "If you have money, then your children will be around all the time. But if you don't have money, they're rarely to be seen. [But you still have your youngest daughter.] No, how can one say that about a daughter; no one keeps daughters." Although she allowed that sons are not necessarily more filial than daughters, it was still her sons on whom her future security rested: "When a son grows up and marries and begins his own family he won't have much money to give to his parents. When we're old, we need to rely on sons for our livelihood, but other than that, the money they bring us will not be more than what [unmarried] daughters give us."

Working daughters need not be given greater authority at home in recognition of their economic contribution, since they will leave anyway. But the opinions of sons must be attended to, for the continuity of the family depends on their loyalty. (As Cohen has indicated, the Chinese family is under "a constant tension produced by the conflict between unifying forces on the one hand, and those making for fragmentation on the other. The major divisive force was generated by the equal rights to the family estate held by brothers, who had the choice of staying together or fragmenting into smaller family units" [1970:xxii].) One ironic result of the employment opportunities open to women (which points at the same time to how successfully daughters are socialized in their natal families) is that many mothers now comment that daughters (married and unmarried) are more filial than sons (married and unmarried), and that it may well be more comfortable to live with one's married daughter than with one's married son.

For the most part, outside employment for women is temporary and fills the years between school and marriage. After marriage women are once again, as in their pre-factory days, connected to the wider society primarily through the family (in their roles as wives, mothers, mothers-in-law). Factory jobs are neither a desirable nor a viable alternative to marriage. Finally, there is an overarching economic and political system that defines where women's opportunities in the labor market lie. Just as daughters have become economically valuable to their families, they are also indispensable to Taiwan's economic growth, but their new role as industrial workers has not brought them a commensurate increase in power.

This book is presented as an ethnography rather than as essays addressed to specific questions, and the material lends itself to a sequence that reflects the chronological order of women's experiences. The book may be divided into four parts. To present the context within which the Taiwan data will be examined, I begin by reviewing issues in measuring improvement in female status. In the remainder of the first part (chapters 2 through 4), I provide background information concerning women and their work in traditional Chinese society so that we might examine how traditional values and expectations govern behavior. I also give a summary of Taiwan's industrial labor force and women's place in it. Part II (chapters 5 through 8) describes the process of finding a job and leaving home, the workplace, and relations in the factory environment. The effects of living away from home and of factory employment on other areas of women's lives (control of income, marriage, self-image) are taken up in part III (chapters 9 through 13). In part IV (chapters 14 through 16) I explore the question of how family structure, female status, ideology, and external and internal economic conditions are interrelated in Taiwan. I conclude with a consideration of the insights the Taiwan data suggest in terms of studying socio-economic change.

1

Measuring Improvement in Female Status

Recent works on the subject have made it clear that participation in production will not in itself elevate women's status in the family or in the larger society. As I will show, the Taiwanese material provides ample proof of that fact. However, we are still left with the questions of how best to define and measure improvement in women's status, and what conditions (in addition to participation in production) are required if such improvements are to be achieved. In this chapter I survey some of the existing literature concerning how to define what constitutes high or low status for women in a given social setting. The questions and issues discussed below form the frame of reference within which the data from Taiwan will be considered.

Since there is as yet no consensus about operational definitions of women's status, this poses a number of problems in measuring women's status both within a society and especially across societies (cf. Buvinic 1976). Some writers are more specific than others; Sandy, for instance, stipulates that her usage of female status refers to the economic and political rights that accrue to women (1973:1682). Others define female status as the ranking, in terms of prestige, power, or esteem, accorded to the position of women relative to the ranking accorded to the position of men (Buvinic 1976:225). The question of what we need to know in order to evaluate the status of women and to develop meaningful indicators of status, in turn raises the question of *who* is making the judgment, that is, who is assessing the prestige of one social position relative to other social positions (Buvinic 1976:225–26). This issue will be taken up again when subjective measures of status are discussed, but clearly, although legal rights may serve as an independent indicator of the position of women, in themselves they may not always accurately specify the status of women within a particular society.

In addition to legal freedoms and property-owning rights, educational and employment opportunities for women are commonly used to show that women's positions in developing countries have improved. Again, in themselves these measures are too simplistic to be useful; that is, even if women were informed about their rights, they may not be able to achieve in practice what they are entitled to by law. In Cohen's study of family organization in southern Taiwan, for instance, we learn that when women marry, they are expected to waive their claims to their fathers' estates to which they are entitled by law (1976:83, also cf. Wang and Apthorpe 1974:40). With regard to women in the labor force, one needs to know the distribution of women and the distribution of rewards in various sectors, in addition to women's absolute numbers in the labor market. Similarly, higher education does not necessarily produce more "advanced" ideas in women about their future roles, especially if women are educated in skills that are defined as feminine and discouraged from learning other skills. At present, therefore, there seems to be little gained by using the "proportion of women in total school enrollment" or "the proportion of women in the labor force" as measures of women's status. Indeed, as Buvinic points out, it is possible to discover the effect of education on fertility without making reference to "status" as an independent variable (1976:228).

Beyond objective indicators of women's position, at least three additional factors need to be taken into account. First, class position can determine women's status. Second, we need to specify whether modernization improves women's position relative to men's or whether the improvements are unrelated to the issue of sexual equality (Bossen 1975:589). Third, women's positions can vary according to stages in the life cycle. In the Chinese family, for instance, a woman's relationship to the allocation of power and her control over the economic sphere, as well as her strategies for achieving her ends, change when she marries, becomes a mother, or a mother-in-law. (Participation in political processes is frequently cited as a key factor in female status; since opportunities in this area are virtually closed to Taiwanese factory women, I will devote more attention to other dimensions that might be grouped under peer relations, personal autonomy, and economic power.)

A woman's ability to maintain ties with her peers has been cited as important in improving her status. Sanday, for instance, mentions female solidarity groups devoted to female political or economic interests (1974:192). It is recognized that membership in task-oriented organizations not only provides a focus for action but also strengthens the capacity of women to act on their own behalf. As will become evident, Taiwanese factory women have little opportunity to develop organizational abilities nor are they given any encouragement in this direction. Even in company dormitories the informal voluntary associations so characteristic of city migrants are not found; instead there are friendship networks that are usually of short duration.

The Murphys, along these lines, draw attention to the effect that economic unity among women can have on their position in society. Among the Mundurucu women's work does lend itself to cooperation, and to the extent that it draws women together and isolates them from the immediate supervision and control of men, it permits a degree of independence (Y. Murphy and R. Murphy 1974:210-11). Nelson seems to be making the same point when she argues that rather than seeing the segregation of men and women as a limitation on women, we should see it instead as an exclusion of men from a range of contacts that women have among themselves (1974:559). Factory work in the Taiwanese setting, however, is not a basis for unity among women and does not structure relations among women beyond friendship. Even if women's organizations existed, the fact remains that unless women are able to act on public affairs through these groups and unless these groups are open to spheres other than the domestic, their effectiveness will be severely limited.

Another criterion used to measure female status is the extent to which women exercise control over their own lives. Friedl, for example, examines the degree of autonomy a woman enjoys in decisions concerning sex relations, marriage, residence, divorce, and the lives her children (1975:7). Beyond this, others name control over movement, over fertility regulation and other life options such as access to educational opportunities. Personal autonomy is conceptually distinguished from the power to control or influence others, particularly those outside the domestic sphere. Women's position rests therefore not only on the degree of household authority held, but on their access to and control over material and non-material resources and their participation in the allocation of resources. Friedl states, "It is the right to distribute and exchange valued goods and services to those not in a person's own domestic unit which confers power and prestige in all societies" (1975:8).

Such control is most often said to be conferred by economic power that derives from participation in production. But as we will see, mere work does not translate into control over the means and rewards of production. Contribution to production is cited as a necessary but not sufficient condition for improvements in female status, but the meaning of contribution to production itself requires greater precision. In stratified societies, for instance, a heavy work load does not necessarily entitle women to a proportionately large share of the rewards of that labor, and their work load may well be a sign of their domination by others.

According to Sanday, in order for an increase in female productive labor to have a positive effect on female status, women must be in the productive labor sphere long enough and in sufficient number to gain control over the products of their labor (1973:1684). In addition, the degree of control women have is determined by: (a) the perceived indispensability to a society of the specific productive activities of women, (b) women's possession of the technical expertise necessary for production, and (c) women's relative control over the means of production and the distribution of the output (cf. Buvinic 1976:236). Sanday suggests that in societies where control over valued resources and production are linked, female power is likely to develop if women are actively engaged in producing valued goods (1973:1697).[1]

The indispensability of women's productive activities, then, can be regarded as one determinant of female status. This alone, however, is not an adequate measure; the performance of household tasks is essential to the functioning of a family but women's role in that sphere does not award them with any prestige commensurate with its importance. One must therefore also look to the meanings attached to productive labor and the valuation assigned to the work women do. As Davin points out with regard to survey data on Chinese women, "it is precisely... the contribution which women are seen by their community as making which is so vital a determinant of their status" (1976:117). She suggests that the low figure in Buck's data for women's participation in production was due to the factor of perception; "women always seem to play an important role in tea cultivation, especially picking, and this work, which was probably seen as 'light,' may have been under-assessed" (1976:120). Likewise, domestic labor tends to be under-valued in most societies. With the separation of the workplace from the home, housework loses its economic value and only the type of work that earns wages is considered economic activity. One writer states that the work of the housewife is devalued because it is not seen to produce surplus value, and thus production within the family is not viewed as integral to the production of commodities (Zaretsky 1973).

In Taiwan the participation of women in the labor force, particularly in light industries, is without doubt regarded by the government as crucial to the nation's economy, but women perceive themselves as easily replaceable, not particularly valued by their employers, and not regarded with respect by the rest of society for their "indispensable" role in the country's development.

Writing about women in trade, Mintz points out that independent economic activity means just that, whereas a salary-paying job does not offer independence upon the woman in quite the same way (1971:266). For instance, a husband cannot safely tamper with his wife's conduct of her trading business, while he may lay serious claims upon her earnings at a job without endangering her performance. Thus, if women have not traditionally regarded their incomes as separate from those of other family members, this could very well limit their ability to save and invest those sums toward their own interest and goals. Advancing the status of women will therefore require that they have access to credit and to information about channels for reinvestment. Their economic independence can be assured only if their income is theirs to control *and* if they know how to best utilize it.

Measures of and constraints on women's productivity are not limited to objective factors such as the policies of employers, the demand for female labor in comparison to the available male supply, or the compatibility of a particular activity with household and child-care responsibilities. Along with these conditions there is the question of what indicators of women's status are perceived as meaningful by the members of the society being studied. Subjective indicators such as feelings of self-worth and self-esteem must be considered in assessing sexual equality. We need to know what the images of women and power are in the domestic and public domains of a society, how women view their own situations, whether they believe they have power, and whether they would accept a portrayal that depicts them as relatively powerless persons. For example, many women acknowledge that they are able to wield indirect or informal power in the family and achieve their ends through manipulation. As one writer indicates, however, such strategies may be effective in the short-run only, and in addition, a person who uses indirect influence is not likely to view herself as a strong person. "The woman's view that she needs to use indirect power to get what she wants will be reinforced, and it is therefore unlikely that her self-concept will change" (P. Johnson 1976:101).

Cultural stereotypes about sex roles (men's and women's respective definition of maleness and femaleness) are important background features. For one thing, they can limit women's occupational alternatives by designating certain occupations as male or female. Here it may be sufficient to note that it is not only division of labor that matters but how this division is interpreted, and what the acceptable limits of variability are. One informant at Western Electronics thought it desirable for women to work outside and said that there is no longer any meaningful distinction between outside and inside for women. She qualified her statement, however, by adding that a woman should not be better educated than her husband, since it would be difficult for him psychologically, and furthermore, her own educational attainment might very well have deprived another man of a place in school or a position in the job market. She also expressed the opinion that employment and mothering are incompatible and do not serve the best interests of the family. Here is an example where the economic activity of a woman is regarded as potentially threatening to the social status of men, and is an instance of the views that become barriers to the development of other role expectations and hinder the enactment of those roles.

Another dimension used in assessing female status rests on the dichotomy between the domestic (private) and the public sphere. Some writers have devoted their attention to the authority women exercise at home and have taken this as an indication that women enjoy higher positions than commonly assumed. While such descriptions may give us a more accurate rendering of family dynamics, the fact remains that much of men's activities are carried on outside the domestic sphere where women, though influential at home, are ineffectual. It is true that wives may manipulate their personal relationship with their husband to achieve a certain end, but as P. Johnson (1976) has argued, the use of such personal power or personal resources is effective only over a narrow range. It limits the user to those areas of influence that are affected by a personal relationship and leaves the person dependent on others, thereby reducing her power (P. Johnson 1976:101–102). As for the working wife, Friedl states that if her income is used primarily for consumption within the household, she may gain a greater say in family affairs, but this remains within the confines of the domestic sphere, and it does nothing for her prestige and power outside it (1975:36).

Other writers have suggested that women gain power and a sense of value when they enter the public domain, i.e., when they are able to transcend the domestic domain and form ties outside (Rosaldo 1974:41). What has not yet been specified, however, is how authority and influence in one sphere are related to power in the other. It appears, for instance, that strategies for obtaining informal power at home may not be effective in the larger society, where a woman's inferior rights do in fact represent her actual position. The entry of Taiwanese women into the public domain has not led to an increase in their power at home (or outside the family). As Friedl points out, unless a woman's ocupation is at a managerial or professional level high enough to enable her to distribute goods and services to persons outside the home, or her income is great enough to be manipulated or exchanged in business, political, or community contexts, her public power will not be significantly altered by the mere fact of her outside employment (1975:136).

I will demonstrate that according to measures such as these, the status of factory women in Taiwan has not been substantially improved by their wage-earning. They are young women (jural minors) who do not expect to be employed for more than a few years; they enter the job market as members of the lower and lower-middle class; little prestige is attached to their work; they do not enjoy complete control over their earnings; and there are no groups designed to promote their economic interests. Finally, women do not view their occupations as activities that would enhance their status in the wider society, but just as a new way of doing what has always been expected of them.

2

Women and the Family in Traditional China

While accompanying two Western Electronics managers on a visit to several factories near Hsinchu, we had become lost in the area. Seeing a young woman by a bus-stop, we drove up to ask for directions; after a brief explanation she offered to show us to our destination if we gave her a lift. En route, we learned that she had been working in factories since she finished elementary school. She first worked in a factory close to home in southern Taiwan, then moved into a dormitory, and later proceeded to move toward the Taipei area, having spent about one year at each factory.

It is perhaps no longer necessary to present evidence to show that the status of women was low in traditional China; their subordinate position in the family and in society has been well documented (cf. Davin 1976, M. Wolf 1972). By and large, women in China did not control the means of production or the distribution of economic resources, nor did they enjoy rights equal to men's in political and religious activities. The oversimplified stereotype of Chinese women as helpless and timid, however, has been laid aside by more refined and careful analyses that have found women wielding not a little power at home, and occasionally, beyond the domestic sphere as well (M. Wolf 1972:42–52, M. Wolf 1974). The following sketch of the forces that shaped women's lives in traditional Chinese society is given to provide some information about the past from which factory women come, and the background that colors their expectations. Furthermore, to answer such central questions as how to define "improvement in status," what indices to use in measuring women's rights, and how certain features of the Chinese family are altered by industrial wage-labor, we must know something about women's lives in the past.[1] My task in this respect is made simpler by the age, sex, and class background of the workers I studied;[2] because they are young, female, and come from families that welcome their economic contribution, one can predict easily enough that they enjoy little in the way of prestige or authority inside or outside the home.

One of the most significant factors determining women's position is a structural one: women are born into lineages and families that do not recognize them as permanent members but rather as "belonging to other people." In the context of patrilineal descent and patrilocal marriage, rights to a woman's labor and to her children belong to her husband and his line, and she earns a place in his lineage only by producing sons for it. Writing about southeastern China Freedman notes that "having few ritual and virtually no economic ties with her own agnates, the married women was forced to cast her interests fully within the group of which she was a member by marriage" (1970:134). But even though a girl's stay in her natal family is in most instances a temporary one, the absorption of a new bride and her loyalty to her husband's family are not taken for granted.[3] Women in their husbands' households are the "strangers within," and even within their natal families they occupy an in-between position. All daughters are expected to marry out and to develop their strongest attachments to a group other than their natal families.

These, then, are pre-determined conditions over which a daughter has no control, and a number of consequences follow from the lower valuation of daughters. First, a daughter may be given out in adoption[4] to be a "little daughter-in-law" (cf. A. Wolf 1975) or to be a maidservant. The logic behind the practice of adopting "little daughters-in-law" is obvious:[5] since a daughter will eventually belong to other people, it makes good economic sense to channel the cost of supporting her into raising an adopted daughter who will stay as a daughter-in-law. The premise that daughters are a losing proposition is also reflected in the rituals surrounding the birth of a girl, an occasion less joyously celebrated than the birth of a son. The gifts sent to a girl's maternal grandparents announcing her birth, for example, are simpler than those sent to announce the arrival of a son (M. Wolf 1972:55). The birth of a boy is also considered less polluting than the birth of a girl: "If the integration into a family is part of what makes birth polluting, then it is reasonable that a boy should be less polluting than a girl. A male occupies a firm, permanent position in his family as a future heir to the family estate and as one of those who will perpetuate descent lines. His integration is therefore in a sense less problematic than a girl's, for she belongs to her natal family only temporarily, until she marries out and becomes part of her husband's family" (Ahern 1975:210).

It is not surprising then to find that common expressions for a girl include "commodity-on-which-the-money-has-been-lost" and "water spilled on the ground" (A. Smith 1970:250). Nowhere is this sentiment as concretely expressed as in attitudes about educating one's daughters, summed up in Arthur Smith's observation: "to almost any Chinese it would probably appear a self-evident proposition that to spend time, strength and much more money in educating the daughter-in-law of someone else is a sheer waste" (1970:202). J.L. Buck in his survey of land use in China in the 1930s indicates that only one percent of females (as opposed to thirty percent of males) had attended school long enough to read a common letter (cited by Davin 1976:72). The introduction of compulsory primary school education in Taiwan (which was extended to lower middle-school in 1969) has, of course, altered the situation;

in 1958 there were only three or four school-age girls in Peihotien, the community in which M. Wolf lived, not attending school (M. Wolf 1972:80). This has not, however, been accompanied by substantial changes in outlook; M. Wolf quotes one mother as saying: "It doesn't do any good for a girl to study anyway. They study, but it is still the same for them after" (1972:81). Realistically, in the past and in the present (though to a lesser degree) the argument put forward by parents is valid: schooling may contribute to self-improvement, but it is of little practical value inasmuch as there are few job opportunities.

In addition to the money spent on raising a daughter, a family's resources are further depleted when she marries and must be provided a dowry. Families other than the most desperately poor are inclined to view a daughter's marriage not just as a drain on the holdings of her father, but on those of her brothers as well. As M. Wolf explains, a dowry is wealth lost forever to a man and his line: "Even if he personally thinks his daughters are worth ten times as much as his sons, he cannot take what does not belong to him and give it to the wives of 'outsiders'" (1972:131). Consistent with this line of reasoning is the fact that women lack property rights, and women can make claims to property only as representatives of a line (e.g., a widow can lay such claims on behalf of her young sons). It is true that a portion of a bride's dowry may be considered as her private property to use as she chooses (cf. M. Cohen 1976), but this is property a woman acquires upon marriage and cannot be regarded as an asset a young unmarried daughter holds and can utilize. Myron Cohen's distinction (1976:72–73) between two jural statuses, dependent and expectant, is important here:

> A jural dependent has no rights within his family ... In the family he is completely under his parents' control ... The "expectant" status relates to the family's obligations to members not yet jurally adult, the most important of which is to endow their weddings ... I am less convinced about the relevance of "expectant" status to women, at least in traditional China; with respect to authority and rights of disposal, the woman's status as a jural dependent seems to have extended throughout the period preceding marriage, although marriage nevertheless was a claim a woman held against her natal [family] ... Jural adulthood is signified by marriage ... A woman commences her jural adulthood as a wife in a new household.

Today in Taiwan a daughter, by law, has the right to claim a share of her father's holdings equal to her brothers' shares, but one wonders about the degree to which young women are aware of this. M. Wolf, in her book *Women and the Family in Rural Taiwan,* reports that the law, at the time of her study, was almost totally ignored in the countryside (1972:204), and Cohen describes how this "legal problem" is circumvented in the community he investigated: women sign away all such claims when they marry or upon their father's death (1976:83).

A "worthless" daughter, however, cannot be confused with the woman whom a family has gone to great expense to bring home as a wife for one of its sons. To the husband's family, the value of this woman lies in her ability to produce sons to continue his line, and it is also this capacity upon which a woman's own security rests. As she gives birth to children (especially sons), she establishes personal security within her husband's household and she is entitled to economic support. M. Wolf has noted that all Chinese women, even young women, seem to worry about who will support them in their old age (1975:124). This observation is borne out by my informants. One of them remarked that marriage marks the beginning of a "bitter" life for a woman, and added, "But not marrying is not the answer either. Later on there'd be no one to take care of you, and it would be lonely."

But until a woman becomes a wife/mother, she is a daughter, and as such is a jural dependent, and she is expected to obey her parents. There are few events requiring a decision on her part during this stage of her life; decisions concerning marriage, freedom of movement, and, as we have seen, school, rest in the hands of her parents.

Until the last twenty or so years a young woman in Taiwan was not likely to have much say as to how she would marry (in the major, minor, or uxorilocal form), or when or whom. Parents made the inquiries concerning a suitable husband, or rather, a suitable family, and with the assistance of go-betweens they took responsibility for arranging the match. For a daughter to refuse one particular match was conceivable, but to reject marriage entirely was not. And an adopted daughter was in a particularly vulnerable position; describing one such woman in the Lim family, M. Wolf writes (1968:77):

> If she refused the marriage . . . she would bring to an end the family's obligation to provide for her . . . [T]he alternatives were too grim to consider seriously, Where could she go, and how could she support herself . . . [A]s the wife of the eldest son, she would have some control over her own future . . . Whether or not Lim A-pou weighed all these advantages and disadvantages, we have no way of knowing. Her decision may have been far simpler. The only respectable thing for a young woman to do in the first quarter of this century was to obey her parents . . .

The same reasoning was echoed in the statements of a woman with whom Jan Myrdal spoke in the mainland: "It is the custom for people to marry. Women marry, even if they are over forty. They can even be fifty when they marry. After all, a woman can't live alone" (1966:241).

Turning to the degree of freedom in movement that young women had, we would do well to bear in mind two points underlined by M. Wolf. The first stresses that while women in wealthy families may have been secluded, women in peasant families were very much involved in interactions with their neighbors and fellow villagers (1974:161).[6] We are also rightly cautioned against accepting descriptions of women's seclusion "in the old days" without qualification: "[One woman in Peihotien] said she had also heard tales of women kept hidden in the 'old days,' but the 'old days' were nearly always in the youth of the storyteller's grandmother" (1972:97). Even this woman, however, acknowledges that as a young girl she was not as free to come and go as women today, and in 1959 M. Wolf found that for women and children the significant dimensions of the world were the thirty-five to forty brick houses and buildings of Peithotien (1968:19). As late as 1959 when factories were beginning to appear near Peihotien M. Wolf could report that parents shared a definite reluctance to allow their unmarried daughters anything like the freedom of movement allowed their sons (1972:97). Until recently, therefore, girls were expected to stay close to home: "except for limited excursions in early childhood and occasional visits to relatives, most Chinese girls never go anywhere to speak of, and live what is literally the existence of a frog in a well" (A. Smith 1970:199). (It is noteworthy that several of my informants used the same phrase—"frog in a well"—to describe their life in factories.)

The contrast between the secluded adolescence enforced by Lao Tai-tai's father and her later years spent "outside" is instructive. Her description of those years provides us with some notion of the prevailing attitudes toward women who ventured outside:

> When I was thirteen my parents stopped shaving the hair from around the patch of long hair left on my crown. I was no longer a little girl. We were not allowed, my sister and I, on the street after we were thirteen. People in P'englai were that way in those days. [This covers the period 1870–81.] When a family wanted to know more about a girl who had been suggested for a daughter-in-law and asked what kind of girl she was, the neighbors would answer, 'We do not know. We have never seen her.' And that was praise (Pruitt 1967:29).

> A woman could not go out of the court [of her house]. If a woman went out to service the neighbors all laughed... I did not know enough even to beg... How could I know what to do? We women knew nothing but to comb our hair and bind our feet and wait at home for our men. When my mother had been hungry she had sat at home and waited for my father to bring her food, so when I was hungry I waited at home for my husband to bring me food (Pruitt 1967:55).

> One year after my mother died... I started begging [she was twenty-two at the time]. It was no light thing for a woman to go out of her home. That is why I put up with my old opium sot [husband] for so long. But now... I had to come out... even though women of my family had never 'come out' before (Pruitt 1967:62).

> [The alternatives to begging were not many.] People urged me to leave [my husband] and follow another man, to become a thief or a prostitute (Pruitt 1967:71).

> [Lao Tai-tai subsequently found employment as a servant and later supported herself through peddling, although] it was truly dangerous for a young woman to be out alone in those days... because of all [the prostitutes], if a good woman goes out she must not go in gay clothing (Pruitt 1967:177).

Women in their roles as wife, mother, and mother-in-law acquire greater decision-making powers and exercise prerogatives unavailable to unmarried daughters. If we examine the sources of the power older married women can wield we can understand why these channels of influence are closed to young girls. That portion of a bride's dowry that becomes seed money for a woman's private use has already been mentioned. With this fund, for example, a woman might be able to exercise more independence in decisions affecting her children. Another means of establishing some influence is through the women's community, a term M. Wolf uses to refer to loosely-knit groups of women in the village that have no formal recognition (1972:42–52). It is in their relations with members of this community that women "develop sufficient backing to maintain some independence under their powerful mothers-in-law and even occasionally to bring the men's world to terms (M. Wolf 1972:37–38). M. Wolf found that the women who had the most influence on village affairs are those who use the collective power of the group to "lose face for their menfolk in order to influence decisions that are ostensibly not theirs to make" (1972:40). If an unmarried daughter is a member of any group, it would be her mother's, and here are opportunities for a girl to learn skills that she would require after marriage. This, however, is not an arena where an unmarried girl can air her grievances; the support of the women's community primarily serves women whose long-term interests are vested in the village. Writing on a related but somewhat different topic, Ahern presents conclusions that bolster this view: the power exercised by women behind the scene is to some extent open to younger women, but it is the older women, themselves mothers-in-law, who set the tone of the women's community (1975:201).

On the subject of women's power, other images come to mind: the "shrews"—shrill and argumentative women—whom R.F. Johnston (1910) saw in his court, women who head credit clubs and make loans (and charge interest) to their friends, and women who control the family's purse strings and manage efficient households. This kind of dominance comes with increasing age and length of residence in a community, and from a woman's careful cultivation of her sons' loyalty. Young women may have little influence over their husbands, much less their parents-in-law, but "older women who have raised their sons properly retain considerable influence over their sons' actions, even in activities exclusive to men" (M. Wolf 1972:41).

Another source of women's power is related to the ritual pollution associated with women's bodies. Lao Tai-tai recalls the strictures to which women were subject because of the potential harm they could cause: "The customs regarding women were very strict in P'englai [Shangtung]...A woman could not visit on the first or fifteenth of any month. She could not when visiting, lean against the frame of the door. She must not stand or sit on the doorstep or even touch it in crossing. To do any of these things might give her *power* over the family she was visiting and so ruin them. Women were not considered clean" (1967:179, emphasis added). As M. Wolf points out, however, little girls soon discover that this "power" can be more of a handicap than a help as they subsequently find more restrictions placed on them. They learn that they are not equals to their brothers, but it is difficult to determine more precisely how women's acceptance of their state[7] (as evidenced by their adhering to the appropriate rules of avoidance and so forth) affects their self-image. In any case the harm that women may inflict excludes them from access to at least one source of authority and prestige: women worship ancestors at home, but men take over this responsibility in public spheres where political and economic benefits are expected to follow, thus in Ch'inan, the community where Ahern worked, there are no festivals for high powerful gods in which women play a major role (1975:205).

Nevertheless, the power that inheres in a woman's reproductive capacity should not be under-estimated. Because the goals of young married women (associated with building a uterine unit) do not coincide with men's ideals concerning family growth, the "*power* women have is their capacity to alter a family's form by adding members to it, dividing it, and disturbing male authority" (Ahern 1975:200, emphasis in original). Again, this capacity does not apply to an unmarried daughter, and in tracing possible parallels between women's social roles and their qualities attributed to menstrual blood (a polluting but life-giving substance), Ahern suggests that in an unmarried girl the potential for harm is minimal. "For the most part unmarried girls identify closely with the wishes of their elders and have little capacity or inclination for disruption. The most that can be said is that when they marry out they disrupt the family's finances and the emotional ties between themselves and others, but these are temporary problems" (Ahern 1975:200).

This summary of some of the factors that determine the general shape of women's lives in rural Taiwan sets the stage for considering what values are instilled as girls are socialized. Knowing the sorts of expectations with which young women grow up is a first step toward understanding their criteria for selecting one option over another.

For having raised her, a child owes her parents a debt which she is obliged to repay by acts of filiality that will continue through her lifetime. For women the most extreme expression of filial piety perhaps can be seen in the daughters who enter prostitution in order to support their parents, and this concept of debt makes the attitudes of neighbors and friends comprehensible: "Villagers are not inclined to see these girls as martyrs since Chinese children are expected to make great sacrifices for their parents ... On the contrary [rather than criticizing her] villagers assume a girl has amply repaid the debt she owes her parents ... when she obeys their command to become a prostitute ... [she has] repaid it more fully than the daughter who remains at home can ever hope to" (M. Wolf 1968:103). It is with this background, therefore, that we should view the recent employment of young women: factory jobs make available to them a more respectable way of repaying their parents. This debt, of course, applies to sons as well, and girls grow up seeing their brothers contribute to household income and learn that to withhold wages is an unfilial act. Wolf cites an instance of villagers criticizing a boy's parents because of their laxness with him: "He contributed a fair amount to the family budget, but his mother made the error of confiding to a relative that she has no idea how much he earns" (1972:27).

Obedience is a valued trait in both sons and daughters, but expectations of obedient behavior and training for it come earlier for girls.

> By the time a girl is of school age she has had much more responsibility training than her male counterpart (e.g., little girls often have the responsibility of caring for baby brothers). She has also learned the pain that follows disobedience, and a few of the ways to avoid that pain. Beyond learning a few chores and some of the behavior that pleases adults, such as obedience, a pre-school Taiwanese girl learns her first subtle lessons about the second-class status of her sex (M. Wolf 1972:66).

> The cost of obtaining submission is not as high in a daughter ... [Mothers] find the training to secure [obedience], particularly in sons, too threatening to relationships they value more (M. Wolf 1972:79).

> Since girls are more likely to be within sight and sound of their mothers than boys, they receive more consistent punishment for expressed aggression. This and the fact that they are generally less active than boys may account for their reputation of being less aggressive (M. Wolf 1972:77).

As the passages above suggest, the lessons taught do not always require explicit articulation. Within the family boys are more secure in their position as sons and can simply demand things. An adult woman's success in protecting her interests, however, depends on her skill in judging the emotions and attitudes of others, skills that she began to develop as a child. Because their standing in the family is less firm and their loyalty cannot be taken for granted, girls are in a sense socialized earlier than their brothers, and even young girls are sensitive to the nuances implied in changes in tone or in expression. To raise the question of sanctions imposed on recalcitrant daughters, therefore, seems almost beside the point. A word or a glance may be all that is required to prod a disobedient girl into compliance,[8] and to ask why daughters do not make issues of decisions that affect their lives is a moot question. M. Wolf states, for example, that "many of the girls were painfully aware of the ambivalence of their families toward spending money on them and even when allowed to continue in school found the emotional strain more difficult than the education" (1972:93). Young girls are quite capable of judging realistically what options are allowed them by family circumstances, and as we shall see the question of continuing school may not even arise. M. Wolf writes that Chinese women learn as children that if their opinion is to be valued, it must be spoken by a man (1974:163), and it should be remembered that there are rarely any occasions when the opinion of a young unmarried daughter will be solicited.

With this type of training shaping the behavior of girls, their predisposition to follow the wishes of their elders and their willingness to meet their elders' expectations of filiality seem reasonable enough results. An outside observer, however, may be left with what appears to be a paradox: how are we to explain the often close relationship between mothers and daughters and the genuine attachment girls feel for their natal families, when we also know that these same girls have heard from the time they were little that they are "worthless daughters" and that girls "belong to other people"? In view of the preferential treatment shown to their brothers, one would not, on surface, expect such loyalty on the part of daughters to exist. The one event about which girls can be certain is that they will marry out, and the knowledge that their stay in their natal families is temporary cannot but color their outlook. Even so, the fact remains that although a daughter (excluding those who marry uxorilocally) has no place in her father's descent line, the only source of security she knows, until she marries, is her family. And indeed, a woman's changing definition of the family given us by M. Wolf (1972:33) shows that this could not be otherwise:

> When she is a child, a woman's family is defined for her by her mother and to some extent by her grandmother . . . those people who live together and eat together . . . But the group that has the most meaning for her and with which she will have the most lasting ties is the smaller, more cohesive unit centering on her mother, that is, the uterine family—her mother and her mother's children. As the girl grows up and her grandmother dies and a brother or two marries, she discovers that her mother's definition of the family is becoming less exclusive and may even include such outsiders as her brother's new wife.

It may be that "when the mother speaks of the future, she speaks in terms of her son's future" (M. Wolf 1972:33–34), but this does not mean that she ignores her daughter. While a father may fret about how much he may spend in good conscience on a daughter's dowry, "the mother has no such compunctions; she has always thought of herself as an outsider in her husband's family and considers her uterine family . . . the people to whom she is obliged" (M. Wolf 1972:131).

On the daughter's part, as she grows older her identification with her mother becomes stronger: "Before the girl is old enough to develop the understanding of her father's problems necessary for any depth in their relations, she begins . . . to discover [shared interests with her mother]. Her father then becomes less her protector . . . and more her mother's oppressor" (M. Wolf 1972:111). A daughter may be aware that she has no permanent place in her father's home, but this does not preclude the possibility of close mother-daughter relations, and several accounts attest to this. Jan Myrdal relates the remark of a woman longing for a daughter she never had: "a daughter is much closer to her mother than a daughter-in-law" (1966:239). Lao Tai-tai regarded her mother as a place of refuge (Pruitt 1967:50), and Johnston states that mothers "are often as devoted to their girls as they are to their boys... It is erroneous to suppose that the old loving relations between mother and daughter are necessarily severed on the daughter's marriage. It is often the case that a young married women's greatest happiness consists in periodical visits to her old home" (1910:247–48). If a young woman thinks about the subject at all she may recognize that her long-term loyalties are focused on her husband's family, but this is a loyalty that develops only gradually. For all a young bride knows, and the same applies to a girl heading for a factory dormitory, she is leaving a warm and secure environment for a houseful of strangers.[9]

3

Women and Work in Traditional China

This chapter deals with the kinds of work that were available to women, particularly to unmarried daughters, in China. It is inappropriate to regard participation in production as a sought-after right because the ideal was not to have to work at all. To speak, then, of acquiring access to the means of production implies a choice that may not have existed; in large part economic circumstances determined whether or not women took part in agricultural or other income-producing activities. In the northern part of China, for instance, women worked in the fields only under exceptional circumstances—if their families were short of labor and were too poor to hire help, and then it was felt to be cause for shame (Davin 1973:78). In a similar vein we would do well to remember that when rental income made it possible for the women in Kwan Mun Hau village (in the New Territories of Hong Kong) to stop working, E. Johnson could detect no feeling of anomie among the women: "From their point of view, the loss of productive work in agriculture has been more than compensated by the relative ease of their lives, particularly the absence of hard physical labor" (1975:219).

Before turning to women's entry into the industrial labor force in China, I will consider productive labor in the agricultural sector and in home industries, and discuss the effects of production on women's roles. It should be borne in mind that non-domestic work was not available to women in all parts of China. In some instances even when a family was destitute, it was not possible for the women to work. In Myrdal's report we read about a woman who left her husband (an opium addict) because there was no money left: "As I did not want myself and our daughter to starve to death, I took a place with a farmer called Sung...I had no pay but food for myself and my daughter. When I was twenty-two, I was sold" (1966:235). She subsequently remarried, was widowed, and was sold again by her husband's family with no mention of her ever working for wages. Lao Tai-tai, as noted in the previous section, was forced to beg because her husband had also squandered his earnings on opium. A town resident, she was eventually employed as a servant and later supported her family by peddling. Aside from prostitution these were perhaps the only courses available to her, and M. Wolf, writing about Taiwan in the late 1950s, could state that the only way a young girl could make a significant contribution to family income was to become a prostitute (1968:61).

Among peasant families, even where women did not work outside for wages paid by a non-family employer, they nonetheless contributed their labor to agricultural tasks, especially during busy seasons. A. Smith writes of women and girls taking turns watching the orchards and melon patches, and during the wheat harvest all available women helped to gather and thresh the wheat (1970:210). Women in the northern part of Taiwan today do not go to the fields on a daily basis, but "most help on occasion with the planting, weeding, and harvesting of vegetables, and nearly all wives take responsibility for the drying of the harvested rice, the washing of vegetables for market, and the gathering of food for family pigs" (M. Wolf 1972:167–68). In a fishing community in Taiwan (K'un Shen) women and children take part in pulling in fishing nets, in addition to the usual weeding and harvesting (ploughing is always done by men) (Diamond 1969:13,18).

The tasks mentioned thus far are either seasonal or secondary in nature, even if vital at times; elsewhere in China women assumed more regular roles in production. In both cases, however, the value of women's labor is difficult to calculate or measure since it was not rewarded by wages. In his survey *Land Utilization in China* Buck estimates that in the southern rice-growing portion of China women performed sixteen percent of farm labor, and in the northern wheat-growing region nine percent (cited by Davin 1976:118). Davin acknowledges that this and further contrasts in other areas[1] are difficult to account for; some relevant factors may have been the differing intensity of cultivation, extent of irrigation, climatic variation with differing labor demands, and soil conditions (Davin 1976:118–19). Sub-ethnic differences played a part: the Hakka women Johnson describes, regardless of their families' economic status, all worked in the fields growing rice and vegetables, raising pigs and chickens, and gathering fuel (1975:218). Today in the Hakka community that Cohen studied, women constitute half of the labor force, with only twelve percent of them involved in non-agricultural occupations (1976:53). Cohen states that the women of Yen-liao in southern Taiwan in fact provide most of the farming labor as full-time workers on family farms (1976:54).

As for subsidiary occupations in China (livestock and poultry raising, basket-making, weaving and spinning) Buck found that such work comprised only fourteen percent of the income of farm families, and women provided only sixteen percent of the labor in this sphere (cited by Davin 1976:22). Larger contributions were possible in areas where it was acceptable for women to be hired out as day-laborers. In Kwangtung, in addition to farm work, women worked as mulberry leaf pickers, as "silkwork maids" working and living in sericulture farms, as fruit pickers, sugar workers (pressing cane) and tobacco processors (Anonymous 1927:568). Tea processing figured importantly for women. Around the turn of the century in the Tamshui area of northern Taiwan, for instance, Davidson states that there were approximately 150 tea manufacturers with the largest firms employing one hundred to three hundred women (the majority of whom were between fourteen and eighteen years old) during the busiest months (1903:385). He estimates that the total number of workers employed daily in a season exceeded 12,000, with earnings amounting to nearly $100,000 per season (1903:385). It is of interest to note that because men often worked alongside women, tea picking became a social occasion of sorts, but one that carried negative overtones similar to those associated with factories:

> [The tea-picking period] is looked upon by these coy damsels as the opening of the social season as it were, and a young sister is brought out with considerable éclat... the coiffure is oftimes a work of art and decorated with... blossoms, while, with her feet bound up in the very smallest compass, she is prepared to dazzle the community (Davidson 1903: 384)... Several thousand Chinese leave their families in China every spring to work in the tea establishments of north Formosa... and the circumstances under which young women are sent from their homes each day to labor with strangers from the mainland, whose highest ambitions [are] the opium dens and brothels of Banka, are not conducive to morality (Davidson 1903:385).

In the Sanhsia region today tea continues to be grown although its economic importance in the area has diminished. Several of the grandmothers of my informants continue to pick tea, work they began as teenagers, and work in which few teenagers can be found now. These women could recall a period thirty years earlier when married as well as unmarried women worked in the tea hills, and that young men would go to meet them there. One woman in her seventies told me: "Each morning after washing the clothes and making breakfast, women would go out to pick tea; if it was not the season they might sort tea leaves at home. Further up in the mountains women raised chickens and ducks, and when they came down to pick tea, they would bring the eggs to sell."

Women took up various other jobs as well. Several of the Hakka women over forty in Johnson's study (1975) were employed at construction sites, and Hakka women, distinctive in their black-fringed hats, can still be seen carrying stones and other building material in Hong Kong today. A small number of the mothers of my informants also had such jobs, and years ago women in the area worked pushing carts containing coal. This often meant pushing heavy loads up grades, and today several of them attribute their present ailments to the exertion that job required.

It was not uncommon among poor families to send their daughters to work as servants, and one writer describes women in Kwangtung who offered their services as "bridesmaids," persons trained in wedding rituals and knowledgeable in the behavior and etiquette required of a bride (Anonymous

1927:576). In the 1920s in Kwangtung the same writer also observed women as ticket examiners on trains and working as waitresses, although the latter occupation was prohibited for a time (by the Bureau of Public Safety in Canton) because it "tended to demoralize society" (Anonymous 1927:577). Another occupation that might be added to the list is that of a religious specialist. Lamson mentions one woman in a village outside Shanghai whose annual income was approximately one third the earnings of a factory girl (1931:1034), and another writer also makes reference to "fairy women" in Kwangtung, women who help people make decisions and who profess to cure diseases. According to this account, although they were banned by the authorities and had to carry out their activities in secret, they nevertheless did a very good business (Anonymous 1927:568).

Before the turn of the century, according to Lao Tai-tai, it was profitable (if not respectable) to be a peddler, for only women peddlers were allowed to enter the homes of the wealthy (Pruitt 1967:175). Diamond writes that many women in K'un Shen engaged in some form of petty trade and peddling of produce; such activities were approved and expected from a housewife (1973:216–17). In present-day Ch'inan, however, a few women claim that their husbands look unfavorably on their wives taking part. One Liu woman in her late forties said, "At one time we raised more vegetables, but my husband refused to let me go out to sell it; he was afraid that I might become involved with another man. He feels that such women do not have a good reputation; their being outside all the time must mean there is another man somewhere."

Women who peddle produce and hire out their labor for a variety of services, like those women active in home industries, are in a position to gauge more accurately the percentage of total household income their wages constitute, and the income derived from home industries appears to have been remarkably high. During the Ming dynasty in Fukien a skilled woman weaver could weave a bolt of cotton cloth every four or five days, which fetched a picul of unhusked rice in the market; since this represented one sixth of the annual harvest from a *mou* of excellent land, there were good reasons to keep women at the loom (Rawski 1972:47). Similarly, in Soochow the model farmer received only forty percent of his total income from rice (and in some other areas this was only eighteen percent) while his wife could earn almost as much through weaving; even after the cost of raw materials was deducted, her contribution to the family income was twenty silver *liang* a year (a hired laborer costs only 13 *liang* a year) (Rawski 1972:55). Another illustration comes by way of Gamble's study (1968) of rural communities in northern China, material that was collected between 1926 and 1933. In one sample area of 453 villages approximately fifty percent of all women over fourteen were involved in home industry of one sort or another (Gamble 1968:287). Most families had a spinning wheel, and girls customarily began at twelve or thirteen, requiring four to five months to master the skill. Gamble estimates that ninety-five percent of spinners were women (1968:298), and women dominated cotton weaving as well, comprising eighty-two percent of weavers (1968:301). Together cloth and thread spinning represented approximately sixty percent of the total income resulting from home industry (Gamble 1968:301). Because the average age at marriage for females in these communities was seventeen (Gamble 1968:41) women as spinners and weavers were important to the household economy of both their natal families and of their husband's families. (Today cottage industries in the Sanhsia area include assembling plastic flowers, mending fish-nets that are manufactured by a nearby factory, attaching hooks to elastic and the like. These are contracted out to women by middle men, and the income is low. Housewives spend what leisure time they have for this work, as do small children, and even factory women when they are home.)

While women may have been able to measure the monetary value of their contribution to production, they were not always the direct recipients of wages, if indeed their labor was rewarded by wages. Elderly women in Ch'inan uniformly responded that as young women all their earnings from tea-picking, pushing carts and so on were handed over to their parents. In other cases women's labor was not paid because they were working on their husband's land or alongside their husbands as tenant-farmers. Information concerning the effects of participation in production on the status of women is scant; the figures given by Gamble and Rawski provide clear evidence of the prominent role women played in increasing their families' budgets, but these data are not accompanied by any discussion of the benefits women may have enjoyed as a result of their labor. Where poor families were concerned, poverty demanded that women join their husbands in the fields, and there is apt to be less differentiation in their economic roles.

C.K. Yang asserts that "among the common people, especially in the South, women's active part in economic production bolstered their position in the family and mitigated the general social discrimination against them" (1969:106), but unfortunately no illustrations are given. Davin offers a similar generalization: Cantonese women who normally worked in the fields were known for their strength of character and were reputed to be tough and fierce (1976:5). Diamond gives further evidence that confirms this view; where a wife's income in K'un Shen was spent on household needs, such a woman had more of a say in household affairs: "compared to women in farming villages, who, if they do so, work on their husbands' lands, the women of K'un Shen are outspoken and aggressive. It is their outside labor which sometimes maintains the household during the months when fishing is meager or impossible" (1969:66). Johnson's study (1975:219) of Hakka female laborers furnishes more specific information:

Women were able to keep at least some of the money they earned; a few women bought fields, and one woman built a house, into which she moved when her husband took a second wife.

Clearly women had a degree of economic autonomy, though it may not have been commensurate with their responsibilities. Because they were willing and able to take jobs as manual laborers, women in need could support themselves, albeit at a marginal level. Desperately unhappy wives or adopted child-brides could run away and earn a living without resorting to prostitution, unlike such women elsewhere.

To cite one more example of how work affected women's position, a Japanese anthropologist collecting material in a Yangtze delta village in the 1930s found that female status was higher among poorer families since these women worked on the farms, made baskets, and did embroidery work (Davin 1976:5). As Davin points out, however, it is noteworthy that even his proof of the "high status" of the housewife, namely that she was able to influence the family head, demonstrates the degree of overall subordination to which women were subjected (1976:5).

These comments underline the need to exercise caution in evaluating "improvement in status" and in pinpointing the factors that confer on a woman the right to control the rewards of her labor. These are subjects to which I will return in the conclusion; here it might be appropriate to reiterate an obvious point, namely, that female status was determined not only by the amount of work they did but also by the type of work they did. With the exception of Kwangtung, women in China played a minor role in directly productive work, and as Yang argues, "In the scale of values, only the labor of acquisition of goods and services or income from primary production was rated high" (1969:140). Secondary chores such as weeding, or tasks that were considered "light," such as tea-picking, therefore, could not be expected to carry much prestige. Women performed indispensable and often laborious chores inside the house, but the processing of food or clothing for consumption, washing, cleaning, child-care, and so on were "rated so low that no man would perform [them] without feeling inferior" (Yang 1969:140). And clearly, in a society where women ideally did not leave their homes to work, those occupations that did admit women were not likely to have paid them well or to bring them social respect. As Davin argues, "It is precisely this, the contribution which women are seen by their community as making, which is so vital as a determinant of their status" (1976:5), and, as I shall show in a later chapter, factory women's own evaluation of the work they do contributes to their low self-esteem.

The role that perception (on the part of family, community, and women themselves) plays in determining women's standing must be stressed, lest we exaggerate the improvements in women's lives following their entry into the labor force. The assessments and predictions made by Lang and Lamson (see below), for instance, seem unwarranted and premature; above all, factory women were, for the most part, unmarried and young. The appearance of factories, however, did mark an important departure from earlier kinds of productive labor. Even though a contract-labor system operated in the early part of this century, eventually the majority of factory women received their wages directly; it was now a simple matter for women to compare the contribution they made to total family income with that of their parents and brothers.

Changes that factories introduced into the lives of young women perhaps emerge most vividly at village level. In one community outside Shanghai one investigator found that all of the twenty-six women between fifteen and nineteen years were working in factories, and twenty-one out of twenty-three women in the twenty to twenty-four age group were so employed (Lamson 1931:1032). Around the same time Fei estimated that eighty percent of the girls in Kaihsienkung village had entered the silk industry (1932:233), and Topley cites a report indicating that, as early as 1904, eleven market towns in the Hsi-Ch'iao-Shun-Te area in Kwangtung had silk filatures, some of which employed as many as 500 to 1,000 women (1975:72). Figures on female workers in the major industrial centers of pre-1949 China are impressive, and while the numbers vary according to the sources, the composite picture they provide is convincing evidence of the prominent role women had in industry for several decades. The following table is one illustration:

Table 1.   Female Labor in Chinese Factory Industries 1914–1920 (%)
(Ho and Fong 1929:29)

Industry	1914	1915	1916	1917	1918	1919	1920
Textile	57	58	59	65	61	62	47
Metal	1	4	1	1	3	2	1
Chemical	12	12	13	12	12	16	22
Food and Drink	35	40	42	31	33	37	43

Child labor comprised a large portion of female workers (Table 2). The textile industry was centered in Shanghai and accounted for the predominance of women among factory workers; in 1927, for example, 58.7% of factory workers in Shanghai were women (Lang 1946:103). One survey taken between 1923 and 1924 in Shanghai shows the same pattern (Table 3), as does one survey carried out in 1929 (Table 4). The high concentration of female employees in the factories of Shanghai is also reflected in the number of women who took part in strikes during the 1920s. In 1922 twenty thousand employees in the silk-reeling factories of Hongkew and Chapei districts of Shanghai struck, and in 1924 twelve thousand women in Chapei struck again (Chesneaux 1968:195,219). In 1928 there were one hundred and twenty strikes in Sanghai with the number of workers involved estimated at 213,966; of these 122,807 were women (Fang 1931:92). The available information for 1929 indicates 37,247 men and 31,263 women took part in one hundred and eight strikes that year (Fang 1931:92).

Women in other areas did not lag far behind. Of the total workers employed by the cotton industry in Kwangtung, 66.95% were women, in

Table 2.   Child Labor (Under Twelve Years) in Shanghai Factories, 1925
(Ho and Fong 1929:29)

Industry	Male	Female
Textile	3,520	16,737
Metal	430	250
Food and Drink	247	318
Miscellaneous	108	290

Table 3.   Female Industrial Labor in Shanghai (1923–1924)
(Chesneaux 1968:74)

Industry	Women	Girls under 12 (%)
39 Chinese-owned Silk-reeling Factories	74.5	15.5
27 Foreign-owned Silk-reeling Factories	55.5	34.9
18 Chinese-owned Cotton Mills	62.8	6.4
24 Japanese and British-owned Cotton Mills	65.9	5.2

Table 4.   Distribution of Male and Female Industrial Workers in
Shanghai, 1929
(Fang 1931:107)

Industry	Male	Female	Children [sex not specified]
Cotton	29,000	62,600	3,000
Tobacco	3,200	8,500	500
Silk Filature	2,150	39,500	10,850
Cloth	4,400	4,500	500
Stocking	2,300	4,150	200
Silk Cloth	3,650	2,200	400
Matches	910	1,500	330
Paper	1,050	1,150	20
Others	30,040	2,400	4,830

Kiangsi—56.74%, in Anhwei—48.99%, in Fukien—46.29%, and 42.43% in Hupeh (H. D. Fong 1932:148). In northern China, however, the number of female workers remained low throughout this period. One writer attributes this to social prejudice against women's employment (Fong 1932:148), but cotton mills and silk filatures did not figure as importantly here as in the south. In Shangtung women comprised only 6.37% of the total cotton labor; in Hopei only 10.97% of the cotton workers were women (Fong 1932:148), with 16.94% in Tsingtao and 2.54% in Tientsin (Fong 1932:116).

Child labor aside, most of these women were young; approximately one half of the 3,500 workers in six cotton mills in Tientsin were between twelve and sixteen (T'ao and Johnson 1928:521); in the textile factories of Shangai, Hangchow, Tsingtao, and Tientsin the average age of the female workers was below twenty (Chesneaux 1968:65). A number of these women were married; social workers of the period decry deplorable factory conditions where babies and small children crowd the floors because there was no other place a working mother could leave her children. This suggests that many such women lived in nuclear households and were recent immigrants to the city. One investigator surveyed one hundred labor families in Shanghai and found that only twelve were natives of the city, and that the average size of the family was 4.11 persons (Fang 1930:869). In most of these families both husband and wife were employed: "after a period of twelve hours of work, the men usually go out for some kind of recreation, and the women attend to their housework" (Fang 1930:866). The demands of housework were one reason why evening classes provided by factories and unions as well as other union activities were poorly attended by women (Kyong 1929:8; Ching and Bagwell 1931:24).

Women were preferred not only because they were already familiar with silk reeling, weaving, and spinning, but also for reasons that still prevail in Taiwan today: women are believed to be more dexterous for certain kinds of tasks, are more amenable to discipline, and willing to accept lower wages than men. It is not necessary here to present the backgrounds of factory women and their working environment in China in the early 1900s. There are, however, a number of patterns that parallel the trends evident in the movement of women into industry in Taiwan fifty years later, and these deserve some attention.

Most of the workers were from peasant backgrounds and tended to be recent migrants to the cities; a Shanghai YWCA survey, for instance, showed that eighty percent of the women in the silk-reeling factories of Wusih came from villages in the outlying areas (Chesneaux 1968:49). With respect to other firms, a majority of workers came from the counties in the rural areas of the province in which the factory was located; a smaller number came from neighboring provinces or even further, and only a fraction were drawn from the population of the industrial center itself (Chesneaux 1968:67). Chesneaux interprets the sums spent on travel expenses as an indication of the links maintained by workers with their native villages (1968:51), but in view of the absence of regular holidays in many firms, it is impossible to estimate the frequency of women's visits home.

Workers were predominantly rural in background, and one form of labor recruitment upon which factories relied heavily was the contract-labor system, although its importance diminished after the mid-1920s. This system operated through the use of an intermediary, the contractor, who recruited labor and who was given complete or partial authority over the workers. Often he paid workers directly or arranged to have the money remitted to the workers' families. (Traditionally, a similar system had been used for hiring seasonal workers in agriculture and for hiring miners.) Even in the free labor market, however, the intermediary played a critical role. Workers were sometimes signed on by a foreman who made a profit on the transaction. Intermediaries were also organized in a systematic manner, and agents from a factory would be dispatched to the rural areas to bring back the necessary recruits. These intermediaries ranged from foremen to janitors and policemen (Fong 1932: 119). The methods used by one factory could apply equally well to some firms in Taiwan today (see chapter 4):

> The first group of workers [for a cotton mill in Tientsin] were recruited from outside districts... especially those parts where cotton mills were already in existence. These [skilled] workers were offered better conditions of work as an inducement, often with free travelling expenses (Fong 1932:118).

Another cotton mill in the same area sent its agents to various districts where they posted advertisements that described working conditions, referred to free traveling expenses, free provision for room, board and clothing, and promised continuing education and pocket-money. As the writer notes, workers were not usually treated so well once admitted into the mill (Fong 1932:119).[2] (These recruitment practices also allowed others to exploit women for other purposes; one writer mentions young women who were lured from the villages around Shanghai on the pretext of placing them in highly remunerative factory jobs, but upon arrival they were sold to brothels [Lieu 1936:169]. Similar accounts and warnings still appear from time to time in newspapers in Taiwan.)

Workers themselves were also sent back to their native districts for this purpose. In the cotton and wool industries in Tientsin, for example, women "section heads" (who supervised fifty or so other women) were routinely dispatched to bring back a specified number of workers (T'ao and Johnson 1928:521). Sometimes the arrangement was more informal:

> Often, a [cocoon] peeler brings her sister or daughter to the filature to help do the work and earn more money for the family. The work requires no training, and there are any number of women living in the neighborhood of the filatures who can do it. Whenever a filatur e needs them, it is only necessary to tell the regular women workers, and they will in turn tell their acquaintances to come and take up work the next day" (Lieu 1940:110).

Much has been written about the supposed disorientation and social and psychological breakdown to which new industrial workers are susceptible (cf. Slotkin 1960). Without denying that some maladjustment does indeed occur, especially in light of the quality of working conditions in China in the 1920s, this is nonetheless an assumption that must be tested.[3] Leaving aside the physical exertion demanded by twelve-hour days in over- or under-heated and unventilated plants, the factory called for other types of adjustment. Three subjects that I want to touch upon here are relations among workers, relations between workers and supervisors, and labor turnover.

Unfortunately, information concerning friendship networks among women workers is sparse;[4] one can only guess at the quality of relations formed among women who shared one work area or participated in union activities or attended evening classes together. We do know, however, that regional loyalties were strong. In one district of Shanghai, for example, marriages between persons from the same province predominated while marriages between persons from different provinces were infrequent (Chesneaux 1968:69). Male workers in dormitories grouped themselves by locality (according to province, district and village) (K.H. Shih 1944:4), a pattern true of women as well. Some formed groups in dormitories based on kinship, while others "having nothing in common by place of origin or kinship, [created] imaginary family relationships, with family names such as 'Pine Tree Which Lasts Forever'" (T'ien 1944:185). Chesneaux also notes that workers, especially women in Shanghai's factories, formed groups known as *Shih-ti-mei* (ten brothers and sisters), and he attributes this to the need of workers to "protect themselves against the inhuman atmosphere of the factories" (1968:123). No doubt the factory left much to be desired, but the variety of social backgrounds that were brought together in dormitories accentuated difficulties in adjusting, a fact duly noted by writers of that period; the complexity and disorder such heterogeneity produces bring to mind similar complaints voiced by factory women in Taiwan.

Depending on the progressiveness of a particular firm, recreational programs may have been provided for its workers, or the workers' union may have offered them. One shoe-makers' union started a library, a weekly paper, and a technical discussion group (Fong 1932:186); a factory in Yunnan established a clubhouse with free entertainment and games for its male workers (K.H. Shih 1944:64) (although it appeared the men preferred teahouses). Storytelling was popular, as was drama, since many workers were familiar with the songs (Fong 1932:186). Chesneaux claims that although workers were short of funds and leisure, they showed great interest in acquiring an education (1968:109). While this may have been true of male employees and young unmarried women, time and distance prevented married women from taking advantage of classes offered. In one silk-reeling factory night classes in English ended after one year due to lack of funds and lack of interest on the part of workers (Ching and Bagwell 1931:23). In Tientsin a school for female workers was established in 1930 under the auspices of the YWCA; there were thirty-six students when the school opened but one month later nineteen remained, the others having left because of household chores and distance from home; of the remaining students eleven were between thirteen and fourteen years of age (Fong 1932:186).

None of the studies cited thus far mentions women who, through evening classes, were able to advance themselves on the job. Women perhaps fared better in silk-reeling factories, because they constituted such a disproportionately high percentage of the labor force and may have had opportunities to become "foremen." Even in the silk industry, however, it was more likely that the better-paying tasks were assigned to male workers. I came across only one study that makes specific reference to women in a position that might be described as a "foreman." (And actually they bear greater resemblance to the unit-leaders of the Taiwan factories whom I discuss later.) In the larger cigarette factories of Tientsin one survey reports "section workers," women who oversee groups of fifty or so other women and who are responsible for seeing that a certain rate of production is maintained and that discipline is kept up (T'ao and Johnson 1928:522). Evidently this was exceptional. In an investigation of the textile industry in Wushih (a district in Shanghai) the writer expresses surprise that foremen rather than forewomen were employed, "since only women are employed for the work" (Kyong 1929:3).[5]

Where the contract-labor system was utilized it no doubt determined the quality of relations between foremen and their workers. Foremen may have been resented, but workers often received their wages through him and owed their jobs to him. The ability of foremen to impose fines on workers for poor performance put the latter at a further disadvantage. The distance between staff members and manual workers was strongly resented, and women wished that there were personal warmth instead (T'ien 1944:188). It was only through years of labor struggle, for instance, that women in the Chapei (Shanghai) silk-reeling factories obtained permission to use the dispensaries run by employers and previously reserved for certain categories of employees (Chesneaux 1968:384).[6]

Other comments, these coming from male workers, would also find wide agreement among factory women in Taiwan: "If the workers are given consideration and attention and complimented on their work by a supervisor, they will do anything. Reprimands and punishments do not help at all... A good supervisor should understand the personal feelings of the worker" (K.H. Shih 1944:58–9). As for the distinction between manual workers and staff employees, if the gender in the following passage were changed, the remarks would duplicate those of present-day Taiwanese factory employees: "[The administrative staff] address workers by name and surname, never adding 'Mister'". These and other small differences give rise to bitter feelings, and grievances, real or imaginary. One worker says when he is alone with an office worker, the latter will talk to him, but when another comes, he will turn his back on the worker" (K.H. Shih 1944:118). It is unlikely that many white-collar employees in Taiwan's factories would feel their dignity lowered if they mixed with workers (Shih reports this in the factory he studied—1944:122); more often than not, the social gulf that exists between the two categories is the result of differing job definitions that allow for little interaction. Women workers then and now, however, do place much weight on "human feeling" in relations with their immediate supervisors.

As for making their opinions known to management, the feelings and opinions held by the male workers in Shih's factory are virtually identical to those expressed by Taiwan's female workers. Shih notes that although the firm installed a suggestion box, few workers ever made use of it; some said that it was just pretense, and most did not take it seriously (1944:125). As this was a government-owned and operated factory there were opportunities for workers to speak to government inspectors, but few took advantage of the possibility, the workers' reasoning being that if they had spoken up other workers "would have stared at them and would have thought that they were trying to make an impression; and if their comments were poorly stated, they would be ridiculed" (K.H. Shih 1944:127).

Employers in Taiwan frequently complain of high rates of turnover among their production employees. This was also a notable feature of the Chinese labor force in the early 1900s. One study found that only one-third of the women in a cotton mill had been there for longer than a year (T'ien 1944:190). In a Japanese-owned cotton mill in Shanghai, 2,150 workers left and 2,417 entered the factory between November 1923 and October 1924 (Chesneaux 1968:86). Of the 2,150 who left, 257 quit to return home,[7] 168 for "domestic reasons," 129 because of a marriage or birth, and 33 because they were dissatisfied, while 280 were dismissed because their work was found to be unsatisfactory, 105 on the grounds of not having worked hard enough, 91 for having disobeyed rules and regulations, and 605 for excessive wastage of materials, this being only a partial listing of reasons (Chesneaux 1968:86).

Chesneaux interprets this high rate of turnover to mean that many workers had "difficulty in adapting to industrial work and to factory life" (1968:86). I do not wish to downplay the obstacles many new workers faced, and the figures given for those who were dismissed lend support to Chesneaux's claim. With regard to the other workers, however, some caution must be exercised in interpretation (excepting those who return home to marry or to give birth): for one thing, from what can be observed on Taiwan today, obtaining a worker's true reason for leaving is an extremely difficult task. But high turnover rates should be regarded not only as an index of problems in adjustment; they also attest to the mobility that workers had, and with respect to factory women this very mobility is new and holds numerous possibilities. It is in this perspective that turnover statistics in Taiwan might be viewed, for many young women do not consider their frequent entry into and departure from factories as symptoms of intolerable conditions but rather, as a way of taking full advantage of a new-found freedom to more or less move where they choose.

In tracing some of the parallels between the female labor force in pre-1949 China and workers in Taiwan, one additional point deserves some comment, and this has to do with the image of factory women in the wider society. In a study of workers in Wusih, the investigator found only a few of the women were native to the area: "The natives are still prejudiced against working in factories, and so do not allow their daughters to enter factories unless they are really economically pressed" (Kyong 1929:5). Such an outlook leads to a surprising reversal in the attitude of parents; according to one report, "none of [the families of the workers], even though they were not well off, wanted their daughter to bring home money. All the parents wished their daughter would not work away from home. They unanimously regarded such work as degrading and a blot on their good name" (T'ien 1944:183–84). The brother of one worker remarked: "Just think, do good women enter such a hole as a textile factory? Such a hole is bound to be full of bad elements" (T'ien 1944:194).

Over the last fifteen years in Taiwan the reservations parents have had about allowing their daughters to enter factories have, of course, evolved into acceptance, but worries about the influence of "bad elements" in the factory milieu remain. New hairstyles and more daring fashions no doubt contributed to the loose reputation that factory girls had (Lang 1946:266), as did newspaper accounts deploring the "breaking down of customary standards of sex morality and restrictions of the relations between the sexes in factories" (Lieu 1936:167). According to another study 107 out of 359 women criminals were factory workers, seduction accounting for twenty-three percent of the "crimes" committed by them (Lieu 1936:170). Today in Taiwan a factory job away from home is sometimes the first step toward other less respectable but better paying occupations, a pattern that repeats a course of development several decades earlier: Lang reports that once women had become factory women other restrictions began to disappear—women began to be employed as shop assistants, waitresses and barbers (1946:103).

Whatever qualms families may have had about sending their daughters to factories, parents were no doubt mollified when it became apparent that their daughters' contribution to household income could be sizable. For instance, as the domestic economy of southern China declined, men had begun to emigrate in large numbers to Singapore, Malaya, and Hong Kong, and Topley quotes one source that reported that "'thousands of peasant homes depended for a large part of their livelihood on the modest earnings of a wife or daughter'" (1975:72). Although women's wages were lower than men's, their contribution relative to total family income was high. Lamson, in a study of four villages near Shanghai, calculated the average yearly earnings for a male worker to be $263.55 and $173.24 for a woman; nonetheless, for the year in which the study was carried out, women earned 48.32% of the total family income (1931:1034–05). Another survey undertaken by Lamson focused on twenty-one working-class families in Shanghai in the late 1920s. There were a total of fifty-eight wage-earners, of whom thirty-six were women, and the distribution of family members' contribution to total family wages is given in Table 5. After averaging the total expenditures for the families and taking a hypothetical minimum needed for an adult male factory worker in Shanghai, in relation to

Table 5.   Distribution of Family Members' Contribution to Total Family
Wages in Twenty-One Shanghai Families (Late 1920s)
(Lamson 1930:1244)

Income Group (Annual)	No. of Families	% by Mothers	% by Fathers	% by Daughters	% by Sons	Total Females %	Total Males %
Less than $100	1[ab]	100.0	-	-	-	100.0	-
$200–$300	4[ab]	49.4	26.4	24.2	-	73.6	26.4
$300–$400	4[b]	25.8	45.6	28.6	-	54.4	45.6
$400–$600	6[b]	19.8	51.9	28.3	-	48.1	51.9
$700–$900	6	5.6	16.7	30.6	47.1	36.2	63.8
Total average		26.3	33.4	26.8	13.5	53.5	46.7

a.   Of these five families, only two had a male head in the family.

b.   In these families, only six sons were recorded, none of whom contributed to family income; one was an apprentice, living away from home, one was twelve years old and attending school, and the remaining four were under six years of age.

his average monthly earnings, Lamson concludes that the average monthly earnings of a male laborer in factories are just sufficient to support himself and his wife but no children, and that a family of four or five members could not be supported on the earnings of the male worker alone (1930:1256).

Child and female labor were, of course, more commonplace in Shanghai than in areas farther north, as a comparison between Tientsin and Shanghai families indicates (See Tables 6a and 6b). One would expect that the markedly higher contributions of wives and daughters in the textile factories of Shanghai, and presumably, of women in the silk-filatures in the south, would confer on them a proportionately greater degree of independence and influence at home than, say, their counterparts in Tientsin. Unfortunately, however, information pertaining to the effects of wage-earning on the position of women does not generally focus on the *amount* of a woman's contribution as a specific variable affecting her status. It would be a safe guess, however, that most parents did not worry unduly about gradations in wages in various factories. The simple fact of gainful employment was sufficient to transform their daughters into economic assets. Fei writes that those who had no adult daughters began to regret it, once factory work became available (1939:233), and another author observes that because of the new economic importance of daughters the adoption and buying of girls were practiced among the working class (Kyong 1939:233). (This leads one to wonder why some families would be willing to give up a potential wage-earner.)

Economic need clearly determined which women were likely to enter factories. In his study of a cotton mill T'ien found that forty-nine percent of the workers were either without parents or without one parent, and that thirty-eight percent were without an older brother or sister (1944:180). But economic circumstances aside, factory employment offered a hitherto unavailable and positive alternative to many women. In T'ien's report a sizable number of

Table 6a.   Average Percentage Distribution of Income per Family per
Month by Income Groups, for Cotton Workers in Shanghai, 1932
(Fong 1932:137)

Income Group	Number of Families	Husband	Wife	Son	Daughter	(Other Males and Females)
Under $20	42	80.6	9.8	1.5	3.8	
$20–$29.99	90	48.2	21.5	9.9	7.3	
$30–$39.99	46	43.7	15.0	10.2	12.4	
$40–$49.99	34	33.8	16.4	10.2	13.3	
$50–$59.99	18	31.9	7.3	12.6	11.2	
Total Average		43.5	15.5	9.9	10.2	(7.4)(9.0)*

*Totals do not equal 100 because of additional income from sources such as boarders, house rent, etc.

Table 6b.   Average Percentage Distribution of Income per Family per
Year by Income Groups, for Cotton Workers in Tientsin, 1932
(Fong 1932:137)

Income Group	Number of Families	Husband	Wife	Children	Brother	Sister
$200 or Under	5	77.60	20.32			
$201–$300	46	84.60	8.75	2.27	0.17	0.10
$301–$400	27	69.31	5.94	13.73		1.99
$401–$500	9	58.36	9.87	14.35	17.16	
Total Average		74.71	8.34	8.23	2.72	0.77*

*Totals do not equal 100 because of additional income from sources such as boarders, house rent, etc.

workers referred to the desire to escape from unpleasant family circumstances as a motivation for going to the factory: mistreatment by relatives (where parents were deceased) and especially by step-mothers, conflict with sisters-in-law, unhappiness with engagements, and constant arguments with husbands and parents-in-law (1944:181). While a factory job may have been only a stop-gap solution for these women, for others wage-earning actually led to improved treatment at home. Lamson finds some evidence that factory workers were given the best food because they were recognized as a steady source of income (1931:1054), and Lang observes that the family began to be friendlier towards the working daughter, and that her opinions were taken more seriously (1946:263).

An evaluation of the impact of factory work and income on Taiwanese women will be taken up in a later chapter; it seems appropriate here, however, to review the conclusions of commentators writing in pre-1949 China. The overall theme is one of greater autonomy and increases prerogatives for the women involved. Wages were paid to the worker directly (the significance of this is duly acknowledged by mothers and grandmothers in Taiwan today), and while most of their earnings were turned over to their families, women did have some pocket money. Fei writes: "If a girl spends a reasonable amount, it will be accepted without interference. But she is not allowed to spend all her wage" (1934:234). Women who lived away from home had more freedom to dispose of their earnings as they chose (Lang 1946:246). Lang reports that in twenty-seven of one hundred and twenty-five families in Shanghai, three of twenty-seven families in Tientsin, and in two of eight families in Wusih, the sons and daughters did not give parents all their wages but kept part and sometimes the entire sum for themselves (1946:158); unfortunately no information is given with regard to family circumstances, although we might note that this is still a small minority.

Evidence of greater independence ranged from outward signs such as style of dress to being consulted more often on family affairs. It seems that most of the pocket money women had went toward improving their appearance; the mother of one woman remarked that her daughter dressed more fashionably than the rest of them (Lamson 1931:1073). Workers in Shanghai, especially, were described as taking pains to keep up with the latest fashions (Lang 1946:262). Because of the amount of time they spent outside and the wider experiences they accumulated (often in a bustling urban-industrial center), girls were believed to be more knowledgeable, were allowed a greater say at home, and were viewed as transmitters of information from factory and city to village. It is also noted, however, that factory women acquired vulgar language, bad manners, and even showed disrespect towards their parents (Lamson 1931:1073). As one elderly man in the village put it, "[with factories] there are more opportunities for women to work and to become economically independent. It gives more freedom to the girls, but as the young people become more powerful they like to have their own ideas which come from outside. They always say to us, 'You do not know this, you do not know that'" (Lamson 1931:1060).

One sector of their lives about which female workers formed definite ideas was marriage. Most studies of the period take note of a later age at marriage; for example, it was twenty-two for women in a 1930 survey conducted in a working district of Shanghai (Fang 1930:879). This was probably encouraged by parents, but in any case daughters now had a legitimate reason for arguing against a particular arranged match. One mother said this of her daughter: "She is all right; she gives me all the money she earns. When I tried to engage her, she refused, saying that she did not want the man, that it is too early for her" (Lamson 1931:1073). A majority of the women Lang interviewed said that they expected their marriages to be arranged by their parents, although some expressed their dissatisfaction with the marriage system: "I am afraid of marriage. It is like falling into a trap. Parents-in-law might be severe, and the husbands rude" (1946:267). Lamson mentions two factory girls who claimed they did not want to marry since they enjoyed more freedom at home as single women, and they also expressed an aversion to having children (1931:1073). Referring to a twenty-seven year-old unmarried worker, Lamson concludes that "girls can [now] refuse to marry if they want to, an unheard of thing not many years ago in these rural communities" (1931:1073–74). (As I shall show later, Taiwanese women also hold ambivalent attitudes about marriage, but none of my informants rejected the idea of marriage.) One girl is quoted as saying, "If we can support ourselves, why do we want to marry? We can be quite free by ourselves" (Lamson 1931:1074). There is no doubt that such a stance could not have been taken before factory jobs became commonplace, and it is tempting to take these comments as the first signs of far-reaching changes. It is true, of course, that without gainful employment women would not have had the wherewithal to consider not marrying or to form marriage resistance movements (cf. Topley 1975).[8] Nonetheless, it is easy to exaggerate the extent of such changes, especially since the attitudes expressed are so radically new. A re-examination of the available data shows that new attitudes may not always be matched by new behavior.

Personal appearance and marriage may in fact be one area over which workers exercised a good deal of control, but in other family matters factory women may have had little say. In Lamson's study, no girls were listed as being in school, although some of them were funding their brothers' education (1931:1035). It would seem that in at least one important sphere of their lives (since education could conceivably improve their future options) working daughters did not enter into the decision-making process. Unfortunately neither Lamson nor Lang furnishes specific examples of those types of family matters where daughters' opinions were solicited. Women who tried to spend less on themselves so they could send more money home (Lang 1946:265) may have done so out of loyalty or devotion, but they also may have done so because they were subordinate to parental authority.

Nonetheless, notions about being independent and positive evaluations about self-reliance were beginning to appear: "To stay at home and depend on one's parents is not good. I am an independent woman now...Life in the factory is more interesting than life at home. I see more of life"(Lang 1946:268). These are statements that could have been made by a Taiwanese factory woman, for whom the concept of "earning money yourself and spending it yourself" also holds much appeal. The point I wish to stress here, however, is that these are not always ideas that factory women could put into practice. To be sure, they were able to spend a portion of their wages, but the amount involved was likely to have been set at their parents' discretion. Moreover, such sums were not sufficient to have allowed an unmarried woman greater control over her future; there were few channels of investment open to her. One worker in a cotton mill, in explaining her reason for leaving, said that a laborer would still be a laborer after working all her life in a factory, that there was no hope of becoming a manager, and that therefore she had asked an uncle to provide her with the means to acquire more education and obtain a better job (T'ien 1944:192). It is undeniable that unlike women in the past, factory workers were able to move more freely and to enjoy at least a portion of their income. Being a wage-earner, however, did not grant these women the right to control their wages, and without this prerogative their expressed attitudes concerning independence cannot be taken to mean that they had achieved higher status.

Various writers have observed that with industrialization and wage employment daughters have become almost as valuable to their families as sons, and it seems fitting to end this chapter with some remarks about this. In 1930 one mother told Lamson: "'To me, girls are better than boys, for my elder son is now seventeen years old, and since his graduation from primary school, I have no money to continue his education, so he just stays at home with nothing to do'" (1931:1074). Moving closer to the present, in *The House of Lim*, M. Wolf describes young men who are too young to begin their compulsory military training and who have difficulty securing employment because their term of duty has not been fulfilled. "Nearly all these young people have stop-gap jobs of one sort or another which bring them a little spending money but nothing that suggests a beginning in adult life. They simply wait, passing the time as pleasantly as they can" (M. Wolf 1968:97). Factories do hire teenage boys as unskilled workers, but it is probably their sisters who have surpassed them in terms of their importance to their families' financial standing.

In traditional China women took part in production because they were forced to do so by economic need. Any increase in power they gained by contributing to family income was limited. For unmarried daughters this meant somewhat greater personal autonomy; for married women it meant a larger voice in family matters. But in no case did participation in production grant women more authority outside the home. As we shall see, these statements apply to Taiwanese factory women as well.

4

Industry and Labor in Taiwan: An Overview

The main island of Taiwan is approximately four hundred kilometers long and one hundred and forty kilometers wide, covering 36,000 square kilometers, over half of which is mountainous and only one-quarter of which is cultivated (Sun 1976:50). Although limited in natural resources the economic growth of Taiwan over the last two decades has been impressive. Between 1962 and 1973 Taiwan's real gross national product increased at over ten percent per year (S. Ho 1975:27), and the rate of industrial growth between 1952 and 1967 has averaged fourteen percent (Silin 1976:13). In 1974 Taiwan recorded a total trade volume of US$13 billion, more than US$1 billion above the level attained by the People's Republic of China, and in its trade with the United States, Taiwan's US$4 billion figure (for 1974) was more than twice that of the People's Republic (Shapiro 1977). Given a scarcity of natural resources and a relatively small domestic maket, the Nationalist Chinese have turned to foreign trade to develop their economy, and exports have grown at an annual rate of nearly eighteen percent from 1953 to 1973 (Hou and Hsu 1976:1). In 1953 total exports of goods and services accounted for 8.6% of the gross domestic product (Hou and Hsu 1976:1), one of the highest such proportions in the world.

Economic aid from the United States was phased out in 1965 and from that time private business investments assumed prominence; the United States has been one of the largest sources of foreign investment in Taiwan, contributing over US$471 million (a 1975 figure) of the US$1.4 billion total since 1952 (Republic of China 1976b). While agricultural production decreased from 23.7% to 17.1% of the net domestic product between 1968 and 1971, the share of industrial production in the net domestic market increased from 30.3% in 1968 to 34.4% in 1971 (Economic Planning Council 1974a:8). Within industrial production the manufacturing sector has grown more rapidly than all other industries; in 1971 manufactured commodities accounted for seventy-one percent of Taiwan's exports (B. Cohen 1975:60).[1] The composition of exports and of imports are given in Tables 7a and 7b.

Table 7a.   Composition of Exports, Taiwan
(Economic Planning Council 1974b:171)

	Value (NT$ Millions)			
Period	**Total**	**Agricultural Products**	**Processed Agricultural Products**	**Industrial Products**
1968	31,568	3,137	6,774	21,657
1969	41,975	3,829	7,089	31,057
1970	59,257	5,083	7,583	46,591
1971	82,416	6,515	9,225	66,676
1972	119,525	8,145	11,822	99,558
1973	170,723	12,855	13,390	144,478
	Percentage Distribution			
Period	**Total**	**Agricultural Products**	**Processed Agricultural Products**	**Industrial Products**
1968	100.00	9.9	21.5	68.6
1969	100.00	9.1	16.9	74.0
1970	100.00	8.6	12.8	78.6
1971	100.00	7.9	11.2	80.9
1972	100.00	6.8	9.9	83.3
1973	100.00	7.5	7.9	84.6

Taiwan's strategy for achieving and sustaining this rate of expansion has been based on price stabilization, low-wage labor, and a series of government policies designed to foster an attractive investment climate. The following quote from an advertisement placed by the Republic of China gives some indication of these incentives:

> The investor may choose a five-year business income tax holiday or accelerated depreciation of fixed assets. In some cases, machinery and equipment may be exempted from import duty, or payment may be made in installments . . . Land and Buildings may be leased or purchased in the already developed industrial estates and in export processing zones, or the investor may choose and acquire a site of his own choosing. Repatriation of profits is unrestricted; that of capital is set at not more than 15% annually beginning two years after completion of the approved investment plan . . . Foreign investment in the fields of capital-intensive and technology-intensive industries is encouraged. However, labor-intensive industries are still welcome (Republic of China 1976a).

Taiwan now has three export processing zones, with 141 factories situated at Kaohsiung, 105 at Nantze, and 43 at Taichung, employing 67,000 workers at the end of 1975 (Republic of China 1976a). "Zones are developed and managed by the government. Red tape is reduced to a minimum. No duties are paid on machinery, raw materials, or components. Streets, utilities and standard

Table 7b.   Composition of Imports, Taiwan
(Economic Planning Council 1974b:171)

		Value (NT$ Millions)		
Period	Total	Capital Goods	Agricultural and Industrial Raw Materials	Consumption Goods
1968	36,222	12,706	21,876	1,640
1969	48,629	18,491	28,019	2,119
1970	61,110	20,863	37,303	2,944
1971	73,942	25,057	45,132	3,753
1972	100,791	32,674	61,597	6,520
1973	145,079	48,618	88,319	8,142
		Percentage Distribution		
Period	Total	Capital Goods	Agricultural and Industrial Raw Materials	Consumption Goods
1968	100.00	35.1	60.4	4.5
1969	100.00	38.0	57.6	4.4
1970	100.00	34.2	61.0	4.8
1971	100.00	33.9	61.0	5.1
1972	100.00	32.4	61.1	6.5
1973	100.00	33.5	60.9	5.6

factory buildings are built and waiting for machinery and workers . . . Loans up
to seventy percent are available" (Republic of China 1976a). Such policies have
lured substantial foreign investment, but critics of the rationale behind the
export processing zones have charged that the technology that is actually
introduced is limited, as it consists of assembly work, with parts brought in
from Japan or the United States (Hsieng 1977:77). Moreover, it is suggested
that workers have not become part of the technological progress that is being
initiated; they are benefiting only minimally in terms of learning skills, and
promotions are few (Hsieng 1977:78).

No less crucial to Taiwan's economic development is the low-wage labor
that is available, and attention is called to this:

One of the most attractive features of the Taiwan investment climate is its inexpensive, hard-
working, and well-educated labor force . . . Taiwan's labor force is generally considered the
best bargain in Asia, if not the world, when efficiency as well as cost is taken into account.
And the island workers are well-disciplined; there is practically none of the costly labor strife
that characterizes the industries in many parts of the world. There are no strikes (Republic of
China 1976b).

In the event of [labor] disagreements, the government steps in as mediator (Republic of
China 1976a).

As one writer put it,

> Instead of exporting its natural resources as embodied in its agriculture and processed agricultural goods, Taiwan is now exporting its most abundant factor, labor... By reducing relative price distortions and allowing its economy to follow its comparative advantages, Taiwan has successfully shifted from a growth based on natural resources to one based on a human resource (Ho 1975:33).

Another economist goes further and argues that the use of low-wage labor is more capable of realizing development of export-oriented production than is the enlargement of investments in plant and equipment (capital-intensive investments) in an economy such as Taiwan's, where a competitive edge in production costs is important (T.C. Liu 1969:81). The prominence of labor-intensive industries in Taiwan's export boom is demonstrated by the following figures: capital-intensive and labor-saving industries account for thirty percent of total production but only 14.3% of total employment; labor-intensive and capital-saving industries make up 70% of total production (T.C. Liu 1969:79). Ranis arrives at a similar conclusion, pointing to the significance of labor-using innovations in the transition from import substitution to export substitution. In Taiwan these innovations have occurred primarily in the textiles, electronics, and food-processing industries, with the use of labor being the most intensive in the electronics assembly industry (Ranis 1973:406). (In 1974 Taiwan exported approximately US$800 million dollars' worth of electronics products, manufactured by some 640 plants with a combined work force of 160,000 workers [*China Post*, 1 October 1974].) Ranis writes:

> According to the general manager of one major electronics firm, the amount of labor used in assembling one television set in a Taiwanese plant is fifty percent greater than that in a plant of the parent company in the United States. In fact, most of the electronics firms interviewed were making efforts in one way or another to introduce labor-intensive methods. While the capital-labor relations in this industry have been generally rising through time, the largest electronics factory in Taiwan has experienced an increase of capital by nine times and an increase of employment by sixteen times between 1965 and 1969... Many of the managers interviewed pointed out that the wage bill was lower in spite of the substantially larger relative volume of employment. (1973:407).

These statements confirm the conclusions of a study of Taiwan's labor supply, which found that real wages have not kept pace with increases in labor productivity. From 1953 to 1973 average labor productivity increased at nearly eight percent a year while real wages grew by only four percent (Hou and Hsu 1976:37). The authors of the study note that "the disparity of the growth rates between real wage and labor productivity has benefited both domestic producers (through higher profits) and foreign users (through lower prices). Through domestic producers, it has helped domestic capital formation; and through foreign users, it has helped export expansion" (Hou and Hsu 1976:37).

They also add that the gap of the growth rates between real wage and labor productivity has been growing steadily.

Even as the number of unemployed persons with a senior high school level of education or higher has been increasing, there remains a demand for and a shortage of unskilled female labor "of the age group 15–24 with an educational background of primary school" (Hou and Hus 1976:39). But at the same time that the government is concerned to keep wages low enough to be competitive, the extension of compulsory education to nine years, the greater availability of education, and the prestige that high education attainment brings all motivate young people (including women) to remain in school longer. This results in greater frustration if they are forced to accept factory employment because of intensification of the qualification spiral for office jobs. It is conceivable that many of these women would be more receptive to factory work if the wages were higher, but apparently this is an incentive the government cannot easily afford.

The government is not unaware of the disparity that exists between what the educational system produces and what the economy needs. A government report notes that due to a lack of "harmonization with education programs, manpower supply has constituted a bottleneck of increasing gravity in economic development" (Economic Planning Council 1974a:22). Since the population of those between fifteen and twenty-one is sure to increase in the coming years, the same report recommends that "the annual enrollment into senior middle schools... be limited to some 75,000. This limitation is in accordance with vacancies in the universities and colleges... A rigid examination system will be adopted and those failing to pass... will be advised to transfer to vocational schools"(Economic Planning Council 1974a:229–30). According to a Ministry of Education survey, unemployment rates as of December 1973 were high for graduates whose educational background went beyond middle school: fourteen percent for college graduates, thirty-three percent for those from vocational colleges (with five percent for those who completed senior vocational schools, nine percent for senior high school graduates, and three percent for junior high school graduates) (Hou and Hsu 1976:13).

As indicated above, however, unskilled women who have not proceeded beyond primary school are still much in demand in the job market. In the early part of 1974, one newspaper in Taiwan reported, for instance, that there were 367,000 factory positions waiting to be filled, sixty percent of which were meant for women (*Chung Kuo Shih Pao,* 17 April 1974). Using figures from an employment guidance center the same article stated that while there were more male job-seekers than female applicants, employers were more in need of women workers, and in terms of age those between sixteen and nineteen were most successful (*Chung Kuo Shih Pao,* 17 April 1974).

To broaden the picture the following section provides a sketch of Taiwan's labor force and the place of women within it. (See Tables 8, 9, 10.) The total population of Taiwan was computed at 15,435,00 in July 1973, and those fifteen years and older were estimated to number 9,002,000, or 58.32% of the population (Taiwan Provincial Labor Force Survey and Research Institute 1973b:11). Those in the labor force (fifteen years and older) number 5,539,000 (Taiwan Provincial Force Survey and Research Institute 1973b:11), and overall, the rate of male labor force participation declined between 1964 and 1967 (from seventy-six percent to seventy-two percent), rose in 1968 to eighty percent and declined steadily to seventy-seven percent in 1973. The rate of female labor force participation has increased from thirty-two percent in 1967 to thirty-five percent in 1972, reaching a rate of forty-two percent in 1973 (Hou and Hsu 1976:7). The proportion of the employed population working in the agricultural sector declined from 42.3% in 1968 to 35.9% in 1971; during the same period the proportion of those working in industry rose from 26.6% to 31.1% (Economic Planning Council 1974a:15).

Table 8.   Labor Force Status by Age and Sex, Taiwan
(July 1973) (In 1000s)
(Taiwan Provincial Labor Force Survey and
Research Institute 1973b:22)

Age	Persons Fifteen and Over	Fully Employed	Under Employed	Unemployed	Not In Labor Force
Male					
15–19	998	419	2	18	487
20–24	447	343	2	12	90
25–29	417	398	4	2	13
30–34	463	453	5	2	3
Female					
15–19	887	488	1	22	377
20–24	694	380	1	7	306
25–29	414	180	1	1	232
30–34	465	217	1	0	247

Female workers are predominant in the manufacturing sector and particularly in the food-processing industry, in textile and garment factories, and in the electronics industry, where they constitute 59.43%, 79.01% and 65.57% of direct production workers, respectively (Taiwan Provincial Labor Force Survey and Research Institute 1973a:17). (See Tables 11a and 11b.) As of July 1973 the average monthly wages of direct production workers were as follows: food-processing, NT$1,868, textile products NT$2,116, apparel NT$1,812, and electrical equipment NT$2,129 (Taiwan Provincial Labor

Table 9. Labor Force Status by Educational Level and Sex,
Taiwan (In 1000s)
(Taiwan Provincial Labor Force Survey and
Research Institute 1973b:24)

Educational Level	Persons Fifteen and Over	Fully Employed	Under Employed	Unemployed	Not In Labor Force
Male					
Illiterate	546	336	4	1	205
Primary	1900	1762	19	8	110
Junior High	625	440	3	8	175
Junior Vocational	100	93	–	1	6
Senior High	341	115	1	6	180
Senior Vocational	424	267	2	13	143
Junior College, University	330	214	0	6	110
Female					
Illiterate	1436	479	6	1	950
Primary	1804	943	3	7	851
Junior High	427	173	1	5	248
Junior Vocational	56	29	0	–	26
Senior High	179	49	1	1	129
Senior Vocational	278	139	2	12	126
Junior College, University	157	72	1	5	80

Table 10. Potential Labor Force by Reason and Age, Taiwan
(July 1973) (In 1000s)
(Taiwan Provincial Labor Force Survey and
Research Institute 1973b:39)

Reason	Total*		15–19		20–24		25–29		30–34		35–39	
	M	F	M	F	M	F	M	F	M	F	M	F
Busy with Housework	1	1589	0	49	0	233	0	244	1	241	0	220
Attending School	540	335	454	294	75	39	7	2	1	1	1	0
Intend to Work but not Seek for	15	31	6	17	2	9	0	2	0	1	0	1
No Intention to Work	20	49	5	2	1	10	0	2	0	1	0	2
Recent Illness/Injury	33	15	4	2	2	2	2	1	0	1	2	3
Others	29	22	10	7	8	9	1	2	0	0	1	0

M = Male
F = Female

*Figures for age groups do not add up to total because some age groups have been omitted.

Table 11a. Employed Persons by Industry, Division, and Age, Taiwan (July 1973) (In 1000s)
(Taiwan Provincial Labor Force Survey and Research Institute 1973b:26)

Industry	Total*		15–19		20–24		25–29		30–34		35–39	
	M	F	M	F	M	F	M	F	M	F	M	F
Agriculture, Foresty, Fishery Livestock Production, Hunting	1056	675	116	77	73	66	87	51	127	85	149	114
Mining and Quarrying	50	7	2	-	1	1	2	1	5	-	10	2
Manufacturing	846	597	229	268	128	154	120	35	106	46	78	38
Construction	267	19	38	2	38	6	36	3	41	3	40	3
Commerce	444	292	44	43	36	51	54	34	61	46	64	45
Transport, Storage, Communication	264	36	10	9	25	11	37	6	45	1	43	5
Finance, Insurance, Real Estate Business, Service	76	42	8	8	7	18	13	8	10	3	8	2
Community, Social and Personal Service	438	316	45	80	36	74	48	44	54	34	47	28
Gas, Electricity and Water	34	3	1	1	2	2	6	-	8	-	8	-

M = Male
F = Female

*Figures for age groups do not add up to total because some age groups have been deleted

Table 11b. Employed Persons by Occupation, Group and Age (July 1973) (In 1000s) (Taiwan Provincial Labor Force Survey and Research Institute 1973b: 27)

Occupation	Total*		15–19		20–24		25–29		30–34		35–39	
	M	F	M	F	M	F	M	F	M	F	M	F
Professional, Technical and Related Workers	158	81	5	7	13	19	28	18	27	11	25	8
Administrative, Executive, and Managerial Workers	117	8	-	-	1	8	8	-	20	2	20	3
Clerical Workers	227	203	7	41	25	97	32	29	35	13	29	12
Sales Workers	418	256	36	32	37	37	59	32	61	44	59	42
Service Workers	149	146	11	50	9	25	11	13	13	15	16	13
Farm, Forestry, Livestock Production, Fishing and Hunting	1038	673	114	77	72	63	86	51	128	85	146	144
Workers in Production, Operatives of Transport Equipment and Laborers not Classified Elsewhere	1319	622	318	281	188	140	177	38	175	49	151	45

M = Male
F = Female

*Figures for age groups do not add up to total because some age groups have been deleted.

Force Survey and Research Institute 1973a:3).[2] In comparison the average monthly earnings of salaried workers during the same period were: food-processing NT$3,973, textile NT$4,265, apparel NT$3,627, and electrical equipment NT$4,221.

The Monthly Bulletin of Labor Statistics provides data on the average monthly earnings of personnel in various industries. In the manufacturing sector, as of December 1972, the monthly earnings of a female worker averaged NT$1,425 (NT$2,106 for female staff worker) while a male worker earned an average of NT$2,268 (NT$3,944 for male staff worker) (Directorate-General of Budget, Accounting and Statistics 1974:116–17). Beginning in 1973, however, these figures in the manufacturing sector were compiled irrespective of sex. Nonetheless, a perusal of the figures given for other sectors reveals that the wages of women in the worker category are always lower than men's wages in the worker category. There is no indication given as to differences in the types of jobs performed, and one would expect that differences would be greatest in the construction and mining sectors. Wages of female workers come closest to (but remain lower than) men's wages in the service sector (Directorate-General of Budget, Accounting, and Statistics 1974:116–17).

Tables 12a, 12b, 13a, and 13b supply information about the number of young people (unfortunately the numbers are not categorized by sex) who discontinued school and who may be assumed to enter the job market as unskilled workers or to become unpaid workers in family enterprises.[3]

The Economic Planning Council of Taiwan provides a comparable set of figures, and citing the increase in the number of youth in the population, it notes that the labor supply grew by approximately 180,000 persons annually between 1969 and 1972 (1974a:14). The Council estimates that during 1973–76 the number of those fifteen years and over will increase on an annual average of 324,000, with an increase of 179,800 persons in the labor force; in addition, it is expected that an annual average of 13,500 persons (9,900 male and 3,600 female) will be leaving the agricultural sector and seeking jobs elsewhere (1974a:228). Although the advantages (lower land prices, accessibility to rural surplus labor) to locating industries in the countryside are stressed by the government, the migration rates for young men and women to cities are high. (See Table 14.) As Speare points out, the similarity of rates in the 15–29 age group when many of the migrants are single indicates that both men and women are responding equally to changing economic conditions. Significant as the female rate of migration is for the 15–29 age group, when translated into actual experiences of mobility and freedom of movement, the rate represents even more dramatic evidence of the changes in women's lives.

The rural areas, however, are important in acting as a cushion when economic recession occurs, as was the case in the latter half of 1974. One study, for instance, found that sixty-four percent of laid-off workers returned to their homes in rural areas, in part to help with farming (thirty-two percent), and also

Table 12a.   Elementary School Graduates, Taiwan
(L.A. Chen 1976:3)

Year of Graduation	1972	1973	1974	1975	1976
Admitted Students (Enrolled Six Years Previous to Graduation)	418,903	428,441	426,167	425,880	416,666
Graduates	389,425	405,320	401,660	402,000	392,800
Drop-Outs	29,478	23,121	24,507	23,880	23,866
Students who Pursue Further Studies	326,438	341,542	354,145	353,760	345,664
Students who do not Pursue Further Studies	62,987	63,778	47,515	48,240	47,136

Table 12b.   Junior High School Graduates, Taiwan
(L.A. Chen 1976:4)

Year of Graduation	1972	1973	1974	1975	1976
Admitted Students	266,734	296,253	312,644	326,438	341,542
Graduates	241,428	248,017	290,804	305,000	319,479
Drop-Outs	25,306	21,074	21,840	21,438	22,063
Students who Pursue Further Studies	172,261	174,971	181,500	187,876	214,800
Students who do not Pursue Further Studies	69,167	73,046	108,500	117,124	104,679

Table 13a.   Ch'itung Li (Sanhsia) Elementary School Graduates

Year	Graduates	Number Who Continue in School	Number Who Seek Jobs
1970	157	72	85
1971	131	67	64
1972	157	94	63
1973	163	101	62
1974	179	117	62

Table 13b.   Sanhsia Lower Middle School Graduates

Year	Graduates	Number Who Continue in School	Number Who Seek Jobs	Others
1971	552	387	163	2
1972	603	407	195	1
1973	653	471	175	7
1974	718	551	156	11

Table 14.   Urban Migration Rates for Taiwanese
(Speare 1974:312)

Age Group	Male	Female
0–14	41.8%	40.7%
15–29	78.1%	75.0%
30–44	58.6%	46.4%
45–59	35.6%	33.2%
Over 60	21.2%	22.2%

because staying in the city was too costly (Wu 1976:13). As one (American) manager from Western Electronics pointed out, "'Most of our labor force is female, and they can always go back home [when production is reduced]'" (quoted in *China Post,* 3 November 1974).

Taiwan's reliance on exports and dependence on foreign trade make its economy especially vulnerable to fluctuations in the world market; later chapters will describe the impact of the 1974 recession on female workers. Here I give some figures to indicate the scale of lay-offs that took place during 1974 in the electronics sector. A spokesman from the TRW Electronic Components Company anticipated a thirty percent drop in the television market from 1974 to 1975, and his firm had laid off one third of its work force in 1974 (*China Post,* 3 November 1974). Two presidents of another television and electronics firm noted a comparable drop in sales volume and did not expect sales to pick up until the second half of 1975; the problem was also exacerbated by large stocks of products that had been piled up in warehouses in the United States (Wieman 1974:52). General Instruments in Taiwan laid off four percent of its 16,000 workers; Admiral cut production by fifteen percent in October of 1974 and laid off 1,300 (forty percent of its work force) workers, and Texas Instruments reduced its 3,700 work force by 1,000 persons (Wieman 1974:54). An American-owned television factory in Tam Shui eliminated its second shift, and while approximately 3,000 workers had been employed in the beginning of 1974 only 900 remained at the end of the year (personal communication). Compounding the difficulties laid-off workers faced, in the same year the government lifted price controls, and in the first six months of 1974 consumer prices rose by fifty-four percent and wholesale prices by fifty-five percent (Ho 1975:37). Most firms indicated that production cuts were temporary measures and that they expected to resume hiring in the following year, and indeed, by mid-1975 the Ministry of Economic Affairs reported that the electronics industry was operating at eighty percent of capacity, textiles at eighty percent, and garments at seventy percent (Industrial Development and Investment Center 1975). More importantly, by 1976 newspaper accounts calling attention to the shortage of factory workers reappeared.

At the same time, however, problems of a different nature have arisen. Increased costs of shipping have worked to Taiwan's disadvantage when products are destined for European and American markets (Wieman 1974:56). More recently the textiles industry in Taiwan has been threatened by a world-wide shift in demand from synthetics to cottons and woolens (M. Liu 1976:60). Taiwan, for example, exports thirty percent of its textile products to the United States, and consumer preferences for natural fabrics have resulted in difficulties for Taiwan's synthetic products sector which makes up eighty percent of its textile business (Ying 1977). Economic recovery has also been slowed by lower wage levels elsewhere (Korea, Philippines, Indonesia, Malaysia). Although textile products constituted thirty-one percent of Taiwan's exports in 1976, the light textile industry was singled out by the government as the "hardship industry" in an otherwise prosperous period (Ying 1977). From the other side, Taiwan's textile and garment industries have been blamed by the United States textile industry for the loss of some 145,000 American jobs in the past ten years (Perlmutter 1977). Figures from the United States textile industry show hourly wages to be US$0.74, US$0.38, US$0.42 for Hong Kong, Korea, and Taiwan, respectively, while in the United States, as of March 1977, the average hourly wage of the textile worker was US$3.85, lowest in the industrial sector (King 1977). Firms in Taiwan, then, have had to witness American workers' demands for more restrictions on import quotas on textiles and clothing. (In one rally in New York against low-wage foreign competition, participants included Chinese women, identified with their local union number and carrying placards in Chinese [Perlmutter 1977].)

For Taiwanese women, what mattered was that after 1975 factory jobs were once again plentiful, and informants' letters subsequent to 1975 invariably mention high work quotas and frequent overtime. A 1976 survey by the North Taiwan Job Placement Center showed that factories in Taipei, Taoyuan, and Hsinchu counties were in need of an additional 70,000 women (*The China News*, 3 May 1976), and reports of such shortages were accompanied by articles denouncing the unethical tactics to which some firms resort in recruiting and retaining their employees (see chapter 5). Another recent newspaper article described one plan under consideration by the government to alleviate this shortage, namely, "that [junior high school girls] be permitted to leave school one or two months ahead of schedule [prior to summer vacation] so they can be recruited earlier" (*The China News*, 23 April 1976).

The same newspaper account also stated that the government intends to "enlist the help of the mass communication media for a persuasive drive aiming at attracting young women to the factories," and to encourage the manufacturing sector to adopt the following measures: "raise pay and improve working conditions, set up new plants in rural areas to better absorb the surplus labor in the farm sector; [and] make efforts to win the loyalty of workers" (*The*

China News, 23 April 1976). This is not the first time that the government has implored industry to take such steps, and the effectiveness of such exhortations seems doubtful. A flurry of newspaper editorials on Labor Day in 1974, for example, all made the same recommendations: to increase wages, improve welfare programs, and to encourage profit sharing (*The China Post*, 2 May 1974). More to the point, one editorial stressed the importance of "the laborers' awareness of their new status and new duties in the enterprises" (*Chung Kuo Shih Pao*, 1 May 1974). The government, of course, is keenly aware of the contribution of female workers to Taiwan's economic well-being, as this excerpt from a speech made by the Minister of the Interior shows:

> Women workers have played an essential role in the course of economic and social development in the Republic of China during the last decade. The rapid rate of economc growth has increased the demand for manpower. It is imperative, therefore, that good use be made of women in order to meet the labor requirement of firms and farms (*The China Post*, 17 September 1974).

It is much less certain, however, that women workers are themselves made conscious of their economic importance to their country's economy. If a positive "awareness of their new status" is to be fostered, women must first be convinced, in part through the actions and policies of their employers and supervisors, that they are indispensable and not merely easily replaceable units in a system. Moreover, they must be convinced (as they are not now) that they are valued by the larger society.

5

The Decision to Work: Where and Why

By the end of her stay in the village of Peihotien in the Taipei basin in the late 1950s, M. Wolf (1972) reports that entering factories had virtually become an automatic step for girls after primary school. With factory employment even more commonplace now many Taiwanese parents and their daughters do regard factory work as a predictable part of adolescence. But however natural factory work might appear to be, it is the outcome of decisions, no matter how casually or informally they are reached. And if we think in terms of the alternative activities that are available to girls of this age and background, there are a number of factors to bear in mind when considering why some daughters are sent to work and others are allowed to remain in school: (1) although "free" education has been extended through lower-middle school (i.e., entrance exams are no longer required to enter junior high school) it still entails fees too high for some families; (2) some families still hold the belief that it is useless to educate daughters; (3) sometimes daughters at this stage in their lives are perceived as being too young to make intelligent decisions; (4) the economic situation of a girl's family may make it necessary for her to work; and (5) sibling order may determine whether a daughter goes into a factory or whether she remains in school. (An elder daughter who contributes to the family may make it feasible for a younger daughter to continue her education, even while notions about education for girls remain unaltered.)

Economic need is the overriding concern and this is recognized by daughters. It would be inaccurate, however, to say that women are forced by their parents to take factory jobs. In fact it is a case where there are few alternatives open to young women whose families cannot afford to keep them in school beyond elementary or lower-middle school. In this context it is virtually inconceivable that a daughter remain idle at home.

One clear-cut pattern emerging from the data is that sons are far more likely to be given the chance to advance to middle school than are daughters, and a growing number of women admit that they work in factories in order to continue their education. In most instances women resume their schooling only after working for a year in order to save a sufficient amount for tuition.

> Kao is from central Taiwan and has been working at Western Electronics for three years. Because there are few factories in her home area, her coming north after lower-middle school was taken matter-of-factly by her parents. Even though she sent remittances home each month she was able to save enough during her first year and began high school in her second year. "If my parents had known that I wanted to work in order to continue with school, they wouldn't have allowed me to come north. They would object because they didn't want me to study anymore. So when I came here I told them it was because there are more and better-paying jobs in the north, and only later, after I started school, did I write home and tell them so. By then there wasn't too much they could do about it. I would prefer to be living at home, but there are only a few small garment factories nearby, and I would have no time for school [because of the longer hours]."

As her comments illustrate, women living at home are more restricted in their choices. Liu only finished primary school and continues to believe that "if there were money available, everyone would wish to stay in school." Her younger sister had completed lower-middle school but high school was out of the question for financial reasons. When Liu herself considered returning to school on a part-time basis and paying for the fees from her earnings, her mother expressed opposition and the matter was dropped.

From a family's point of view factory employment for a daughter springs from economic necessity, but some women have translated economic obligation into an opportunity to see the world outside.

> Chen's parents were initially opposed to the idea of their youngest child being so far from home (Chiayi in the south), but her father eventually consented to her coming to Western Electronics. "I worked for one year in Tainan and then stayed home for about half a year, taking sewing lessons. At home one depends on one's parents for everything, and there is a lot one can't learn at home. My mother predicted that I wouldn't be able to take it for very long up here by myself but I wanted to prove that I could manage on my own." Chen intends to return to Chiayi eventually but said, "I just want to acquire more experience and see more of the north; the more one sees, the better." After a few months at Western Electronics she resumed dress-making lessons in her spare time, explaining that even though she had not finished lower-middle school she did not think that it was a practical thing to do since three years are such a long time. "I'm not sure how much difference it will make as far as finding a better job is concerned, but dress-making skills would be more useful."

The attraction of the world outside is such that young women from the south, who are expected to do a substantial portion of farmwork, are quite willing to turn over a sizable amount of their earnings to their families so that other agricultural laborers might be hired to take their places. How these women fare away from home is discussed in the following chapters.

Entry into the industrial labor force has therefore become a fairly predictable and automatic step for many young women in lower- and lower-middle class families in Taiwan. Women, however, interpret this common experience in different ways and their comments quoted above convey some sense of this variation. There are daughters who understand their jobs primarily in terms of fulfilling family obligations and whose expectations from their jobs and wages are correspondingly modest. There are others who simply accept their economic responsibility to their families and turn their attention to the social opportunities and excitement to be found outside. Working-students perhaps have the clearest sense of purpose of all factory women but they exhibit markedly ambivalent attitudes about their work: at the same time that they claim to value self-reliance, they also wish that they did not have to manage their education on their own. Their goals make their stay in the factory more palatable, but making the adjustment in the interim comes hardest for them.

In this section I present alternatives to factory work that are open to women with limited education and discuss the types of considerations that enter into a decision when women choose factory employment over other occupations.

There are three levels at which decisions must be made, and the choice of a factory represents an accommodation of various interests and priorities. At the broadest level parents and daughters must select a particular line of work (factory work versus other occupations). With that resolved it becomes a matter of choosing one type of industry over another and deciding on a particular firm.

But for women who belong to farm families the possibility of factory employment may not even arise if their labor is required for agricultural production. Unlike women in the north, those in the central and southern portions of Taiwan customarily take part in agricultural work. Stereotypes abound concerning the division of labor in the south, and for these reasons women consistently express a preference for marrying in the north.[1] The following comment is representative of sentiments widely shared by women in the north:

> I hear that many girls in the south leave home without their parents' permission. I can't say I blame them since a woman's life is so much more 'bitter' there. Not only does she have to work in the fields and labor in the sun for hours, but she has to cook for other field hands as well.

Since there are in fact relatively few industrial centers in the central and southern regions (with the exception of the export processing zones) women who take up an occupation other than farming are generally required to leave home. As many of them say, "If a girl remains home she would have to help in the fields."

It is easy to understand, therefore, why the appeal of factory work is greatest for women from farm families in the south. But these same women are also the most restricted in their ability to take up factory jobs. First, they may be needed at home to provide additional agricultural labor, and second, because a factory job usually demands that a woman leave home, her family may be even more reluctant to acquiesce to factory employment.

It is at this level, where an occupation must be selected, that parents are insistent about having daughters abide by their decision (if the subject comes up for discussion at all). Liu Su-fong, for instance, had held a number of jobs during the nine years she had been working. When, in her view, layoffs at her factory were imminent she considered taking up barbering, and had asked to apprentice with a Liu woman who runs a small "shop" (in her living room) in Ch'inan. She regarded barbering as a skill that would offer her some independence, but her idea met with strong opposition from her entire family, and she subsequently abandoned her plans. Chuang, a high-school graduate, said, "I always talk [job changes] over with my parents first. They are not likely to object to a change such as this [she was in another electronics firm prior to her job at Western Electronics], but they would object if I were to enter a working environment that is too complex, such as a restaurant."

Factories, more than other work-settings (restaurants, shops, buses), are perceived by parents as offering some measure of supervision. The semblance of order created by rules and regulations in the factory is also viewed positively by women themselves. In addition, they have other reasons for not entering other occupations open to women of their backgrounds. These include being a maid, a waitress, a busgirl, a salesgirl, and other service-related jobs.

Being a maid is probably the only occupation which, while "respectable," is lower in status than that of a factory worker. Factory women say that the position of being a maid is one level lower than that of a factory employee; "to be a maid sounds very bad." One woman gives this assessment of the present situation: "today factories are everywhere and there are so many factory women that working in a factory has become very commonplace and quite acceptable for a woman." While factory workers are expected to listen to their supervisors and have relatively little say about their duties, the work of a maid is described as even more "bitter" and demanding. A maid's work is more "bitter" because her movements are even more restricted than those of a factory employee, and she is continually at someone's beck-and-call. Employers (specifically wives) are said or assumed to be condescending, and many women are unwilling to tolerate this. The wages a maid earns are not appreciably higher than those of a factory woman (particularly those in the textile/garment industry) and working hours are also longer for a maid. As one factory worker put it:

> Even if your employer wanted something late at night, you would have to get it for him. Whereas in a factory when you get off work, the time is your own and you have more freedom. If you work as a maid and happen to have a good employer, then it might be all right, but otherwise it amounts to selling your whole self.

One factory worker who had once been a maid quit because she found it too uncomfortable to be left alone at home with the head of the household when his wife was out. One factory woman describes the situation this way: "Some factories will not hire married women, so it happens that young unmarried women are precisely suited for such jobs. Now most maids are middle-aged women or young aboriginal women from poorer areas who don't mind working so hard."[2]

The working hours of waitresses and salesgirls are also long and irregular; a woman who works in a shop or restaurant has a different schedule from most of her friends and has little free time for herself. These are also described as "bitter" jobs with long periods of standing and frequent overtime. It will become apparent that women do not choose a particular occupation solely on the basis of high wages. Most women are aware that shopgirls and waitresses (with commissions and tips) earn a good deal more than they are able to in a factory, but a more important consideration is that those jobs require that a woman deal with the public, and it is this that most factory women prefer to avoid. As one factory woman explained, "the best part about working in a factory is that one does not need deal with strangers: in fact you don't need to spend much time or expend much effort in dealing with people at all. Here, once your work is done, that's all there is to it. This kind of work is simpler." The following comes from another factory employee:

> Even though my family isn't very well off I would rather not work as a shopgirl. Most people regard salesgirls the way I do—it's work no one really wants to do. It is only women from the south, eager to become more fashionable and to live in the city, who might be interested, but then their reputation isn't as good.

One woman who had worked in a department store said, "unless a person has actually worked as a salesgirl, she's not likely to know what a woman must put up with. A person has to deal with all sorts of people, and many customers can be very aggravating."

The same type of comments are repeated in reference to women employed as busgirls: "a person can never tell what kinds of people she will run into in such jobs. Such situations are too complex. One so often sees passengers who are rowdy and who argue with the busgirl, refuse to pay the fare, and who make trouble. Surely earning a bit more money isn't worth going through that every day." One former busgirl explains why the turnover rate among busgirls is so high:

> Most girls have no idea what the job actually involves. There are constant arguments with either the driver or the passengers. You have only two days off a month but you are never sure when they will be, and although the pay is much higher than what I'm now earning [in the factory], girls who are in such work have a reputation of being loose in the way they behave. It is for this reason that many people consider it a low-prestige job.

Women do distinguish, however, between different lines of buses, and some factory women express interest in applying for positions with bus companies that have long-distance routes and that provide more "high-class" transportation for their passengers. Yet because a high-school diploma is generally required for such positions (and for that of a train attendant, which is even more desirable), many women are not eligible.

Factory workers express an even stronger dislike for the environment in which waitresses work, an atmosphere invariably described as complex and disorderly, qualities that characterize urban public places. It is believed that once a woman goes to work in a restaurant, it becomes very easy for her to learn bad ways, and people assert that this is the most common route to prostitution. In the eyes of some women being a waitress in some establishments is a short step away from prostitution: "Male customers are often rude, make jokes at your expense, and make improper advances. It's very hard to take, but what else can you do if you don't want to offend them." One factory worker mentioned two former roommates who went to work in a Taipei restaurant: "the kinds of people a girl encounters in such places aren't good people. Just like a salesgirl, being a waitress may look all right on the surface, but underneath the situation is actually very disorderly. In restaurants there are men who tease or take advantage of the girls." The image many factory workers hold of waitresses runs along the following lines: "Women who are waitresses don't really care about what happens to them: they don't have much self-respect. They're on easy terms with men and act improperly. Younger women, especially, are easily deceived and will pick up bad habits very quickly if they remain in such jobs." One woman went further and added: "there's so many jobs: why would a girl choose that kind of work? One may earn less and the work may be harder, but at least one will live a happier life."

If factory workers do give thought to other employment possibilities, they may give more consideration to those of hairdressers and dressmakers than those named above. Here, choice is primarily a matter of personal interest. Working in a beauty salon entails long hours and prolonged standing, and using chemical solutions that some women claim are harmful to the skin. Dressmaking, on the other hand, requires months of sewing lessons. In both cases, however, women believe that they would be acquiring a skill, and even though some factory workers say they have no interest in either field, they do appreciate the advantages of having a skill to offer. Women who work in garment factories are well aware that the tasks they perform constitute only one part of the many steps that comprise the entire manufacturing process. Although experienced workers earn more than those less experienced (since they are paid by the piece), women do not consider that such experience gives them skills in any independent sense. One woman, for instance, reasoned that sewing lessons are more practical and worthwhile than completing middle-school since she would be earning money while others are still in school; moreover, there is no assurance that middle-school graduates will be able to find white-collar positions. In this line of work women distinguish between merely "adding labor" and using skill; "in a garment factory all you ever learn to do is to put clothes together but not how to cut. There's no chance of getting ahead because you're not learning any particular skill." Towards the end of 1974 when layoffs of workers were becoming more frequent, some garment workers remarked upon another advantage dressmakers enjoy: "they don't need to worry about being laid off or not being able to find another job."

The same can be said of hairdressers. Women begin by performing very limited and simple tasks and receive minimal wages during this "apprenticeship" period, eventually progressing to more advanced and time-consuming tasks. As with dressmakers, it is not surprising to find two or three women (especially in the countryside) who rent their own shop and manage their own business, taking on additional workers as customers increase.

One other line of work that factory workers are likely to consider seriously involves operating the large knitting machines that are now a familiar sight in the "living rooms" of houses in Taiwan's villages and towns. It is most often a family enterprise, with one or two members of the family renting the machines and receiving supplies on a contractual basis. Young men are also employed for such work, but women are drawn not only from neighboring families but also from further points in the south. Because workers are paid by piece and may work for virtually as many hours as they wish, wages can be very high, and this type of work appeals to women who can tolerate the schedule and long periods of standing. Wages are low initially as women learn how to operate the machines, but they think of their training as endowing them with a skill that they are able to take with them.[3] Some women consider the working environment in such family businesses too confining and isolated, while those who operate the machines declare that they prefer the more personalized and informal atmosphere the home setting provides.

Having discussed why factory work is in some ways preferable to a number of other occupations, something should be said about the factors that enter into the choice of a particular factory. At this level of decision-making, parents are likely to exert their authority if the decision involves a substantial wage differential and if it involves the possibility of living away from home.

The idea of having young daughters working outside and perhaps some distance from home was a major cause for concern on the part of parents some years ago (M. Wolf 1972). Such reluctance has lessened in recent years, but this is not to say that parents are never opposed to their daughters leaving home. Once the decision to work has been made, there may be some attempt to reduce the impact of the factors that generated opposition in the first place, perhaps by selecting a factory close to home. (I discuss this more fully in the next chapter.)

One category of women not likely to be allowed to work far from home are those who are only daughters (or the only remaining daughter at home) and where there are no daughters-in-law at home. As one mother said, "having one daughter living outside is enough; I want [my younger daughter] to stay home." Young women are themselves sometimes reluctant to leave home if it means that no one would be left at home to help their mothers or provide them with some companionship, and a number of workers at Western Electronics justified their dormitory residence by assuring me that they had sisters-in-law at home.

Not surprisingly, the younger a daughter is the larger her parents' say will be in the selection of a firm. Parents are not always well-informed about different companies but they are more knowledgeable than a fourteen year old, and it matters little that this information may not be of a first-hand nature. Looking back to their first jobs, women had this to say:

> I went to [company X] after elementary school because my family had some relatives who were working there, and since I was so young, they felt it was better for me to be with relatives.

> Going to [company Y] was my father's idea; being just out of primary school I really didn't have many choices anyway, and so I just went there.

> When I finished elementary school there weren't many factories in this area, and it was decided by my mother that I should go to the fish-net factory because it was one of the larger ones and because there were other girls from the village working there. Being so young I had no idea where I wanted to be, and so I just went to work there. At that age [thirteen] a person really doesn't know anything, and even for the next few years, even though I knew the pay was low, I was too young to do anything about it and so just stayed on.

While most parents have never seen the inside of a factory, they are aware that one can earn more working in a garment factory than in an electronics factory; they know which companies provide transportation, and know which firms tend to have frequent overtime, etc. Such information is easily obtained from other parents and simply from observing the comings and goings of factory girls in the community.

Women's own opinions about the merits of different firms take into account the products factories manufacture, because these often establish relatively inflexible constraints to which women must accommodate themselves. (I should note here that virtually all my informants were employed in the textile, garment, and electronics industries.)

Women recognize that it is virtually impossible to have jobs that entail light tasks and that bring high wages as well, and they are realistic in their expectations: "A person can always find a job that pays more, but the work is bound to be more 'bitter' too." From the experience of friends and from first-hand knowledge women are able to weigh the advantages and disadvantages of various industries. Textile and garment factories, as a rule, offer higher wages than electronics factories (roughly NT$3,000 to NT$4,000 in the former compared to NT$1,500 to NT$2,500 in the latter).

A young woman who enters a garment factory without previous experience, of course, will not attain this level until she acquires some expertise in sewing. Generally, very young women (those between thirteen and fifteen) are assigned to miscellaneous tasks for a period of six months to a year, during which they are paid a straight monthly salary. When a woman is sufficiently familiar with the work, she is then assigned to a machine, and thereafter her wages are calculated according to the number of pieces she completes.

Less attractive, however, are certain kinds of working conditions found in most textile and garment factories. Hours are longer (ten per day during busy periods are not uncommon); overtime is more frequent; there are fewer days off, and these often come at irregular intervals. Such work is also described as being less stable when compared to electronics firms. Depending on a company's volume of business, women in garment industries may be expected to work overtime for many consecutive days, or may not be called in for work at all. Women in these firms complain of being overworked during rush periods and being idle at home during slack periods. There is a set scale of wages according to which workers are paid during slow periods, but the amount is substantially less than they would normally earn. For these reasons women argue (if they happen to be in electronic or other factories) or concede (if they are employed in garment factories) that higher wages in theory do not always assure a worker of a guaranteed, consistently higher paycheck each month.

Women employed in electronics companies often complain about the "bitter" quality of their own work, but they are quick to point out that they fare better in some respects than their counterparts in garment and textile factories. The working environment typical of the latter is said to be worse because poor ventilation frequently results in air that is heavy with lint and cotton dust, which in turn may lead to respiratory problems. (Residents in Ch'inan prescribe pig's blood for cleansing the lungs of such lint and dust.) Moreover, operators of textile machinery often must stand for the better part of their work-day. These occupations are considered more arduous and more demanding also because many textile plants are in operation twenty-four hours a day, and one common pattern has workers alternate on a weekly basis, working the day-shift for one week, the evening-shift the subsequent week, and the third shift the following week.

As might be expected, women in electronics factories claim that, compared to textile or garment factories, their work is lighter and that they enjoy shorter and more regular hours, and that these compensate for their lower wages. On the other side, women in textile or garment firms have much to say about the occupational hazards associated with the electronics industry, and their concerns are not totally unjustified. Most of their worries center around the fumes that soldering produces, and the harm the fumes can cause was well publicized several years ago when the deaths of several female workers were attributed to such work-related hazards. These deaths instigated several investigations of factories conducted by governmental agencies and stricter regulations concerning safety. While defective equipment or faulty facilities were presumably corrected, not all women are convinced of this. Newly hired workers in electronics firms commonly voice their dread of being assigned to a soldering position, while those who in fact work in such positions rationalize that it is harmful only if undertaken for long periods. There are others, however, who, if they are unsuccessful in obtaining another assignment, will go to another factory. As one of them explained:

> I'm not willing to do soldering, even if it does mean more money. [Some factories offer a $100 monthly bonus as inducement.] It's the same as giving my life to the company. [She then mentioned a recent death reputed to have been caused by soldering fumes.] There are many girls who are afraid of the same thing, but newspapers generally don't print such stories anymore, probably at the request of firms because they know that no one would work for them.

Work that involves the use of microscopic equipment (for assembling computer parts and watches, for instance) is considered cleaner than work in other electronics factories. The air is said to be far better, and there are no unpleasant odors. Its attraction, however, is reduced by the belief that such work is harmful to one's eyes, and it is a particularly tenacious and wide-spread notion that leads to turnover problems. Women, of course, make gradations in terms of preferences in the tasks they are assigned to perform in electronics factories. If one is fortunate enough not to be placed in soldering or on an assembly line (with a moving belt), women state that a job in an electronics factory can indeed be lighter and cleaner than other factory jobs, because "a person just sits all day."

Shorter hours and more regular (albeit lower) wages, however, are not sufficiently appealing to some women, who are deterred by what they consider to be the "bitter" aspects of electronics plants. In addition to the possibly harmful chemicals in such a factory these women claim that it is difficult to become accustomed to a moving line: "such a worker has no freedom; she cannot walk around, read, eat, or rest since she's always tied to the line."

The number and regularity of working hours matter not only because of wages and reasons having to do with physical stamina, but they are important to those women whose primary incentive in taking up factory work is to earn money for their school fees. For most of these women the longer hours and frequent overtime demanded by textile or garment factories make jobs in those companies impractical. Working-students prefer electronics factories because the work is thought to be less taxing; as one of them said, "work in electronics factories cannot really be described as 'bitter.' Besides, if a person wants to attend school, she must find a job that is relatively light." From another worker: "For most of us working-students who came not for the job but for school, our choice in jobs is limited by considerations of time and physical energy."

I now consider the question of where women work from the perspective of employers, and describe their attempts to attract workers.

From speaking with factory women, one might conclude that the majority of them obtain their jobs through "introductions." These "introductions" are highly informal and may mean no more than having a friend already in the factory who is willing, at most, to accompany a newcomer to the personnel office. (Such an impression is not without foundation: one survey of industrial labor concludes that the labor market is still highly personalized in Taiwan; fifty-four percent of clerical workers found their jobs by way of relatives or friends, and the figures for service workers and production workers are forty-nine percent and sixty-four percent, respectively. Only 2.3% of all employed persons located jobs through government employment services and 1.7% through private employment services [Hou and Hsu 1976:31].) Factories, of course, do rely heavily on such personal ties as a source of new employees, and the practice of rewarding an employee who brings her friend(s) with a bonus (anywhere from NT$50 to NT$200 on the condition that the new recruit stay for a stipulated period) is not unusual. Given the labor shortage management must also devise other techniques to insure a steady labor supply. Obviously, the needs of a firm such as Western Electronics are far greater than small enterprises, and it must resort to more systematic and formalized methods of recruitment.

To take the simpler enterprises first: the men and women who operate knitting machines in their homes throughout Sanhsia, for instance, either live in the immediate area or come through the introductions of friends and relatives. Should additional workers be required, word of mouth suffices, with the network extending as far as the home areas of currently employed workers. When a tea-processing plant in Ch'inan began its operations five years ago, the owner deliberately chose to recruit his workers from two districts in the south which he knew to be isolated and virtually without factories. Since the jobs are available on a seasonal basis, the prospect of finding steady workers from the north or immediate vicinity was slim (since they could locate more permanent positions), and to make the job more attractive the factory offered (in 1974) the relatively high wage of approximately NT$100 per day (for twelve hours of work a day). In the beginning recruitment was a house-to-house procedure, and at present, although only a few of the fifty or so women who come north in the spring are actually related, they all come through the introduction of another woman, with the latter receiving a bonus of NT$200 for each new worker she brings. At New Year's the company sends train fare for those who intend to make the trip, and at the end of the work period the company provides buses for the journey home. Just prior to the fall season the manager contacts the most experienced woman and tells her how many workers are needed, and she then informs women in the area. Other tea-processing firms in the area occasionally approach the Ch'inan company for additional workers, but they too rely primarily on their own contacts in the south.[4]

Further down the road from the tea factory, about a ten-minute bus-ride away, is a Chinese-owned electronics factory, a subsidiary of one of the largest Chinese firms on the island. This plant, which I have named Advance Electronics, employs approximately 600 women. As the breakdown by place of origin indicates (see Table 15), over one-half of the women are from Taipei county. Recruitment at this factory proceeds through several channels: newspaper advertisements, dispatching company representatives to local lower-middle schools and further south to rural areas where, in addition to school counselors, company representatives meet with local administrators or any other influential person with whom they share a special relation (*kuan-hsi*). According to the personnel manager no money is exchanged for this service (more on this below) although, he added, "some companies have been known to do this."

Table 15.   Place of Origin of Female Production Workers at Advance Electronics (April 1974)

Taipei	31	Nantou county	9
Taichung city	3	Changhua county	10
Keelung city	7	Yuenlin county	34
Kaohsiung city	3	Chiayi county	54
Taipei county	332	Tainan county	9
Ilan county	10	Kaohsiung county	4
Taoyuan county	23	Pingtung county	9
Hsinchu county	7	Hualien	11
Miaoli county	35	Taitung	13
Taichung county	5	Kinmen and Matsu	3

Virtually all parts of Taiwan are represented in the employees of a factory the size of Western Electronics. These workers come in response to posters, newspaper advertisements (and receive reimbursements for their travel costs), and are sent to the factory by government-run employment centers. Drawing heavily from middle school graduates for its workers, Western Electronics' recruiting schedule begins in earnest in April, when company representatives begin their forays into selected areas and pay their annual visits to school counselors, principals, and teachers: "It is important not to let one's connections get cold." Needs for the coming year are discussed with school administrators, and then information about the company (wages, accommodations, fringe benefits) is presented to the students through pamphlets, slides, and short talks. Western Electronics enjoys an advantage in that its name and products are well known and familiar and they help in creating a lasting impression. In May Western Electronics sends buses to schools in its immediate vicinity (Taoyuan) to bring students to the factory for a tour of the plants and dormitories. This is also the time when many girls are registered at the personnel office, although the office continues to be swamped with new workers throughout the month of June. The latest group to arrive (in July) are often those women who, having failed high school entrance (or junior college) examinations, decide to enter a factory and perhaps to make another attempt in the following year.

Western Electronics focuses its recruiting efforts on four areas in particular: Nantou, Ilan, Hualien, and Yuenlin counties. As the personnel manager explained, these are not especially prosperous areas and few factories are located there. Further south the export processing zones draw off many women, and unless Western Electronics is able to offer exceptional benefits women are more likely to work closer to home (especially if it happens to be a first job). Less attention is directed to the Taitung area in the east; to begin with, its population is smaller, transportation to Taoyuan is less convenient, and besides there are fewer schools. As for Taipei there already exist many factories competing for labor; Taipei residents, moreover, are accustomed to a somewhat higher standard of living, and are therefore not as willing to settle for a lower wage. Women from the four counties mentioned above are believed to have a higher capacity for enduring hardship (to "eat bitterness"). As one personnel manager told me, "If the company environment and the dormitory facilities are better than what they know at home, these girls would be very willing to stay."

Schools are an obvious and logical place to seek potential workers, but there is another reason why this strategy makes sense to employers, one that is particularly relevant with regard to unskilled male employees. The third shift at Western Electronics, for instance, comprised entirely of young men, has the highest turnover rate and absenteeism (ten percent is the weekly average) of all three shifts. But this shift is also plagued by more serious difficulties: materials and supplies are stolen with regularity; disciplinary problems are greater in number (smoking and eating on the job, throwing materials, etc.), and workers and occasionally supervisors are harrassed by young employees who belong to gangs (with names such as "Black Dragons," or "South Gate"). Gang members will "ask" others to do their work for them, will "ask" for "loans," threatening to "fix" those who do not comply. To eliminate some of these problems Western Electronics has been reducing the number of non-students and replacing them with students. These young men, who will attend a nearby high school, are accompanied to the factory by one of their teachers who continues to supervise their behavior, and any disruption they cause at work jeopardizes their position in school as well. (In July 1974, just under forty percent of the male workers on the third shift came to the company under such an arrangement.)

Conversations with personnel managers invariably begin with references to the current labor shortage (late 1974 was an exception), a problem exacerbated by high labor turnover. (According to one study turnover is highest in the manufacturing sector, where thirty percent of total employed persons stayed on their jobs for less than twelve months [Hou and Hsu 1976:20].) As one employer at another large television factory told me, "Since 1970 the situation has become one where it is the worker choosing the factory rather than the companies selecting their workers. Five years ago we were looking for high school graduates and women who are above average in height; now, as long as they have some degree of literacy and are of legal working age, we accept them. But even though we've broadened our qualifications to this extent, we are still short of workers." The following comes from a manager at Western Electronics:

> With so many firms trying to attract workers, some companies start out ahead because they have special relationships with school personnel. Some, especially the smaller firms, make gifts to the school. Meanwhile the available pool of labor becomes smaller. It is therefore important to develop and maintain *kuan-hsi*, and yet remain within the bounds of what's legal.

One should bear in mind that the recommendation of one factory over another by a school principal or teacher carries much weight in the rural areas because neither students nor their parents are apt to be knowledgeable about factories far away. How then do school employees deal with the various company representatives, all of whom are vying for workers? This is the response of one Western Electronics manager:

> Those who have special ties with the school counselor or principal are in the best position; they may be relatives, or may have been classmates, or may have been in the army together. Gifts may be offered to ensure that the commitment of a number of students will be met, but companies like Western Electronics try to stay with more proper methods, although entertaining them with dinners is legitimate and necessary. So we are dependent on those who we hope have the welfare of the students in mind, and trust that they will think of the quality of working conditions in the different factories... Then there's also the problem of trying to deal with school personnel who belong to various cliques, Mainlanders, Taiwanese, and so on.

In the comments of persons who are familiar with recruiting practices, such as Western Electronics managers, there are insinuations of wrong-doing and unscrupulous tactics on the part of "other" companies. Even group-leaders at Western Electronics could tell me of women hired by other factories to enter Western Electronics with the express purpose of luring Western Electronics workers to their own companies through enthusiastic descriptions of higher pay and better working conditions. As Taiwan's economy began to recover from the recession of late 1974, signs of a shortage of female workers reappeared, reminiscent of the situation prior to the layoffs. Statistics from the Employment Guidance Center in April 1974 report that there were more male than female job-seekers but that employers preferred women workers (*Chung Kuo Shih Pao*, 17 April 1974). One factory manager was quoted as saying in another newspaper article: "Boys are clumsy. They break up things and aren't fit to work on electronic components. They also ask for higher pay" (*The China News*, 3 May 1976). One newspaper stated in mid-1976 that the largest factory on Taiwan, General Instruments, needed six hundred women, a large garment and textile concern outside Taipei required three hundred additional women, a toy factory in Hsinchu was short five hundred women, and a plastics firm in Taichung needed two hundred women (*Lien He Pao*, 3 May 1976). A survey in 1976 by the north Taiwan Job Placement Center showed that factories in Taipei, Taoyuan and Hsinchu counties needed 70,000 female workers (*The China News*, 3 May 1976). Under these conditions, conventional practices such as rewarding workers who bring their friends, entertaining school teachers, and sending scouts to the countryside offering sums of money to village leaders for directing young women to a certain firm no longer seem to suffice, and there are indications that some firms resort to more questionable schemes. In addition to using "talent raiders," newspaper accounts write of:

> Employers who ask taxi drivers by train stations to be on the lookout for girls getting off with suitcases; the factory pays the taxi-fare plus a commission to the driver if he brings a girl to the factory (*The China News*, 3 May 1976).

> In the countryside around Tainan factory recruiters arrange to have the diplomas of elementary school graduates withheld unless the girls enter their factories. This, the newspaper report charges, is done with the cooperation of school officials who are actually working on behalf of outside interests (*Chung Kuo Shih Pao*, 10 July 1974).

> In a Changhua factory it was discovered that part of a woman's pay is withheld as "savings" by the employer; if the factory suspects that she is going to another factory, she won't get her "savings" back (*Lien He Pao*, 3 May 1976).

> "A factory near Taipei has its girls' dormitories guarded like barracks. There is a patrol who questions visitors at great length for fear they might be . . . scouts [trying to lure workers to another firm]" (*The China News*, 3 May 1976).

Although the government expresses its indignation at such irregular practices through newspaper editorials and the like, it also recognizes that a shortage of workers means that factories cannot operate at full capacity and that work orders cannot be filled. Its response has been to "persuade more girl graduates of junior-high schools to join industrial plants to combat an acute shortage of factory hands" (*The China News*, 23 April 1976). The same article states that "the government is planning to enlist the help of the mass communication media for a persuasive drive aiming at attracting young women to the factories" (*The China News,* 23 April 1976). Unfortunately, no specifics are given about what the content of such a campaign would be; it would be of great interest, for example, to see whether the government emphasizes the importance of the contribution that female workers are making to the nation's economy. But whatever form the government's appeals and exhortations take, they seem at odds with the motivations of the women themselves, who do not always consider themselves fortunate in having found a place in a factory.

In summarizing the process of seeking factory employment, there are a number of structural constraints on women's autonomy that should be noted. First, parents play a prominent role in the selection of an occupation and, frequently, of a particular firm for their daughters. This is especially true in cases where women are entering the job market for the first time. Distance from home and wages are primary considerations in parents' minds. Even where parents do not exert complete control over women's access to jobs, the influence of a network of relatives and neighbors is important in directing women to certain companies. Women are apt to enter factories where sisters, cousins, and neighbors are already employed. (I return to this point in chapter 7.) Plentiful jobs make it appear as if daughters have a wide range of options when they seek employment, but as I have shown, parents restrict these opportunities and make certain that their daughters enter only a limited number of occupations and firms. Parents, for instance, often prevent a daughter from accepting a job that would require her to live in a dormitory. (I discuss their reasons for doing so in chapter 6.)

Second, where parents are not able to direct their daughters to certain jobs, because of lack of knowledge or because of an absence of factories in their home area, we find that schools channel women into particular factories. In this respect, the function of school principals and counselors is not too different from that of labor-contractors of the 1920s in China who played a key role in recruiting workers (see chapter 3). Even though school principals and teachers, unlike labor-contractors, generally lose control over women once they are in factories, the relative ignorance of young women and their propensity to follow the advice of school administrators in fact give the latter the power to commit an entire graduating class to one firm rather than another. Thus, a woman's first job might well be determined by which school she attended and by the nature of relations between school personnel and company recruiters.

The government is a third structure that channels women into one sector of the labor market (although not to specific firms), as shown by its willingness to allow lower-middle school graduates to begin their summer vacation earlier so that they may enter factories sooner (see chapter 4).

In combination, then, kinship structures, schools, and government policies exert pressure, directly and indirectly, on women and thereby restrict their autonomy in deciding where they will work. Women, of course, do make job changes, but this is a prerogative that only comes gradually, and even then women are not free to work *wherever* they choose. As the next chapter shows, one important reason is because many parents do not permit their daughters to live away from home.

6

Residence of Factory Women

Factory women in their mid-twenties can recall a time when they were not permitted to work in factories because they were situated "too far"from home. Since then notions of distance have been revised, and women who live in the more isolated regions of Taiwan have no choice but to live away from home if they wish to take up factory work. The majority of these women, along with their parents, look upon company dormitories as acceptable substitutes insofar as some supervision exists; dormitory regulations, curfews, bed-checks and the like convey an impression of order that allays the worries of parents.

A small minority of women who find even these regulations too restrictive elect to forego free or very cheap company housing to rent furnished rooms on their own. Aside from the added expense (approximately NT$200 to NT$300 a month for a room that is shared by one or two roommates) there are other disadvantages: locating accommodations close to the factory is not always an easy task; landlords not infrequently rent rooms in one building to both men and women, and rooms may be divided only by thin partitions; landlords are often none too attentive to cleanliness and the condition of dwellings.[1] The lack of supervision and the proximity of male and female tenants cause many women to characterize the habits of those who rent outside as disorderly, and residents in Ch'inan and Ch'ipei express disapproval at the casual mixing of male and female workers who rent rooms in the vicinity and who congregate at the fruit and ice shops during summer evenings.

Policy differs from company to company as to which workers are eligible to live in dormitories. In general a firm that employs several hundred workers provides transportation for employees living within a certain radius of the factory; those who live farther away must see to their own transportation (an unlikely choice because of added commuting time and cost) or live in dormitories. In some cases a firm will choose to establish a plant in an area where a pool of workers already exists (e.g., Western Electronics' satellite plant in Ch'ipei), thereby saving the expense of constructing or leasing housing. On the other hand, there are firms (though fewer in number) that urge all their production employees to move into company residences in order to reduce tardiness and to eliminate transportation costs altogether.

Occasionally, the matter of deciding whether to live at home or in a dormitory involves only the factor of distance. A handful of informants had made several job changes that took them from home to dormitory and often back to their families again as they worked closer or farther from home. For a far larger proportion of women, however, other considerations enter into the decision, including the composition of a woman's family. Daughters who belong to households in which there are "enough" family members to manage the work load are in a clear advantage; most often this means the presence of sisters-in-law or younger sisters. Sickness or death can alter such arrangements abruptly, as can the departure of a brother and his wife. Chen, who had been quite happy living in a dormitory, returned home to Ch'inan when her only sister-in-law died. Another worker in Ch'ipei returned to live at home to take care of her ailing mother because her younger sister worked longer hours in a garment factory.

Yang Su-ying, who has one older married sister and three unmarried brothers at home, does much of the cooking and other daily chores after she returns from the factory. As for the possibility of living away from home, she said: "I've never been in a dormitory before, and I wouldn't mind trying it. But I doubt that my mother would permit it. Actually, living in a dormitory would be nice since there would be no housework to do."

If one factor can be singled out as the overriding concern in determining whether a daughter is allowed to move into a dormitory, it is the widespread belief that young women who live on their own are more likely to succumb to bad habits and learn bad ways. The initial reluctance of parents to send their daughters to factories described by M. Wolf (1972) no longer exists, but the conviction that young people are susceptible to unhealthy influences and become less filial is tenacious and lingers on.[2] In large part the basis for these reservations is an economic one,[3] since a woman who lives outside is certain to have added expenses, with food being the major item. One woman remarked, "My mother is worried that if I live outside I'll spend my money whenever I see something pretty." As long as a daughter remains at home, her parents are able to exercise some control over her time, her activities and whereabouts, and spending "too much money" is a key part of the definition of learning bad ways.

The worries of parents are not without grounds. Yang Chiu-lan's mother is commenting on her elder daughter who works and lives in another city:

> When she first began working she turned over all her earnings to me, but now that she's been working outside for a long time, she doesn't seem to listen to what I say. She now keeps about $400 to $500 for herself and gives the rest to me [each month]. Living away from home, she spends more money too.

The same comments were frequently heard from many mothers in Sanhsia. One woman, for instance, found a job for her daughter in a nearby family-owned knitting business because with her daughter living at home, "there's not much for her to spend her money on." One grandmother was particularly adamant on this issue and one of her grand-daughters came home after a few months spent in a dormitory not too far away. Her grandmother explained:

> It isn't good for a young girl to be far from home; it is too easy to learn bad ways. She may go out at night with friends, spending all her earnings on 'playing.' If young people aren't supervised it becomes too easy for them to do such things. With them at home they can be looked after, and that goes for their health and eating habits too.

Similarly, a woman in Taipei refuses to permit her younger sister, who works as a maid, to enter a factory. "If she goes into a factory that means living in a dormitory, and then it will become all too easy for her to make the wrong type of friends; once they're off work they'll go downtown and meet even more undesirable types."

In some cases, compromises are reached; most frequently, in situations where a woman lives within a reasonable distance from the factory but for whom transportation or school and work schedules create some inconvenience, dormitory residence is an acceptable alternative. Parents whose daughters must leave home exceptionally early to catch a bus or who must walk some distance in the evening after working overtime are likely to approve a move into company dormitories.

Availability of transportation and lower living costs at home mean that a worker's wages are left more or less intact each month, while a woman who lives in company housing is forced to use a sizable portion of her income on daily expenses and is subject to the influence of peers who might lead her to spend even larger sums on herself. These considerations are reflected in the findings of one study of commuting patterns among factory workers in two export processing zones in southern Taiwan. In his sample, the investigator found that 81.5% of female factory employees in the Kaohsiung Export Processing Zone and 82.9% of women in the Nantze Export Processing Zone with families living in Kaohsiung county commuted (the corresponding figures for male workers are 75.5% and 83.3%) (Wu 1976:5). The reasons for commuting are listed in Table 16. Daughters, therefore, are more likely than sons to remain at home in accordance with parents' wishes, with lower living expenses a major factor in the decision. Another set of findings from Wu confirms that in most cases daughters are allowed to live away from home only if commuting is impracticable (see Table 17). These figures indicate that with respect to women in the sample, the desire to experience city life or dormitory life is not as strong as one might expect, and the reasons women offer for preferring to live at home or in company housing are outlined below.

From their own experiences in a dormitory, from what other workers tell them, or from visits to dormitories, factory women have some knowledge or

Table 16.   Reasons for Commuting to Work, Male and
Workers in Kaohsiung County
(Wu 1976:8)

	Male (%)	Female (%)
Living Costs Cheaper at Home	55.4	33.0
Company Bus Service Available	2.7	17.8
May Help with Farming, Housework on Days Off	16.2	12.6
Family Factor; Parents Prefer at Home	10.8	21.3
Personal Preference; Rural Home Rather Than City	6.8	7.8
Others	4.1	1.7
Non-Applicable	4.0	5.8

Table 17.   Reasons for Living in the City, Male and Female Workers
Whose Families Live in Kaohsiung County
(Wu 1976:10)

	Male (%)	(Female (%)
No Company Bus Service	23.8	19.6
Residence Too Far	42.9	52.9
More Comfortable in City	19.0	7.8
Fare Too High	0.0	7.8
City Life More Attractive	4.8	0.0
More Liberal Living Outside	4.8	0.0
Others	4.7	0.0
Non-Applicable	0.0	11.9

have formed opinions of what dormitory life entails. The most frequently cited reason for choosing to remain at home is that "it is more convenient; one can do as one pleases at home." In addition to the cost of eating outside the food that is available in stalls or in the company cafeteria is said to be less tasty and less varied. "In the dormitory every time you eat it means having to spend money, and you have to go out for it too." The lack of privacy in many dormitory bathrooms, and the shortage of closet and desk space are less important but may be equally annoying.

    While most women acknowledge that one has greater freedom in a dormitory, a number of dormitory residents and women who live at home point to curfews and regulations about cleanliness in rooms as indications that .ife in the dormitories is also subject to restrictions. Most women welcome rules about maintaining a neat room, since the close quarters magnify any disorderliness, and they tend to be critical of dormitories in other factories that are lax in this respect. Nonetheless, workers complain that occasionally the rules are carried to excess; clothes and other belongings not put away, for instance, are confiscated for several days. Part of the rationale behind regulations such as these is to reduce the high incidence of thefts, a problem that appears to plague many factory dormitories, and supervisors admit that they are rarely able to deal with the problem successfully. Not many workers are exempted from the experience of having belongings stolen, and women regula.ly take the precaution, for example, of watching (or take turns doing so) their drying laundry on the roof-deck.

Thefts and messy rooms contribute to the image of dormitories that many women have, and those living at home commonly cite this as their reason for having no interest in dormitory life. Aside from the fact that dormitory rooms tend to be crowded (on the average between six to twelve in a room), group living is regarded as inevitably noisy and disorderly.

> With so many people together, all of different backgrounds and temperaments, it's certain that there will be a lot of bickering and arguing. And because some women are very "loose" in their behavior, a person can very easily be influenced and change her own standards.

Women also explain their reluctance to move into dormitories by pointing out that should they fall sick or require assistance in other matters, there would be no one to take care of them. "Leaving home isn't a good idea because there is no one who can take care of you if something goes wrong. In the dormitory you can go to the dormitory supervisor but she has too many people to look after."

Some discomforts of dormitory living are minor and can be tolerated if a woman feels she has no alternatives, but even the attractions are not always clear-cut:

> It's more comfortable at home; there are no problems about meals, there's no shortage of water, and so on. When I listen to those who live in the dormitories it seems that a person has more freedom at home. But when I'm home [the speaker had lived in both] I feel I had more freedom in the dormitory. Sometimes if I come home late my mother would scold me. But then in the dormitories you can't be out past eleven [p.m.] either.

To be sure, there are women who view a factory job as a means whereby they can escape from an unpleasant situation at home and who are apt to find dormitory life a welcome alternative. The attitudes of these women represent one end of a continuum of reactions toward leaving home, and at the opposite end are those women who unhesitatingly assert that if jobs can be had in one's home area, "everyone would rather live at home." For these women this preference is taken for granted, and if they must live in a dormitory they insist that on their visits home (which never occur frequently enough), they are on even closer terms with their families.

With greater length of time away from home ambivalence may increase; on the one hand there is the companionship of friends to enjoy, and on the other, homesickness continues. One particular conversation with Hwang began with a long discussion about the importance of leaving home and learning to be self-reliant, and yet after covering several other subjects, she ended on an equivocal note:

> If the job were the same I'd prefer to live at home since a person really never gets over being homesick. When I go home now I feel very close to my family, although after a while I begin to feel bored; talking with members of one's family is not the same as talking with friends, and I begin to miss my friends here at work. [Hwang had worked in Western Electronics for three years.]

Hwang resembles many factory women in her uncertainty; although she may not have resolved her own ambivalence about leaving home, she and many others share the notion that coming outside constitutes a valuable experience. This section focuses on the expectations that women have about their new independence and on those positive aspects of leaving home that draw them to cities and factories, however unrealistic their appraisals may eventually prove to be.

Despite the higher cost of living in the north women from the central and southern parts of Taiwan continue to seek factory jobs in the north. The elder brother of one Ch'inan informant runs a knitting business at home and employs three sisters from the south. My informant explained:

> From talking to them [they live with the family] you can really tell that girls in the south have much harder lives in terms of the work they are expected to do. So they're willing to come up north even if it means long hours at a job like this. [She herself works in an electronics factory.] There, families are eager to get their daughters married earlier and so women who want to take things easy for a while longer come up north to work. [In this particular case one sister began sewing lessons and stayed in the Sanhsia area, but her two sisters were told to return home to help with farmwork.]

One woman from the south, who came north to work in a factory and who later married a Sanhsia man, had this to say:

> Where I come from, many people don't allow or don't like to see girls go north because they're not likely to return to their own village again. [Pointing to herself as an example, she continued:] The north is more fun, and a woman who marries north will have a more comfortable life; she'd be better off. Women in the south are very capable and can handle many household chores as well as farmwork, but if they settle here they wouldn't be willing to do such work again; after all, that was the point of coming up in the first place.

Motivations such as these explain the willingness of women from the south to take even seasonal jobs such as those provided by the tea-processing plant in Ch'inan. The hours are long and the dormitories can hardly be considered attractive, but for a handful of women each season this represents an opportunity to look for other jobs that will enable them to remain in the north.

The most obvious benefit a woman gains by leaving home, of course, is the prerogative to spend her time as she chooses. At one extreme are those women who literally "tour" Taiwan as they travel from firm to firm; in most instances, however, freedom of movement refers simply to increased control over one's time. Chen Chiu-lan's family lives in an area where there are few factories (Hualien on the east coast) and she came to Western Electronics after lower-middle school. During a conversation about the dormitories she said,

Compared to other dormitories the ones here are pretty nice; they're fairly neat and less disorderly than most. The only drawback is that meals are less convenient than at home. But I have more freedom here; at home my mother doesn't like me to go out very much, or she says that I have to be home at a certain time. Even when I'm home on vacation I usually have to stay home; my mother claims that otherwise I'd be running around too much.

Once women have moved away from their families, subsequent job changes and travel to other areas are more feasible. But it is the first move that parents control most closely. The next case is somewhat long, and the speaker is perhaps more independently-minded than most women; I include it as an example of the transition that may take place:

When Chen Ling-fong first left her home in Hualien [because there are few jobs to be had there] she went to Taipei where she stayed with her father's brother's family. For almost three months she stayed at home, not daring to go out by herself in the city. She took a job in an electronic factory and shared a rented room with some other workers since there was no dormitory provided. [This is true of most factories in Taipei.] "I really enjoyed myself then, being on my own, and being able to do what I wanted. Often we would call up some friends to come over to dance, although the landlord complained about the music and we would have to stop." Her next job was that of a busgirl with a Taipei bus company: "One good thing about the job was that all our rides were free, so I've been all over the city, and my friends and I could go out all the time." After a year she returned home for two months only to return to Taipei again, this time to a garment factory. She didn't care for her job assignment and went to visit a friend employed at Western Electronics; it was under these circumstances that she decided to remain and work there. "It's good for a person to come out and see more; people are still very conservative at home and there isn't much to do; for instance, people still object to girls swimming. I don't understand how some people are able to stay at a job for several years; for myself, one year in any place is about all I can take. My mother keeps saying that I run around too much and as a result I never learn anything useful."

Hsu, another Western Electronics employee, who is in other respects a filial daughter (she makes regular remittances home and is not extravagant in her personal spending habits), said,

The dormitory isn't that comfortable but I'm not used to being at home anymore. It's not that my mother is overly strict; it's just that at home I wouldn't feel right about going out. At home you can't do as you please.

The process by which some women come to adopt outlooks such as these is described in the following chapter.

7

Adjusting to the Factory Environment

Girls as a rule have next to no opportunities for cultivating friendships with one another. The readiness with which under favorable conditions such attachments are formed and perpetuated shows how great a loss is their persistent absence (A. Smith 1970:250).

[The] problem [of teenagers] seems to be one that was classic in the West before "teenager" became a separate status with its own mores, values, and accepted behavior patterns. They are neither children nor adults and are paralyzed by uncertainty when a new situation requires that they be one or the other (M. Wolf 1972:94).

In this chapter I provide a sketch of factory dormitories and the circumstances in which women find themselves upon leaving home. No less than the fact of wage-earning, the atmosphere of and the relations formed in dormitories and in the workplace can have a significant impact on the behavior and attitudes of factory women.

Few young women are likely to have had reason or the opportunity to travel long distances alone prior to their first trip to a factory. It is true that the definition of a safe and permissible distance to travel is a relative one, but it should be remembered that even half or the entire length of the island is a far longer journey than most of the *parents* of these young women will have occasion to make. Traveling companions, then, mean security not only for the women themselves, who have had little preparation for such an experience, but are reassurance for their families as well. Some of their apprehensions are borne out by the following incident.[1] A young woman from the south, traveling alone, arrived in Ch'inan asking for directions to Taoyuan. Seeking the main Western Electronics plant there, she had, instead, been directed by mistake to the Western Electronics satellite plant (which has no dormitory) in Ch'ipei. By this time it was evening and the woman had no recourse but to hire a taxi to take her to Taoyuan. (The brother of one of my informants volunteered to take her on his motorcycle but was prevented from doing so by his mother.) Her departure left some of the Ch'inan residents wondering out loud how her parents would have been willing to allow a young woman to undertake such a "dangerous" venture on her own.

Employers offer a wide variety of housing to their workers, ranging from several rooms in buildings adjacent to the factory rented for employees to apartment-like dwellings accommodating several hundred persons. The former are typical of the living arrangements in which shop-girls and waitresses are found, and there is not likely to be any formal supervision. The dormitories I visited in the Sanhsia area are generally three or four-story buildings where two or three middle-aged women are hired, on rotating schedules, to serve as dormitory supervisors. At the other extreme are the large complexes of buildings characteristic of the largest factories and the export processing zones, where in addition to a full-time supervisory staff, recreational facilities and programs are available. On the premises of Western Electronics, for example, there is a large cafeteria, a recreation center that houses a lounge equipped with televisions and radios, a library, a snack-bar, a beauty salon, an auditorium, ball-courts, and rooms where folk-dancing, sewing, or typing classes are held. In comparison the dorms in the Sanhsia area are vastly simpler structures, with more modest facilities to match. Dormitory rooms, however, are similar in their furnishings; in the three-story buildings and in the larger complexes alike, most of the rooms I saw were occupied by six to twelve women, occasionally more, who shared the use of a small table, locker-type closets, and bunk beds, with bath facilities on each floor.

At Western Electronics two women are employed as "dorm mothers" for each of the eight women's dormitories, and they alternate every other day working and living in their respective buildings. Each supervises the 300 to 400 residents in the building. Given the numbers it is understandable that most of their time is taken up by room checks (for neatness), bed-checks at night, and that their duties only rarely include counseling. Workers do not perceive dorm supervisors as counselors, and they acknowledge that it is a formidable task for a dorm mother to learn their names.[2]

Workers are assigned to different buildings according to their shifts, and there is some attempt to place working-students together on the same floors. Thus the quiet and deserted appearance of the dorms during the day (or early evening, depending on the shift) changes dramatically when several hundred women return from the factory in the afternoon or at midnight, all of whom must share the available facilities. Until a room on each floor was designated as a study-hall in the Western Electronics dormitories at the end of 1974, working-students were particularly hard-pressed for time, trying to squeeze in a few minutes of homework before lights were turned off.

The presence of a factory of Western Electronics' size has meant an expansion of opportunities for small merchants, and the path between the plants and the dormitories is now lined with family-owned and operated noodle-stalls, fruit and ice shops, fabric and dress shops, all catering to the workers who pass by several times a day. More recently, modern two-story apartments have been built behind these paths, housing similar businesses on the ground-floor, with the owners and workers renting rooms on the second. In addition, vendors display their goods (clothing especially) regularly on pay-day. Besides offering greater variety and an alternative to factory meals, the noodle and fruit stands also provide some factory women with part-time jobs. These small shops are also important as socializing areas where workers may gather to sit and talk away from the dormitories, and where occasionally one can spot one worker teaching another how to dance to the accompaniment of Western music.

The behavior of new hires during the first weeks following their arrival demonstrates that many discover that managing on one's own is not as carefree as they had previously imagined and find it a sobering experience besides. It is not unusual to find new recruits leaving within days of their arrival, only to return to the factory (or another firm) some days or weeks hence. Aside from dissatisfaction or disappointment with the work assigned them or intimidation by supervisors, the following cases point to problems most frequently encountered by new workers at Western Electronics.

A group of six classmates from Nantou county, just out of lower-middle school, complained to their trainer that they were running short of money to pay for their meals since they had only brought with them NT$200 each. One admitted that her red eyes were a result of being homesick; another claimed that a skirt was missing. With an advance to tide them over and their meal problem thereby solved, the three of them decided to stay on. When the trainer accompanied them back to their dormitory room she discovered that their three companions were also in the process of packing. When they learned that their three classmates were remaining after all, they, too, began unpacking.

One woman from the south returned home after one week at Western Electronics. She said that since she had friends from home who were coming, she had joined them out of curiosity ("to look around") more than out of any serious intention of working. Within a week, however, she discovered that she did not have enough money to spend on food, was homesick, developed stomach pains, and did not care for the dormitory where, she had heard, belongings get stolen. Being from a farm family, she said she could work helping at home.

Four workers who arrived and left together offered roughly the same litany of complaints by way of explanation for their departure: homesickness, "not feeling well," not getting enough to eat because they were short of cash, finding the dormitory too noisy to sleep, thefts (from soap to clothing), and worries about the effects of working with microscopes.

In spite of such inconveniences a majority of women obviously do make the adjustment and overcome the difficulties listed above.[3] The support that companions provide has already been underscored: "In the dorms what matters most is having friends; otherwise things would be very hard for a girl alone. Girls nowadays, unlike in the past, want to see the outside, and as long as they have companions it will be all right."[4] One working-student described to me how she and her classmates had designated two of the other girls among them to act as "parents" since they were thought to be more mature. "When we had problems we would go to them; it helps to have someone to talk to." Several others characterize the atmosphere in their rooms as warm and family-like, but this is far from being a typical pattern. One woman who had just depicted her own unit as family-like, for example, was quick to add that such ties did not extend to those next door or across the hall." From another worker, "A person is really only acquainted with those women in the same room. Sometimes I don't even recognize those who live next door because I don't see them at work. Besides, each person minds her own business."

Activities with peers and time spent in school ("school keeps you busy so you have less time to be homesick") alleviate homesickness, and trips home every Sunday are not uncommon for some dormitory residents. One worker recalled returning home three times a week when she first came: "later, after I had made more friends I didn't mind being away from home so much. I became more accustomed to not having my parents around." A genuine attachment to one's family, however, seems to persist for most women. There are workers who have lived away from home for two or three years and yet continue to make weekly trips home. "If something came up, such as overtime, and I was not able to go home, I wouldn't feel right for the remainder of the week." More planning is required for those women whose homes are further south. There are few extended holidays that make a round-trip of eight to ten hours worthwhile, and the two or three trips home a year are awaited eagerly even though the journey is often an uncomfortable one. Unable to afford the faster trains and not having the time to stand in queues to purchase seats early enough, some are forced to accept standing-room on a trip of several hours duration.

Newly hired women are primarily concerned about not being separated from their companions in dormitory assignments, but seem sufficiently relieved and pleased to find roommates who come from the same region of Taiwan, or who are also students, or who speak the same dialect.[5] Sharing a common place of origin may facilitate familiarity among strangers but it does not seem to be of any lasting importance as a basis for building more enduring bonds.

The Taoyuan vicinity and its adjacent districts have a relatively high concentration of Hakka, and a word about relations between dialect groups is appropriate here. Since many Hakka speakers are comfortable using Taiwanese it is to be expected that those who feel ill-at-ease tend to be the Taiwanese themselves, and resentment is most acute when a woman also happens to be new on the job. A Ch'inan woman recalls that the beginning of her stay in a Shulin dormitory was particularly trying because the other women in her room were all Hakka. She said, "It was hard enough making the adjustment since that was my first time away from home, but [their presence] made things even more difficult. I finally asked to be switched to another room, telling the dormitory supervisor that I would quit otherwise." A Western

Electronics worker's account echoes the same sentiments: "When I first moved into the dormitory there were only five of us in the room but the other four were Hakka. This was not very pleasant. Usually people in the dormitories get along fairly well, but those who speak different dialects tend to stay together, and being in one room it's very easy to be left out. It really isn't right to [speak in another dialect] when there are others present. You wonder what they are saying that they don't want you to hear." One Western Electronics dormitory resident remarked that since there was only one Hakka speaker in her room, the latter rarely had a chance to use it, but she went on: "But there's still a distinction; they [the Hakka] get along better with each other and when they're together they speak Hakka."

While it is probably true that new Hakka-speaking employees feel more at home with other Hakka women, friendship networks do not seem to be drawn entirely along sub-ethnic lines. Such a tendency exists to a greater degree among aborigine women (even though most are also at ease using Taiwanese),[6] and among the few Mainlander women in the factory, but this point should not be exaggerated. Comments about relations among those speaking different dialects were volunteered in only a few instances, and it is not an issue with which women are preoccupied. In the case of the Mainlanders I suspect that the distinction they draw between themselves and the Taiwanese is also based on differences in educational achievement. Chang, Cantonese and a high-school graduate, for example, had this to say about the worker who sat next to her: "Her Mandarin is only fair so we don't talk much [even though Chang speaks Taiwanese well]. My friends are mostly Mainlanders, since I feel we have more in common and more to talk about." (The implication is that if her coworker were better educated her command of Mandarin would also be better.)

One distinction that cuts across regional and dialect differences is that between working-students and those not attending school. Aside from practical considerations (similar schedules, the need to have some quiet for homework, etc.) working-students are insistent in their preferences for being placed in rooms with other students, although these are voiced only to one another. Complaints about noise and too much distraction to allow any concentration are frequent among women who happen to be the only student in their rooms. The following account is representative of the experiences of many workers:

I've even thought of leaving because I can't get used to the conditions here. My job tires me out, and then when I return to the dorm at night there's not enough water [for a shower] and that means waiting. With all those people that means not getting to bed till after one [a.m.], and I have to be up at seven for school. And worse, I'm the only student in my room; the others play the radio and there's no way for me to study or read. I've spoken to the dorm mother once but am hesitant to go again. There's nothing for me to talk about with the other girls. I'm concerned about school and that doesn't interest them in the least. [She was later reassigned to another room and remained at the factory.]

Her last comments point to another reason why newly hired student-workers actively seek out others like them; having just arrived in a new area they are dependent on older working-students for information about the tuition, curriculum and reputation of neighboring schools.

In this section I describe the transformation of an initially naive recruit into a woman more knowledgable about society outside. Women themselves hold stereotypic images of the end result. When I asked one worker whether she detected any differences between the women entering the factory now and the women who were her companions four years ago, she portrayed herself and her coworkers as having been more compliant and obedient: "We did what we were told. But girls nowadays are better able to take care of themselves; they are more assertive. They don't always do what they are told, and in fact, may even talk back." She attributed these qualities in part to television and to the opportunity to live outside; "young people are exposed to more these days." This exposure, of course, begins the instant a woman enters her first factory, and in the remainder of this section I use material collected at orientation sessions at Western Electronics to illustrate the range of ideas and attitudes a worker may hear, notions that she may not adopt but of which she will nonetheless become aware.

At one orientation session a young woman stood out in the ease with which she spoke of her past jobs. She gave no sign of hesitation or shyness (which is the norm), and when the subject turned to hobbies she mentioned with enthusiasm her interest in swimming and dancing. Later, during a break, two other newly hired women, just out of school, told me that they had been startled by the speaker's bold admission about liking such "daring" activities as dancing and swimming.

From a woman who had worked at an electronics factory before but who had lived at home during that time: "I wanted to become independent rather than to rely on my parents. The biggest problem now is money, that is, trying to save enough of it. It's boring at home, and besides, it's not good to be dependent on your family; it's better to come out and be on your own. You learn more about society that way."

This woman was formerly employed at a garment factory but came to Western Electronics so she could attend school: "After working a while you realize that going to school is still the best."

"I often think to myself that after so many years [of putting myself through] school, to have to come and work in a factory is hard to take, but I do need the money to continue my education since I can't rely on my family for that. I still have many younger brothers and sisters at home."

Another speaker displayed a more carefree attitude: "Actually I've been here [at Western Electronics] before; I left because I wanted a change of scene. My next job was that of a scorekeeper in a Taipei bowling alley, but that kind of work environment and Taipei are too complex and so I left. But in any case I want to travel all over and see Taiwan."

This woman is a Mainlander, self-assured in her manner, and showed very definite ideas about her own position: "I take school very seriously and want to be a good student. I like movies but other than that I don't go out much. I'm a girl of the present generation, not of the past. It's just that I can't go out all the time because I don't have that much money to spend, and then there's school besides. And now with a job there will be even fewer chances to play...I hope someday to work as a translator of English."

In work and social contexts women encounter in their peers a comparable mixture and range of aspirations, expectations, and values, and in a cumulative fashion such exposure produces in a large number of women ambivalent feelings about being independent.

For instance, the most frequently heard characterization of large factories and dormitories is that they are too complex, and the consensus is that this disorderly environment is conducive to improper behavior, an image held by some dormitory residents and non-residents alike.[7]

You see all kinds of people at this factory [Western Electronics]. It's a very complex situation. Everyone may look the same on the job in their uniforms, but once they're off work, some women are even more made-up than movie actresses. [Where do they go?] To night-clubs and dance-halls. Girls who work in smaller factories are probably more innocent, being exposed to less, not like the conditions here.

In the next dormitory building sometimes you can see four girls [in the room across from the speaker's] close the door and take out bottles of liquor and cigarettes. They don't seem to care if others find out. I think the factory environment is partly to blame; with so many people around how can the dormitory supervisors look after everyone?

Because the company is so large you can see all types of people, good and bad. Some treat the dormitory as if it were a hotel, as just a place to sleep, since they are out most of the time anyway. You can see a lot of delinquent types. For the rest of us [students] the dormitory is like a home away from home. My mother was worried that I would learn the wrong kinds of things, but a person must have self-respect.

Thefts are common in the dormitories; sometimes you discover that you never even receive packages sent to you by family or friends. I've had money stolen four times, but it's hard to find the ones who're responsible. Sometimes, women who are leaving the company and are moving out of the dormitories will take someone else's suitcases with them. The dormitories are a very complex place where you can observe all sorts of people. Some are very loose in their behavior; they don't seem to care how they act; they drink, they even smoke. Have you ever seen pregnant women in the dorms? I have. And there are some who work in bars and dance-halls. There are fewer who do so now that there is a new rule: if a woman doesn't return to the dormitory a certain number of times, she must move out. Some women may look young when they come but they may already have been out in society for a long time, and may already be quite experienced. And then with so many women living in one place, there's always some argument going on.

The behavior these speakers describe is of course not applicable to all women, but they regard the context in which they live as sufficiently complex to consider it necessary to be on guard, lest one also learn bad ways. (High school graduates and students are inclined to believe that less educated workers are more susceptible to such influences.) In one episode of a daytime television serial I saw, a definition of the term "learning bad ways" was given in almost these exact words: "A young woman who comes to Taipei and 'learns bad ways' means that she takes up drinking, smoking, and dancing." Why this is apt to happen is hinted at in the following remarks:

Speaking of the casual mixing between men and women who work in Ch'ipei Western Electronics plant and who live on their own, one woman said, "Without supervision of any sort the behavior of those girls can quickly become 'loose and casual.' They just want to have some fun, but because some of them are so young, they can be easily deceived by the young men they go around with." [In contrast I might include here what the speaker herself said with reference to going out: "I would like more opportunities to play but when I think of how much it costs, I'd rather not go. Earning money isn't easy, and it's better to be thrifty."]

[Another worker makes a similar point:] Young women today are changing quickly, often without really knowing what they're doing, without any specific goals in mind. For example, they rush to keep up with the latest fashions; once they see something they hurry to get it without thinking whether it's right for them. There're many girls who behave this way, and not having had much education is one reason. When they first come the girls are well-behaved but they pick up things in a short time. They emulate others and just follow whatever they see. In the evenings some even go to work in clubs and bars, while others become friendly with boys who belong to gangs. But then what else is there to do in the dormitories besides going out? And it's just a matter of one girl taking along another and so on.

An older worker (twenty-three) provides an example:

The girls who are just out of school are obedient and timid; it takes a more experienced worker like myself to "educate" them. For instance, if you ask them what they do with their earnings, they invariably say that they send their wages to their mothers. When I suggest that they keep some money for clothes, they only reply that their mothers will have dresses made for them! As for me, I still take money home, but I retain some for myself—for going out, movies, and clothes. Although sometimes there are girls whose appearance and behavior change very quickly. When those two first came [pointing to two workers nearby] they wore long skirts, flat shoes and socks; now look at them with their makeup, miniskirts, and they're always changing their hairstyles.

Having companions is frequently cited as essential in easing a new worker's adjustment, but friends are also a decisive influence on a woman's subsequent behavior. The following excerpt from a conversation between two workers demonstrates this. (Chen is sixteen and commutes to work; her friend, T'ao, a year older, lives in the dormitory.)

Chen: When we go out to play, it's usually just a group of girls; it's less convenient with boys around. [Why?] Well, for instance, if you go swimming it's embarrassing wearing something so skimpy.

T'ao: I don't think there's anything wrong in going out with boys; we're all about the same age and are merely friends; there's no harm in that.

T'ao   [a little later]: There's a generation gap between us and our parents. They're at least twenty years older, but so much has changed, and we have different perspectives on things. We are of the present generation. If a mother objects to her daughter smoking and she insists on doing so anyway, what can a mother really do about it?

Chen: Most girls who smoke are the girlfriends of hoodlums.

T'ao: That's not really true. Some girls smoke and do so in an acceptable lady-like manner. Girls in Taiwan have changed a great deal in recent years; they are more vivacious and outgoing. For example, before, you rarely saw couples holding hands in public; now it's not uncommon.

Lee has worked and lived in a dormitory in the south, and her job at Western Electronics meant her first trip north. Our conversation had turned to swimming, a new sport for many rural women:

> I'm still not brave enough to try and learn. The swimsuit styles are too revealing. At home we almost never hear of girls going out to swim. When we go out it's usually to the movies, shopping or hiking. My friend didn't learn how to swim until she came up here. Girls in the north are more daring, and this kind of environment is a big influence on the changes in the behavior of girls who leave home.

School can be an important element in determining who one's friends are and comes to function as almost a preventive measure:

> [From a working-student:] It's all a matter of time—with school there's little time to do anything else. Those who are not going to school have more opportunities to go out and spend time on streets and make friends who are apt to be a poor influence.

Yang, having worked at Western Electronics for three years, began with the recurring remark that all types of persons can be found in the factory. Speaking with regard to herself, she continued:

> Since I've been on my own for quite some time, it's not likely that I'd be led astray; or, take someone like my roommate—since she's going to school she hasn't got the time to learn bad ways. It's the person who becomes bored from having free time that is more susceptible to undesirable influences.

To cite more examples of the range of conduct that compounds the complexity of the factory environment, one could include those women who manage (usually with the cooperation of a friend already there) to move into the dormitories at Western Electronics for a short period but who never report for work. Having registered at the personnel office they are entitled to a place to stay without charge while they go out and play or look for a more desirable job. Should the dormitory supervisor ask, they are ready with the explanation that the personnel office has not finished processing their papers. Then there are instances of female workers who become involved, sometimes unknowingly, with married men; once, a dorm-mother took it upon herself to open the mail of a worker whom she suspected of having such a relationship. In another case the man's wife came to the dormitory demanding that the dormitory supervisor dismiss the worker so her husband would no longer be able to find her. Returning to the dormitory on warmer evenings one sees young men on their motorcycles waiting at the gates, and one article recently reported a new game: the men toss their motorcycle keys onto the ground and each woman rides off for the evening with the owner of the key she has picked (C.C. Yang 1976:66). Security guards claim that some of the women who ride off with these men are actually headed for second jobs or dance-halls. Such charges are not always easy to disprove or to confirm but from hearsay and observation, rumors of this nature add to the aura of disorder that women associate with large factories in urban settings.

A newspaper editorial that appeared on Mother's Day holds parents responsible for juvenile delinquency: "While some youths succumb to the 'bad' influences in society, others remain entirely unaffected. The determining factor . . . is the influence of the parents"(*The China Post*, 12 May 1974). This is an opinion that many young women hold as well:

> [A factory worker describes her former classmates who are now employed as salesgirls in a Taipei boutique:] The shop rents a place for them but they prefer to have their own place because if they're out late, the landlord would inform their boss. Their present landlord doesn't care what time they come in, so it's very easy to learn bad ways. Things would be different at home where our parents would look after us; no landlord or dorm-mother would do the same.

> [About roommates at Western Electronics who keep late hours:] Now if they were at home their parents would not let them go to such parties; that kind of behavior wouldn't be allowed. A girl who is away from home can easily deceive her parents because they can't see what she's up to.

> [Yang, speaking about her roommate who eventually left school and her job at Western Electronics:] Being away from home her parents couldn't keep watch over her activities. If a person writes home and says everything is fine, how are her parents to know any better?

Parents are not without recourse and do make their disapproval known. Whether or not parents do in fact take action to correct a daughter's behavior hinges, of course, on their ability to acquire reliable information about her activities. How often a working daughter returns home and the gossip of neighbors who have daughters employed at the same factory are some clues that parents have. What is of most concern to parents, however, is the amount of money a daughter sends home, and as increasing portions of a woman's earnings are diverted to clothes and recreation, her parents can easily surmise how her leisure time is being spent. Mothers in Sanhsia who have daughters living in dormitories complain that the longer their daughters are away from home, the less money they remit; and yet it appears that so long as the fluctuations are within reason (i.e., so long as half of a worker's income is sent home, with the exception of working-students), this is accepted, albeit grudgingly. Perhaps the most extreme measure taken by parents is to tell a daughter to return home, although such a step is not always initiated under drastic circumstances. (Women from farming families may be asked to return home simply to help during busy seasons.)

By way of summarizing women's attitudes about living away from home I present the feelings of three workers on the subject:

Taipei is a good place to go if you want to play, but I wouldn't want to live there. People aren't as trustworthy as people at home [in the south]; Taipei people are more slippery, and human feelings run stronger in [the countryside in the south]. Whenever there's an opportunity for a trip home I get so excited about the prospect that I can hardly sleep, and I can think of nothing else. [The speaker, Liu, is a student and has been at Western Electronics for three years.]

If it's been a long time since I've seen my family, it's not too bad. It's after returning to the company from a trip home that is the most difficult, and I have to get used to being away from my family all over again... Now whenever I'm home I feel as if I were a guest: it's a strange feeling. But even though I've been living on my own for about five years I still get homesick sometimes, especially during holidays or festivals.

[In contrast, Tseng, who is in her third year at Western Electronics, admits that she goes home only once every two or three months.] I know that's not very often considering that my family is so close by. But now when I'm home I feel somewhat distant from my family. I also feel restless at home; there isn't much to do. I can't go out—that wouldn't look right. I don't know what to do with myself at home. Maybe I've been outside too long; I'm more accustomed to the dormitory. At home there's no one to talk to.

There are a number of easily identifiable factors contributing to this divergence in outlook: a woman who must leave home because there are no factories in the local area brings with her expectations quite different from a woman who welcomes the chance to leave an unpleasant family situation or farmwork, and the goals of a student are likely to orient her perceptions in yet another direction. This very range or combination of attitudes about being away from home shapes the perceptions of all women in the factory. A woman who has Tseng for a roommate could just as easily have Lin for a roommate, and hear the opposite sentiments expressed.

Why women would have cause to be ambivalent about being independent is apparent by now: the idea of managing for oneself is a novel and popular one, and the dormitories that make the realization of that possible carry their own attraction (the availability of companionship). Women declare that "a person can't grow up and become mature if she remains at home" and that "it is a good thing to leave home and be exposed to more." The appeal of an abstract notion of self-reliance, however, is offset by having to cope with homesickness, a condition only partially mitigated by having friends at hand, and by the discovery that dormitory life can be routine and monotonous. Furthermore, with free time on one's hands and with one's parents absent, a girl soon hears how easy it is to learn bad ways; autonomy has its pitfalls as well.

Obviously, for some women there is no ambivalence: these are individuals who actively seek and exploit the freedom that living away from home affords them. (Workers such as Chen Su-fong, who made the most of the mobility that her job as a busgirl allowed, are an example.) For these women freedom of movement in a literal sense on a day-to-day basis and over a period of years is highly appealing. In another category are those workers for whom increased personal autonomy comes by default. Not particularly attracted by the possibilities that follow from leaving home, these workers find themselves living in places distant from home because jobs could not be had there.

Occupying yet another position is a more far-sighted group, mostly students who conceive of themselves as making their own way. Their plans have direction and they couch their present circumstances in more positive terms. Persistence and determination, bolstered by the prospect of a white-collar job that a high-school diploma will bring, are not untypical: "In the beginning it was hard being on my own; everything was unfamiliar and I was by myself. But I was the one who wanted to come. It was 'bitter' working and going to school at the same time, but I stuck with it because if I went home, after all the fuss my leaving created, people would make fun of me." Often it is women in this category who are able to list the virtues and merits of leaving home and of learning to take care of oneself, and yet a few moments later, state without reservation that they would prefer to remain at home if the same job were available and if they could continue with school.

Considering their poor prospects for vertical mobility on the job, it should not be surprising that, with the exception for working-students, female workers rarely talk at length about their future and goals. I am not suggesting that they do not give any thought to it; on the contrary, one could argue that they perceive their options all too clearly. Rather, there is the notion, stated in very general terms along with references to fate and destiny, that matters will simply take their own course. In the meantime (i.e., in the interim between school and marriage) the *idea* of being independent has wide currency and is capable of imparting positive connotations to what is otherwise a lackluster job. Above all, women uniformly state that once a person is accustomed to and resigns herself to a particular set of circumstances, the situation becomes tolerable and acceptable. The passivity indicated by this attitude reflects the relative powerlessness of these women over many areas of their lives: they need to work but have limited qualifications, and they are placed in jobs where, as the next chapter shows, they exercise virtually no control over the tasks they perform.

8

Relations in the Workplace

From ethnographic accounts of Taiwan we already know a good deal about the background from which the majority of factory women come. However, we have less information about the nature of the work situation they enter, and it is this industrial organization and the interaction taking place within this milieu that make up the new experiences the female worker confronts. With regard to the working women themselves, it might appear that the most radical change resulting from their wage-earning would have to do with their status in the family. This is a central and complex question that I take up in the next chapter. My purpose here will be to describe how factory women experience work and how these experiences alter their perceptions of factory work.[1]

My premise is that the experience of work might well be equally as important as the fact of earning an income in affecting a woman's status or her understanding of it. The focus of my study was not decision-making processes and relations at the managerial level, and this chapter does not purport to be a survey of industrial relations as practiced in factories in Taiwan, nor do I claim to be able to describe styles of management peculiar to these factories. Statements about managers, company policies, and supervision, therefore, are admittedly from the point of view of the women workers. The subject of this chapter has to do with patterns of relationships formed at work, the interaction of women with their peers and with their superiors, and their views of management.

Rightly or wrongly, much of what women workers learn in the factory and the conclusions they form about interpersonal relationships and about "how to be a person" are generalized to the larger society outside. Chang, who had worked in a factory for two years, had just made some remarks about being homesick, and she continued:

> You can learn things in the factory that you can't learn at home. The most important is learning how to get along with people. People at school are 'simpler', whereas in society you see all kinds of people; it's more disorderly. At home it's no problem getting along with people, but here outside, such as in the factory, you have to be very careful in how you deal with people; sometimes a very small matter can offend somebody.

The way in which factory women define and apprehend the work situation and relations at work is, of course, determined in part by positions they fill in the company hierachy. By examining the interplay of organizational constraints and informal processes, I hope to say something about how the orientations women bring with them are reinforced or transformed into new attitudes, and how these attitudes constitute the social context in which women work. It is also from such an assessment that concepts such as "work commitment," "work involvement," and "job satisfaction" may be more satisfactorily explored.

I began with a brief description of the socialization process by which newly hired women gain some familiarity with the factory and of the roles they make up. I then consider relations between women workers and their supervisors, and how women characterize these relationships and supervisory roles. The next section reviews workers' perceptions of management.

The orientation session for newly hired workers (men and women are trained in separate sessions) at Western Electronics consists of a two-day program that includes some technical training (intended more for reducing anxiety than for actually promoting proficiency) and a tour of the plants and factory premises. The orientation program is led by one of three trainers who were formerly assemblers themselves.

All the trainers could recount to me anecdotes about new hires who came to Western Electronics thinking that they were joining a toy company or a computer parts company. The ubiquity of the Western Electronics name in television advertisements and on billboards makes such errors unlikely these days, but many women entering Western Electronics are still apt to hold inaccurate notions about wages and benefits. The central purpose of the orientation session is to correct these misconceptions, beginning with the proper pronunciation of the company name, and running through a gamut of company regulations on hours, time cards, legal holidays, leaves of absence, welfare benefits (recreational facilities, dormitories, medical insurance, transportation), and most important, the pay scale. Considering that no one takes notes during the entire presentation, it is hardly surprising that most new workers remember little more than how much they will earn and their work schedule. Yang works in one of the largest garment/textile factories in Taiwan and had this to say about familiarizing oneself with a new company: "The more you know—about wages, about how often you get paid, about meals—before you go to work, the better. But not all girls think of making inquiries beforehand. Even then you still only get a general idea of conditions in a factory, and the picture isn't going to be very clear. Only gradually do you learn more from your coworkers." Chen, who is employed in the same firm, agreed: "A person finds out about company rules, wages, and procedures gradually from the girls who work with her. As for how much is deducted for medical insurance and so on, you know only by looking at your pay slip; the same goes for union contributions. Actually, no one pays much attention to these little matters; the only thing we notice is the net pay." Similarly, when I asked Lin, who works in a Western Electronics satellite plant outside Sanhsia, about the company union, she replied:

> I know I'm in the union but don't know much else about it, and everyone knows because you can see the deduction on the pay slip. I heard it explained once, but I didn't pay much attention, and even if I had been listening, I would have forgotten long ago.

During the time I was at Western Electronics an experimental program called Termination Assessment was devised, and it was designed to follow new workers for a period of two weeks. If a new worker resigned within that period, efforts were made by personnel in Industrial Relations to ascertain her reasons for leaving. It is generally not an easy task[2] to persuade a young woman to give her "true" reasons for leaving a company;[3] nonetheless, an examination of some of the reasons new workers offer illustrates the discrepancy that may exist between a worker's expectations and what she actually finds.

> Three women from central Taiwan claimed they had been deceived by the recruiter the company had sent to their school, and came believing that meals and the dormitory were provided without charge. In addition, they were dismayed to discover that Saturdays are regular work days, and by this time they were running out of money as well.

> This woman had worked in the Kaohsiung export processing zone previously, earning NT $3,200 per month. She had tired of her job, however, and wanting a change of environment, decided to come north. When she learned of the wages she would be receiving at Western Electronics during orientation, she decided to leave the next day.

> This worker had been a group-leader in another factory before she was laid-off in a series of cutbacks in workers. Claiming to have earned well over NT $3,000 per month there, she stayed at Western Electronics for eight days and left after having found another job.

> When first asked by a trainer why she wanted to leave Western Electronics, this woman said that her father had written asking her to return home. Only after much probing did she admit to being out of funds, again, thinking that meals and the dormitory were free. She wrote home asking for money, but none was sent. At the time she spoke with the trainer she had no more money for food, had had no breakfast, and had packed her belongings but had no money for a train ticket. (Subsequently, the trainer arranged for a temporary loan from the company, and she stayed on.)

Women who view a factory job as an opportunity to play or as a "fun thing to do" but who have never visited a factory may be ill-prepared to make the adjustments required of them.

> When we first came to be trained, everything was so different; the room was carpeted, it had air-conditioning, and it was quiet. Then when we actually began to work in the plants, finding out what work was really like came as such a disappointment. The plant is dirty, it's

always noisy, and it's usually too warm. It's so different from what I used to think about when I was in school. At this job each worker isn't even like a person but resembles a machine more. Before, I could not have imagined myself using tools such as these.

This description comes from a trainer:

Before, at home or at school, these girls always had a teacher or parents to look after them, and at first, many become dependent on the trainers. Sometimes they don't take their work seriously, playing with the parts, and then are not able to fill their work quotas. And then when their group-leaders or foremen scold them, they're ready to quit then and there.

Chen, a new worker from Chiayi, admitted that she was prepared to quit on several occasions:

In the beginning I wasn't at all used to my work, and I could not keep up with the others. Then the foreman would always come by and say something, telling me to hurry up. This was very hard to take, since I wasn't doing it on purpose; everyone wants to do as much as possible, and so it's embarrassing to be yelled at. But then if you want to come out and be independent, you must be prepared to "eat bitterness"; once that period is over, things are better. In any case, that's just the way things are if you are a [manual] worker.

The unwillingness of many new workers to speak up and ask for information only exacerbates their difficulties. A group-leader cited the following case as an example of how reluctant some newcomers are to speak up:

A girl on my line burned her hand with her soldering iron but didn't even tell anyone. She was afraid she would get into trouble and would be scolded by her supervisors. It wasn't until the next day when I noticed the swelling that I sent her to see the nurse. That's how it is with many of them who come to work for the first time; they're young, they don't have their parents here, and they don't have the nerve to say anything.

Given the rather rigid authority structure of schools, the timidity of new workers should not be surprising. The new worker at Western Electronics, however, encounters a hierarchy of titles and positions that has far more gradations separating her and her coworkers from other company personnel. There are three plants at Western Electronics, two of which manufacture television parts and sets, with the other producing solid state components. The figure on the opposite page is a simplified chart of plant organization.

The majority of new workers are assigned to assembler positions, and inspectors, testers, quality control workers, and group-leaders are generally promoted from assemblers. Women with high school diplomas from vocational or technical schools, however, are most quickly placed in tester and quality control (QC) positions. Group-leaders (who receive an additional NT $250 per month) may have to supervise up to thirty assemblers, but the average

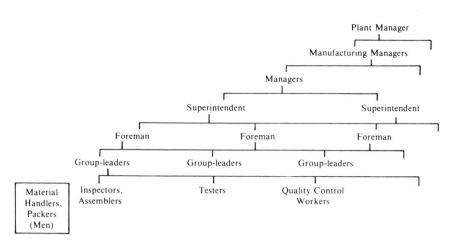

number ranges between fifteen and twenty women. Foremen are responsible for approximately eighty to a hundred workers, and they in turn report to superintendents.

Given the size of Western Electronics it is not remarkable to hear women announce that they do not even know who the managers in their plants are. Perhaps more revealing is the fact that when staff members in the personnel office discuss problems in supervision that contribute to a high turnover rate among assemblers, only references to group-leaders and foremen are made. Although factory women do form definite overall opinions of managers and superintendents (all of whom are lumped into the *lao-pan* [boss] category), direct contact is limited to group-leaders and foremen, who, almost by default, come to represent or are perceived as extensions of the company management. In conversations with women about supervision, superintendents are rarely mentioned, and the few unsolicited comments and responses to questions about superintendents are consistently vague and similar in content.

> A superintendent might know the names of some of the group-leaders in his section, but there's no point in even talking about managers. When girls see a manager coming, most will turn around and go off in the other direction. A superintendent may have something to say to a group-leader, but never to us workers.

This statement comes from a group-leader:

> When most girls see a manager or a superintendent come by, they quickly act as if they're very busy at work. The girls are more afraid of the superintendent, because he's the one with the authority to get rid of them.

The distance between a superintendent and the women is perceived to be so great as to make any conversation virtually inconceivable.

Images of foremen that emerge from workers' comments are clearer in outline, and women hold firmer opinions about what a foreman can legitimately do and about what they might wish him to do. To begin with, foremen know the names of the women on the lines they supervise; "he should know our names; after all, it's part of his job to know how well each person does. But this doesn't mean that he is well acquainted with us." A foreman is almost always in his section or nearby, but actual contacts between him and the women in his section are infrequent. According to the workers it is from their observations of him and how he interacts with their group-leader that they learn about the kind of person he is. Under ordinary circumstances a worker with a problem will take it to her group-leader, and if the latter is unable to solve it, the group-leader consults her foreman. "Although we don't speak to him much, the effects of things he says and does will filter down to us."

Unlike the trainers who are more solicitous of the new worker's well-being, foremen tend to be perceived, at least initially, as no-nonsense, strict supervisors whose sole concern is meeting production quotas.[4]

Yet at the level of general expectations and in terms of his role, a foreman has to be "mean" and strict. "A foreman has to be mean, at least some of the time, or else no one would listen to him." This statement comes from a worker in a radio factory: "Our foreman is too 'casual' with some of the workers, and now as a result there's almost no girl who is scared of him." Tseng, the only forewoman in Western Electronics, remarked that many women still find it odd that she holds such a position: "Many feel that a foreman should be a man, and that any woman who does a foreman's work must be a very mean person indeed." With a bit more probing, however, it becomes apparent that for some workers this is merely a stereotype, and some women acknowledge that often this is only a facade. Chang, after a month on the job, described her foreman as "not really a bad person; sometimes he'll joke around with us, although not all the time, because that way no one will be afraid of him." Wu, as one of three female trouble-shooters in the factory, speaks from a somewhat special standpoint, but her characterization resembles that of other experienced workers:

> Our foreman will sometimes ask us to work more slowly because it looks bad if the superintendent catches us just sitting and talking. But nobody is really scared of him; he can't even control the girls on the lines, how can he expect us [testers and trouble-shooters] to listen to him; so when we finish our work, we just read, or talk, or take a nap.

These comments, however, do not permit us to ignore frequent complaints from workers that their foremen are too strict. Su, having worked at Western Electronics for five years, is one of a handful of women who have worked their way from an assembler's position to that of a trouble-shooter. In discussing the causes of a high turnover rate she includes, among other factors, the tendency to be overly strict.

> Sometimes, especially when they are under a lot of pressure themselves from their superiors, foremen demand too much from the girls; they expect everything to be perfect. Many workers see their foremen as being too concerned with following regulations to the letter. Many workers find this hard to take, and if there're other jobs available, they think, 'Why should I have to put up with this,' and so just quit on the spot.

Obviously, Su's explanation does not invalidate the statements made by the other women, statements that reflect an air of indifference toward their foremen. But together these observations indicate that the relationship between a worker and her foreman is not a simple one, and that the expectations women have of their foremen are by no means unambiguous. Clearly, workers also judge their foremen differently according to their own positions and temperaments, but some of the elements that have a bearing on how satisfying a worker considers her relationship with her foreman can be sorted out.

Factory women invariably address their foremen by title, since to call them by name (Mr. So-and-so) would connote a familiarity that does not exist. (Foremen address workers by name. I know of only one instance where a worker occasionally addressed her foreman by name, and she was described by her coworkers as "chasing" him.) The sex difference complicates any expressions of familiarity and helps to maintain some distance between a foreman and the woman he oversees. As one group-leader said, "There's no point in taking our problems to the foreman; we're all women and he's a man. I think it's best if we can work things out by ourselves." From another group-leader, "It's hard being a group-leader; the girls come to you with every little thing; they don't go to the foreman because he's a man." The age of a foreman is also thought to affect his style of supervision. Older (above forty) foremen are viewed as tending to be laconic sorts, more stern in demeanor, and more distant.[5] Chang compared two foremen with whom she has worked:

> My first foreman is now a superintendent, but when he has time he may still come over and talk for a while. As for our present foreman, he hardly speaks at all. When he first came to this section, he might occasionally come by and say something, but he rarely does that anymore. If anything is up, he tells the group leader who then tells us. But it's probably because he's an older person, and doesn't talk as easily with us girls.[6]

Chang's reference to the limited interaction between a foreman and his workers is easily confirmed by casual observation in the plant; a foreman is often seen hovering over the assembly lines, but little exchange takes place between him and the workers. This is largely a consequence of the organization of work in the plants, and women are aware that organizational requisites restrict contacts between foremen and workers. "There's very little contact between a foreman and the girls; there're just too many people. Our foreman supervises sixty workers, and besides, there is no time for talking and getting acquainted." Moreover, with the group-leaders as an intermediary between the foremen and his workers, there is little need for a foreman to pay too much attention to any one worker so long as she is doing an adequate job. There are workers who interpret this as a preference on the part of foremen to interact only with other foremen or group-leaders, prompting many women, when the subject is raised, to state flatly, "the only time he comes to us is if there's a problem or mistake. When there are few rejects you won't find him coming to say something nice."

Even though this kind of statement is heard frequently, workers might still wish that the situation could be otherwise. Unlike the Japanese work groups Ronald Dore describes in which the foreman and his workers together constitute a team (1973:250), the foreman in Western Electronics stands clearly and separately in a vertical relationship vis-à-vis his workers. I suggest that on the one hand, there is a desire among many women to see expressions of concern and human feeling on the part of their foremen for his workers, and on the other, a desire not to be "bothered," since the foreman is a supervisor.

Obviously, these somewhat conflicting and ambivalent expectations are not easily fulfilled, and admittedly, informal relations between a foreman and his workers constitute a precarious and ill-defined area for him. If he expresses genuine concern in a worker's welfare, it may be misinterpreted by the latter as unwelcome attention. Since women rarely have need to seek out their foreman, the burden of establishing the "proper" kind of relationship rests upon him.

> Actually our foreman is pretty nice; he isn't overly strict and he kids around with us. And he also said, 'If there's something on your mind, don't be afraid to come and see me.' But what difference does saying that make; who would actually go see him on her own?

One obstacle to better communication is that women are unable, in any direct fashion, to make their wishes known and to articulate their expectations to their foremen. The following comments show how a foreman must be able to sense, for each worker, what is legitimate for him to do, because an act that is inconsequential in his eyes may carry more serious implications for a worker.

> Liu is employed at the Western Electronics satellite plant and recounted a case of a fellow worker who left the factory: "The reason she gave was that during all the time she was working there, six months, the foreman never spoke to her, and so she felt he looked down on her. All of us thought this was very funny and had a good laugh about it; who does she think she is?" Later in the year Liu herself left the company; when production on her line was stopped she was switched to another section (cleaning) where she found she could not tolerate the smells. Ostensibly, this was her reason for leaving. But she went on, "I suppose I

might have been able to get used to the smells; after all, other women do, but our foreman made no attempt to persuade me to stay, so why should I have made the effort? This foreman seems to think that if you want to leave, it's not worth the bother to talk to you about it. If he did try to talk me into staying, I would have, because this would show he had some feelings."

Chang, a worker at Western Electronics, had this to say about a foreman and the women he supervises:

Of course, each person likes to know that someone is concerned about her. For example, when my younger brother came to Taipei my foreman asked about him and what he was doing here. But this would depend on the girl herself; some don't like to mix work matters and personal affairs. For instance, a worker might be an adopted daughter, and she would not like to talk about her family. She would find a foreman's questions annoying, as if he were prying. In any case, a foreman is most concerned with production.

Group-leaders in particular, since they must deal with both foreman and workers, are most apt to appreciate that a comfortable, friendly relationship between foremen and workers has much to do with improving work performance.

If a foreman would talk with the girls—and not just about work-related matters—then everyone would become better acquainted, and the quality of work would be higher. It's important for him to be on good terms with all the workers, and not just the group-leaders.

For another worker expressions of concern in themselves carry more weight than whatever tangible results might be gained.

If you're a foreman and your work is going well, you still couldn't be considered successful in your job if you're not on good terms with the girls in your section. [How would a foreman go about doing this?] He could be more easy-going, more approachable, make himself easier to talk to. The wrong thing to do would be to stress the distance between him and the workers. When he has time he should talk and joke with the workers; this way better relations will develop. He needn't ask about personal matters, but could just show some concern in your work, or ask you about school. Sure, he may not be able to solve any problems for you, but this way the girls would feel that he cares.

Most women who had an opinion on the subject agreed that it would not do for a foreman to suddenly initiate a more familiar relationship; they suggest instead that he ought to begin by complimenting a worker on her performance or taking an interest in her work, and only later, proceed to more personal matters. Examples of concern that workers gave show that such expressions need not be about major issues; inquiring after a worker's health after she has been ill, or taking the trouble to notify her family if something should happen, asking a worker about school examinations—all these are taken by women as indications that a foreman has "human feeling" and takes a genuine interest in the welfare of his workers.

But even these illustrations are somewhat exceptional, and further examination reveals that few workers can claim a "close" relationship (even by the modest expectations noted above) with their foreman or find it conceivable. If a worker and her foreman converse at all, more than likely the subject is production.

> Most foremen would not know much about our families or friends; of course, as far as family matters are concerned, everyone tends to keep such information to herself and generally won't volunteer much. Besides, we go to our foreman only when there's a need to.

> It's hard enough to know another person on your line, so it's even more improbable that a foreman would know anything about a woman's family or really understand her.

As I proposed earlier, it is a fine line that divides attempts to "understand" a person from what are considered improper and unwanted advances. A foreman who ask "too many questions" is clearly out of bounds, and he becomes a nuisance. Older, more experienced workers could describe, either from their own experience or from hearsay, foremen who were too friendly— such as one who had a habit of patting everyone on the shoulder (considered too forward), and another who liked to talk when his workers would have preferred to be left alone.

> Our foreman is always trying to take advantage of the girls. He's a very slippery person; that's why girls who come to work cannot be too trusting.

> He was always trying to get one of the workers to go out with him, but no one was willing. And he was always interested in things that didn't concern him, or would try to join our conversations. So we girls just didn't pay any attention to him, and there was nothing he could do.

(It works the other way as well; women who are on familiar terms with their foreman are accused by their coworkers of "currying favor." Since favoritism is viewed as an inevitable fact of work relations, there is consensus that women who "know how to talk" come out ahead.)

I have suggested that factory women assign greater value to having a foreman who will maintain warm relations with his workers and are less preoccupied with the possible work-related advantages they might obtain from such relations. This is supported by their awareness of the limits of what a foreman can acheive on behalf of his workers. As one worker said,

> No one pays any attention to our opinions. We could tell our foreman but it's not likely that he would speak to those above him for us, besause he does not want to jeopardize his job. You can't blame him; everyone wants to move up. He's afraid that he might be considered too much of a busy-body.

Although this might be frustrating, it does not appear to be difficult to accept.

What causes greater discontent is a foreman who underlines the distance between his position and the workers', a foreman who flaunts his higher status. (A typical example: a foreman comes upon two workers or group-leaders who are resting and orders them back to work. Later they accuse him of taking pleasure in ordering them around.) Because women perceive it to be the foreman's responsibility to instill some human feeling into relations between himself and his workers, even a casual remark or gesture can lead a worker to accuse her foreman of "putting on airs." According to one group-leader, "some girls would greet their foreman, but all it takes is just one time if he happens not to respond or acknowledge a girl, and she'd think that he looks down on her." The sensitivity of many women concerning their status as manual workers and their low educational level makes them especially prone to such interpretations. As one trainer remarked,

> Some girls may be on friendly terms with their foremen, but if he should ever yell at them, their reaction is very strong and more intense than you might expect, since they assume that he looks down on them because they are only primary or lower-middle school graduates.

She continued, drawing on her own experience as a group-leader:

> I admit now that I was wrong to think that way, but as a high school graduate, I didn't want to associate with primary or lower-middle school graduates, but preferred to talk with other high school graduates and the foreman, since he was better educated.

Hence, even casual remarks that are misconstrued as brush-offs are felt keenly.

Although a foreman is not categorized as a member of the managerial class, he is not regarded as a laborer either, and giving orders is viewed as a legitimate exercise of authority. The situation, however, is different for a group-leader; on the one hand she resembles the assemblers she supervises in that they share a similar background, and in all likelihood she was once an assembler herself. Yet on the other hand she differs in that she supervises them. The group-leader's social identity as a worker and the definition of her job therefore generate some ambiguity about her status, as the following case demonstrates:

> A woman returned to her dormitory room after work and immediately began to complain to her roommates that her group-leader had refused to permit her to take a day off. "All I was trying to do was do *her* a favor by telling her ahead of time; otherwise, I could have just not come to work at all. Who does she think she is, acting as if she's got all the authority."

It should come as no surprise, then, to find that factory women are frequently ambivalent about becoming group-leaders themselves. Part of this confusion is of a superficial sort and can be cleared up if one specifies whether a woman is talking about her *particular* group-leader or if she is commenting on the *role* of a group-leader. Nonetheless, it is worthwhile to examine the bases of these

ambivalent responses, insofar as such an effort may provide some clues as to
how to begin to measure job commitment and job satisfaction (since becoming
a group-leader is a promotion). More simply, a group-leader's job-description
furnishes some indication of the contrast between the timid, unassured woman
entering her first factory and the woman who, perhaps after a few months,
oversees a group of fifteen to twenty other women like herself.

During the time I spent at Western Electronics there were three women
trouble-shooters (the rest being men) and one forewoman,[7] and inside the
plants these were the highest positions held by women. Older workers told me
that four or five years ago there were more opportunities for assemblers and
group-leaders to be promoted as the company's expansion created a demand
for more clerical workers, and they could point to women in the offices
(including the three trainers) who were formerly assemblers. The prospect of
such mobility, however, no longer exists, and even though the company has a
policy of "promoting from within," all agree that few openings materialize. The
status of group-leader, then, is the best that an assembler could hope to attain,
and when I asked assemblers about positions to which a group-leader could be
promoted, the answers either indicated that there are none or alluded to "the
way things were four or five years ago." As one working-student put it, "Here I
feel as if I will always be a group-leader; even if I had more schooling it wouldn't
be any use; there're no chances for promotion beyond group-leader." As some
would add, the opportunity to become a group-leader appears only when
another departs. The tendency to flock to new factories reflects the belief that
one's chances for promotion are better with a growing company.

New workers generally address their group-leader by title, but after a few
days, call her by name as other workers do, a practice that group-leaders say
they prefer. One group-leader said, "I would feel funny hearing someone call
me 'group-leader;' it'd be as if I were a level higher, so I ask them to call me by
name." It is understandable that a woman who is herself a group-leader might
wish to downplay her status. Most assemblers, however, and a number of
group-leaders speaking in other contexts will acknowledge that there is some
distance in status between a group-leader and an assembler. "The group-
leader's position is a little higher than ours because she supervises us;" "it's not
quite the same because our jobs are different." Yet this is a distinction that is felt
to be specific to the work situation; "it's not something you would feel away
from work or that you would take with you off the job." Nevertheless, the title
itself does carry some prestige: "Being a group-leader just sounds a lot better
than being an assembler; if you tell someone outside the company that you
work as a group-leader, it sounds better." One group-leader, who in an earlier
conversation had much to say about the difficulties of her job, later said
without prompting, "I often do feel myself fortunate to be a group-leader, and
at my age too [nineteen]." To one woman a group-leader is still a "factory girl,"
although "she is one level higher than we are."

While a group-leader may insist in the abstract that all women are workers and that she does not want to be treated as a group-leader, to be re-assigned to an assembler's position after having been a group-leader is not easily accepted. In the fall of 1974 production of several models was terminated, and a group of group-leaders was switched to other sections as assemblers. Although their wages remained the same as before, the move was a distressing one to most. "After all, the positions are different; before, you were the one telling people what to do, and now someone else is giving you orders." In another case at the satellite plant, a group-leader (A) was sick for three weeks and returned to find another worker (B) in her place. The situation was awkward for both women and their foreman, with B feeling that since A was her former group-leader, she could not be expected to supervise A; A, on the other hand, felt she could not bear to remain on the same line and was subsequently transferred to another line.

To many women, however, the added prestige that the title group-leader bestows seems rather empty, and even the extra NT$250 do not seem compensation enough for what they regard as a thankless job. A new worker is apt to notice only the more comfortable and superficial features of a group-leader's day; "I certainly wouldn't mind being a group-leader; all they do is walk around and talk, and they don't have very much work to do." A far more frequently heard assessment, though, is that a group-leader's work is light, but her responsibilities are heavy.

By definition a group-leader's job requires her to deal with people and she is constantly placed in the position of being an intermediary between workers and their foreman.[8] Together these aspects of a group-leader's duties create the complexities that cause some workers to think twice before accepting the promotion. In the opinion of the one woman who has been both group-leader and forewoman, it is the former who has the more demanding job: "Foremen do not always have to deal with every worker directly, but a group-leader has to cope with all matters relating to every worker." As another group-leader put it, "if you have to deal with people there are bound to be more problems."

It is said that being in the middle makes it difficult to "be a person" because meeting the demands imposed by both sides usually means offending one group. The following summarizes the group-leader's predicament:

> Being a group-leader isn't easy. If you follow company rules to the letter you'll have all the girls against you; no one will like you. But if you bend the rules too much, you're in trouble with the foreman and the superintendent. You can't please both sides. But many workers are still interested in becoming a group-leader; you can't blame them—everyone wants to climb up, only they don't realize how bitter the job can be until they actually begin the job.

What appears to be one primary source of a group-leader's dilemma is that while group-leaders are expected to perform supervisory tasks that are similar (in nature if not in extent) to those which foremen carry out, group-leaders lack (or they feel they lack) the right to exercise such authority. They seem to feel that their title alone does not legitimize their exercising such prerogatives. A group-leader cannot treat her workers in the way a foreman might and remain an effective group-leader for long, yet she must also answer to her foreman. Almost always, a group-leader was once herself an assembler, and her relationship with the workers differs from that of the foreman.

> It's easy for a foreman to scold us group-leaders, but what methods are we to use to get the girls to listen to us? If a group-leader does what a foreman tells her to and resorts to his methods, the girls won't stand for it and you would have an even more difficult situation. Sometimes when a worker's performance isn't good enough, a foreman will want to get rid of her, but how is one supposed to say such things?

> The foreman is only interested in how many pieces we finish, but as a group-leader, it's difficult to criticize your workers since you know them so well, and since we were all doing the same job once.

An assembler can usually count on the inspector on her line to catch her mistakes, whereas a group-leader is held accountable not only for the quality of the assembled parts (which also leads to conflicts between group-leaders and quality control workers) but is held responsible for the conduct of the workers on her line as well. "Everyone's faults fall on your shoulders, and if something goes wrong the foreman comes looking for the group-leader and not the other women." "Being the person in the middle doesn't get you any appreciation; if you're too friendly with the foreman the girls will talk, but if you're not on good terms with him, he might accuse you of being uncooperative."

However seriously some group-leaders may take their responsibilities to their supervisors, maintaining smooth relations with the workers under her is considered an even more challenging task. A group-leader's greatest worry is to find an uncooperative worker on her line, and in a group of fifteen to twenty there are bound to be one or two women who do not like the group-leader, or who see no point in exerting extra effort since wage increases are not dependent upon performance. According to the trainers a new group-leader is apt to have a particularly frustrating time because the workers know she is inexperienced; "some of the smarter ones often manage to finish their work faster and find time to walk around, to play, or slip away to the dormitories, and so on." Such women can also be a poor influence on their coworkers. "Some women do not hesitate in talking back to the group-leader, and when you have workers gossiping about a group-leader, they can blow a small matter out of proportion, they can turn white into black, and they can accuse you of playing favorites." For a group-leader to scold workers, however, is counter-productive: "This only makes them more angry, and they will create even more problems for you."

Faced with a worker who is not performing diligently group-leaders must find their own solutions, and they emphasize the importance of encouraging their workers rather than merely scolding them. Some group-leaders consciously exploit the closer relationship they have with assemblers. One group-leader claimed that "workers are more afraid of their group-leader than their foreman because there are more contacts between them, and so some feeling develops. A worker who does poorly, therefore, might feel very embarrassed towards her group-leader, whereas it matters less with a foreman since he and she don't have much of a relationship anyway."

A group-leader's strategy of making her own job easier by making an effort to better understand her workers does not succeed in every case. Special circumstances create other problems. Older women, for example, are thought to be difficult to supervise because the age difference makes any assertion of authority an awkward task. "A group-leader has to try to be a little more polite in speaking to them; after all, they're old enough to be our mothers." One group-leader's solution is to ask another older worker to speak for her, so as not to embarrass the older woman. The educational level of the group-leader relative to that of her workers is also a sensitive point that may disrupt work relations. A number of group-leaders at Western Electronics and at other factories, being primary or lower-middle school graduates themselves, are inclined to attribute problems in supervision to this factor; "that girl thinks that because she is a high school graduate, I have no right to supervise her." Indeed, the statements from workers who have completed high school confirm a group-leader's apprehensions. "Our group-leader only completed the second year of lower-middle school, so she isn't very mature at times, and her behavior is childish sometimes."

The importance factory women place on educational level and the fact that a promotion from assembler to group-leader status does not hinge upon educational level undermine a group-leader's self-assurance and prevent her from acting as she might wish. Most workers would concede that group-leaders are more experienced, but there are those who see little else in the way of special qualifications that legitimize the status distinction.

> So what if a person is a group-leader; she isn't that much higher than the rest of us.

> In my section the group-leaders all get together and talk and they can do as they please. But if we talk even a little, the group-leader will come over and scold us. To be a group-leader isn't that big a deal; even an elementary school graduate can be one, yet they still feel so superior.

One high school graduate feels even more strongly:

> Education isn't a very important factor in becoming a group-leader. Many are only elementary or lower-middle school graduates; it's just that they've been here a long time. Having to listen to them is hard to take, but then what can you do?

As might be expected better educated workers are nearly unanimous in asserting that a person's educational level should be taken into account when a promotion is considered, while workers with less schooling emphasize the greater relevance of actual working experience.

A none-too-thorough understanding of company policy concerning the selection of group-leaders and the very few openings that become available also promote ill-feeling (that is sometimes misdirected to the group-leader herself). A group-leader may recommend workers for promotion but the final decision is made by the foreman and occasionally by the superintendent. Selection is based on a combination of factors: seniority, quality of performance, and "leadership abilities." The fact that such evaluations are often subjective in nature inevitably leaves much room for accusations charging favoritism. Given the very large number of women who are bound to be passed over, it is not surprising to find that women can readily point to reasons that explain why some workers are quickly promoted while others are unfairly left behind. There is a strongly felt consensus among factory women that knowing the right people is essential for attaining any desirable job.

> They say that seniority counts, but I've been here over two years; it's all a matter of having the right connections.

> There aren't many openings anymore; all the promotions I know of depended on connections. If one foreman knows another foreman well, and a worker is on good terms with one of them, she can pull strings or use her influence to get a better position.

Thus, although women may at times deny that they attach much value to a group-leader's title, in other contexts it appears that women do make fine gradations among themselves according to criteria such as one's work status or one's educational level. The friction that such distinctions may generate between workers and group leaders represents only part of a larger pattern of discriminations that can interfere with the maintenance of smooth relations among workers in a factory. (I discuss these distinctions more fully in chapter 12.)

The majority of factory women look upon the relationship between company management and themselves as a straightforward one involving an exchange of cash for labor; furthermore, recognizing that they fill the lowest level in the organizational pyramid, factory women do not consider it their place to demand special attention. In addition, most of them perform repetitive tasks that quickly become monotonous. For many women, therefore, the most rewarding aspect of a factory job is of a social nature—the opportunity to meet new people, to make friends, and to enjoy the interaction such ties make possible. At the same time, there are facets of the work situation that interfere with the formation of friendships; women soon discover that getting along with people was a simpler matter at school.

I do not claim that the prospect of satisfying social relations is the primary consideration when women are choosing among several factories, but only that with time these bonds with coworkers take on greater meaning and bring more gratification than other aspects of their jobs. The following comments made by a worker from another television factory are typical:

> For most girls the best part of work is probably knowing that they can come and talk and be with friends. With this sort of work it'd be impossible for anyone to just sit there for eight hours; talking makes the work easier to tolerate.

Feelings among workers developed over time may be sufficient reason to induce a woman to stay; another group-leader explained:

> I've thought of quitting several times when I'm upset, such as when I have arguments with the foreman, but then I'd think about having been here so long and about my friends here. If I change jobs, everything would be new and strange, and I would have to adjust all over again. If I ever leave this place this is what I'll miss—the friends I have and not the company.

It is not an uncommon view among factory women that the most anxiety-provoking part of "becoming accustomed" to a new working environment has to do with learning to deal with a new set of people. "Making friends takes time; even if the work were the same you never know what interpersonal relations will be like, and even if the job paid more, it wouldn't be worth the trouble." Women therefore value stability in their work situation and the security that comes from being among familiar people. Working against this, however, are a high turnover rate and the rotation of workers from dismantled production lines to new lines.

References to self-interest in specific workers (or in a class of employees) translate at the broader level to charges of opportunism on the part of the company management. In the view of factory women the clearest manifestation of this is the company's "take it or leave it" attitude; women claim that only rarely are efforts made to persuade a departing worker to stay. "The company is only concerned with what's good for it at any particular moment; when they need workers they'll even offer a bonus if you introduce someone to work here, but when you're no longer needed, they make it so that it's very hard for you to stay on."

Although the cases women could cite are not isolated to this period, charges of opportunism were heard most frequently during the 1974 recession when many factories were forced either to close or to reduce their work force substantially. The number of employees who were actually laid off at Western Electronics was small in comparison with other factories,[9] but the threat of layoffs and the knowledge that jobs could not be had elsewhere produced a quick and visible change in the work style of factory women at Western Electronics. Reading, eating, and napping on the job were definitely frowned upon in the past, but during this period the high anxiety that many women felt was reflected in a new conscientiousness.

There was a more specific reason, however, that brought on this display of conspicuous diligence. Although impending layoffs became a central topic of discussion, few workers had accurate notions about the criteria by which workers would be selected to stay on.

> The company should have a specific policy stating which workers will be laid off, such as by seniority or by quality of performance. Instead, what the company does is to make it hard for you to stay on; it amounts to forcing you to leave; that way, they don't have to pay you any severance compensation. For example, things have become much stricter (no books, no food, no loud talking, no walking around) so that if you're caught violating even a small rule, they have reason to dismiss you. Another method of forcing workers to leave on their own is by reducing the number of buses (and routes) for commuting workers, so that those who find it too inconvenient now to come to work will just have to quit.

To be sure, this particular three month period did heighten workers' propensity to detect purely instrumental motives on the part of management, but for many women the supposed policies of the company during the crisis only confirmed what they had known all along. ("In any case, all factories just use our labor to make money.") The small amount of the annual increases, for instance, signifies to many women that the company has no strong interest in retaining its more experienced workers, since new workers come at a "cheaper price."

It might appear that the opportunistic practices of the company would result in alienating many members of its labor force. Without denying that resentment is created, however, such an assumption still warrants further examination because job satisfaction must be gauged in terms of expectations and in terms of perceptions of "how things really are." Here, there may be reason to suggest that the gap between the two is not always a wide one. More experienced workers, in particular, characterize the relationship between management and themselves plainly and predominantly as one involving the exchange of cash for labor.

> There're so many levels in the company, and we're at the bottom; others may not even know what goes on here. But then no one forced us to come here, and we're here only to do the work the company pays us to do.

> All I feel is that the company [a garment factory] has the money to employ me, and I will work for them to earn that money, to do just what is assigned me. But as for myself I don't see this work as necessarily benefiting my future in any way. For now, only the wages matter.

An awareness that the "obligation" between employer and employee is primarily an instrumental one[10] does not deter women from trying out different factories in the hope of finding still better working conditions, but it does set limits to one's expectations. Added to this is the knowledge that without a high school (or college) diploma, truly better jobs are out of reach, that a comparable position that pays more is bound to involve more bitter work, and that cumulative on-the-job experience does not guarantee a woman a higher rank at another firm.

Given a fairly realistic appraisal of their standing in the job market and of the instrumental tie between themselves and any particular firm, one might suppose that factory women reason that their expectations must also be modest, commensurate with their low positions. Although there is data that would bear this out, to leave the matter here would leave much unsaid. The following remarks are an appropriate illustration.

> Of course, our expectations cannot be too high but the company should recognize that the efforts of the workers are very important. After all, if the products are good, it's the workers who made them that way, not the managers. But we get no praise and no encouragement. All the company seems to care about is saving money, and their attitude seems to be, 'if you don't like it here, there's nothing to stop you from leaving.' For example, the new schedule [longer hours on weekdays and no work on Saturdays] is especially hard on students, but for those who only have a year of school left before graduation, all they can do is try and put up with it. No one pays any attention to our opinions, so we girls just talk among ourselves and let it go at that.

The reminder that one's expectations cannot be too high, therefore, clearly does not prevent a worker from wishing that things might be otherwise, and perhaps in part it is the tension between these attitudes that stimulates some women to make their way from factory to factory.

The cynicism and passiveness revealed in the quote above are typical reactions, insofar as voicing complaints and taking action to correct them are concerned. There is perhaps more agreement on this subject than on any other issue among factory women. The consensus is that as mere assemblers, for the most part, the opinions of factory women would not count for much, and rather than seeing themselves as constituting the largest category of employees in the factory, individual women state instead, "There're so many people in the company, why would they listen to us? We're just one among many." Although some workers can argue forcefully that they deserve more recognition for the work they do, they can in the very next moment admit that they would not dare to be so presumptuous as to present criticisms to anyone but each other. Even a worker in a small company that employs about twenty women (producing serum for vaccines in the community of Ch'inan) expressed a similar view: "It's true that we have meetings, and I admit it sounds better than other factories. But if we were really to speak out about our dissatisfactions, we would only be reprimanded." The attitude of a majority is one of resignation; in their outlook "things have always been this way and are not likely to change." For others, submitting suggestions is a futile effort because there are no effective channels for voicing complaints. In the words of one woman,

Whom would I tell? Besides, what would that accomplish? Everyone wants to move up; if we tell the foreman, he's not going to tell the superintendent since the foreman himself hopes to become a superintendent someday, and the superintendent is even more afraid of the manager.

As for the union representatives,[11] while a number of workers were able to explain to me that the purpose of the union is to protect workers, few could tell me who their representatives are. The idea that a woman could seek out union representatives is inconceivable to most women, and some gave a more specific reason for not even considering doing so:

The way I see it, the managers of the company are the ones who run the union, and they have the final say. Their interests and ours are different, and naturally they'd look after their own concerns and would not give much attention to what we want.

The way the system works now, the union only knows the opinions of the foremen and the people above them and hears nothing from the women workers themselves, so how can they do anything for us?

It is not surprising, therefore, that for many factory women, being able to do their work in peace, without being bothered and without running into problems, takes priority over seeking improvements in company policies. One group-leader's advice to her workers is not to take anything too seriously: "I tell them they only come here to earn some money, so it's not worthwhile if you let things get to you." A woman may be dissatisfied with certain features of her job or with working conditions, but in the end she is more apt to shrug and say, "I do my work and the company pays me for it; what else needs to be said?"

When given the opportunity some women do indeed have much to say about the improvements they would like to see, although they are a long ways away from acting on those ideas. Mention has already been made of the desire on the part of workers to receive some sign of appreciation from the company management. Women claim that managers know and care only that work quotas are filled, but do not acknowledge the special efforts that may have gone into meeting a deadline. Working students claim that they must cope with rising tuition fees and examination schedules and wish for some special consideration. A wage-scale that is adjusted according to seniority rather than merit leads many women to conclude that good performance does not count and usually goes unrecognized. Women consider it unfair and frustrating that efficient workers are given the same compensation as less conscientious workers, and as one woman said before leaving Western Electronics: "The company gives no recognition to a good worker; it need not be a big reward, but at least it would be an indication that the company appreciates extra efforts." As the following case illustrates, appreciation need not be expressed in monetary terms, and this is the only instance I came across in which a worker (in a company numbering several hundred workers) volunteered such a positive opinion of her employers. (The firm is a garment factory outside Ch'inan owned by three brothers.)

> The [bosses] are very good to us workers; they'll come over to our work areas and talk with us. They even remember the names of those who have been here longer. There is a suggestion box in the plant, but the managers are so nice to us that the foremen don't dare make any trouble for us.

My impression is that the atmosphere this woman describes is more commonly found in family-run enterprises such as knitting businesses,[12] and I suspect that many women at Western Electronics would find her view naive.

Women state that it is best if the company were to establish, on its own initiative, programs for the benefit of its workers. However, they do not always regard existing amenities or welfare benefits as adequate or as suiting their needs. (One important exception at Western Electronics was the designation of one room on each floor of the dormitories as a study hall for students; previously, limited desk space and early lights-out in the rooms severely reduced study time for students.) Factory women are aware that only relatively large firms such as Western Electronics have the resources to fund and maintain the variety of welfare and educational programs and recreational facilities that fall under the heading of "fringe benefits," but their appreciation of these is not borne out by a high participation rate.

Except for the quality of a company's dormitories, considerations such as the availability of medical coverage, company-sponsored outings, sewing classes, etc., are not the deciding factors in determining whether a worker remains in one company or whether she opts for another.

> It's true that the welfare programs in a large company are more varied, but what are the actual benefits you enjoy? For example, you can only participate in the birthday parties here once a year [Western Electronics arranges birthday parties for workers according to month,i.e., one party per month], and if you don't get a prize in the drawing, you end up with nothing. If it's a choice between such programs and more money, I would rather have the money, it's something you can take with you.

Similarly, singing contests, popular at several large factories, are criticized as wasting funds that might be put to better use. Other than serious illnesses, medical coverage for workers sometimes appears to inconvenience women rather than to assure them of adequate care. Women claim that they are given inferior treatment and are subjected to the rudeness of doctors and hospital personnel who "don't like to see our workers' insurance slips [since the fees are smaller]." Frequently, therefore, women say they must spend their own money to obtain proper medical attention.

Hence, in the opinion of some factory women a good deal of a company's programs exists only for show, much as the union and suggestion boxes are provided for the sake of appearance. Other examples cited as evidence of such practices range from charges that ventilation units, designed to remove soldering fumes, are retained even though they do not function effectively to charges that examinations for clerical positions within the company are only a matter of "going through the motions," since the proper connections often determine beforehand which workers achieve the promotions,

Added to these suspicions is an often imperfect understanding of company policies, leading some workers to conclude indignantly that the company is always trying to "put one over on us."[13] Rumors about the contrived means by which the firm would dismiss workers rather than lay off workers are one example. Not all women are equally predisposed to believe such rumors, but at times even more serious charges are made. One group-leader at Western Electronics heard that a wage increase had already been approved by the American managers, but somehow the funds were still "in the hands of Chinese managers; the things they tell us aren't true, and they're trying to deceive us." (Sometime later a wage increase for group-leaders was approved, although I cannot say for certain how the two developments are connected.) A woman in a large garment factory said,

> In a large company you only know the few people near you, and there're hardly any contacts between the [bosses] and the workers, so there would be lots of matters workers would not know about. Recently, for example, managers and office personnel appropriated for themselves a sum of money intended for us workers.

Part of the problem stems from the difficulty of disseminating accurate information on a myriad of subjects to all workers in a factory the size of Western Electronics. A Western Electronics worker who had spent four years in a smaller electronics firm stated that in the latter "a worker has more opportunities to know and has a better idea of what's going on in the company, whether the company is having financial problems or whether it's doing well. Having such information it's more likely that a worker will feel that what is good for the company is good for workers as well." Company bulletins are issued, of course, but often these appear too late to correct the distortions rumors produce, and the impact is weakened. Or, in the case of company examinations, one personnel manager admitted, "Sure, there's a promotion-from-within policy; the problem is that there is no communications supervisor, so how are women to know when and what positions become open?"

Factory women therefore appear to vacillate between resigning themselves to their low-status occupations and to modest expectations on the one hand, and feeling that they deserve recognition and treatment with more concern on the other. Because human feelings run both ways, it is not surprising to hear from trainers and group-leaders that when workers leave a firm, they give little thought to whether the timing of their departure will inconvenience others, or to whether they have any sense of obligation or responsibility to the company (as might happen in a smaller firm). Instead, women merely follow their own inclinations.

Economic necessity, a woman's educational background and the job market, low expectations regarding the intrinsic interest an assembler's job holds, and the expectation that women generally work only for a few years until they marry[14] all shape the orientations toward work women bring with them when they enter a factory. Factory women's perceptions of work, therefore, involve factors that go beyond the nature of their tasks, and the satisfactions they find derive in large part from the social context they themselves create and may not have very much to do with the company itself. But at the same time there are elements in the work environment (e.g., the playing up of status distinctions) that reduce the chances that a woman's high expectations concerning social relations will always be met (see chapter 12).

Women also value recognition from their companies, but their modest expectations of their employers reflect their outlook toward wage-earning in general. Women are aware that they and their employers stand in different structural positions; moreover, women have little control over the decisions that affect them, making company policies susceptible to misinterpretation. But in the view of many women, expressions of concern on the personal level are lacking as well, and these need not be imcompatible with management's interest in achieving its own aims.[15]

I do not wish to exaggerate the importance women place on such expressions of concern; surely, the tendency to dwell upon what is *deficient* in the company can make expectations in this regard seem higher than they actually are. Rather, it appears that factory women's understanding of their work is more heavily influenced by three components: the temporary nature of their work, the fact that their social identity comes to be defined as "only a factory girl," and a lack of awareness (or in any case, no articulation) of the fact that they make a substantial contribution to Taiwan's economic growth. Perhaps more revealing is this statement from a worker who had been discussing working conditions: "But then, like many things, if one doesn't have a choice,one should just try and adjust, and once a person becomes accustomed to something, then things will be all right."

We see therefore that women's distrust of management does not produce worker solidarity, and that, in fact, an emphasis on rank and status can disrupt relations among female workers. I shall return to these points in chapters 12 and 13.

Control of Income and Women's Position in the Family

Factory women view the social environment in which they work and in which some of them live in positive and negative terms, but for their families it is their daughters' incomes that are most important. Families in which a father and two or three daughters share the responsibility of supporting the family are not uncommon today and are a measure of the enormity of the change in the economic contribution factory women are able to make, the expectations of parents with regard to their daughters' earnings, and the consequences this new economic capability has for working women.

The mere fact of wage-earning has not conferred upon daughters the right to control their incomes. Because it is the family's interests that are being served when a daughter goes to work, decisions about the proper disposal of her income are in the hands of the family head. Women in dormitories allot approximately half of their earnings to requisite living expenses, but this is not equivalent to having the power to control one's wages. It is true that women are allowed spending money, but with the exception of working students, these sums are not large enough to improve their future options.

A summary of expenditures should be outlined before beginning a discussion of control over earnings. Wages vary according to the type of industry and individual firms, but on the average women in electronics factories earn between NT$1,500 and NT$2,500 per month, and textile/garment workers can earn up to as much as NT$4,000 per month.[1] A transportation allowance is often included in the base wage, as is a meal allowance.[2] Most dormitories are available without charge, with some firms occasionally charging minimal fees for bedding and maintenance (NT$50 per month at Western Electronics). It is food that constitutes the largest expenditure for women living in dormitories; NT$20 per day is not an extravagant amount to spend on food, and unless a woman restricts herself to a vegetarian diet she is likely to allot anywhere between NT$700 to NT$900 a month for meals. Since this sum amounts to almost one half of a new workers earnings, it is not surprising to hear that daughters are sometimes told to return home to work in a nearby factory (if one exists) or to work in the fields.

Students must save enough for their tuition and other school fees. There have been several increases in tuition for senior high school in recent years, reaching a high of approximately NT$2,700 per term in one school in the fall of 1974. (It should be remembered that working-students are only able to work, in most cases, in electronics firms because garment/textile factories demand longer hours; they must therefore balance greater expenditures with a relatively lower wage-scale.) Women estimate from a low of approximately NT$200 a month to NT$400 per month for personal expenses (recreation, small purchases, and transportation home), not counting clothes or meals. A few calculations make it evident that working-students who live in dormitories have a difficult time either saving or sending home more than NT$200 to NT$300 a month. As one of them said, "With school it's hard to send money home, but then with less time to go out we also spend less an amusements."

When workers, particularly those on their first jobs, are asked what they intend to do with their earnings, the standard answer is that the money will be sent homes to one's parents. In fact, of course, the matter is not so simple, and it is really a question of how much a woman is expected to and is able to contribute. For instance, one newly-hired woman left Western Electronics after several days because her family deemed the wages at Western Electronics too low and urged her to go elsewhere. Additional concrete examples provide a preliminary picture of what a daughter's contribution can mean:

In the Hwang family in Ch'ipei each of the three daughters (all of whom live at home) contributes NT$1,500 per month, even though their earnings differ. According to the second daughter, "the amount was not decided by our parents; each of us brings home the same amount because as sisters, it's not good if one brings home less." There is an elder brother who works only sporadically and two younger brothers still in school.

With an older brother in the army and two younger brothers of middle-school age, the earnings of two Chen daughters living in Ch'inan add a substantial portion to their family's income. The older daughter's monthly wages at a garment factory average NT$2,600 while her younger sister's wages in an electronics factory are close to NT$2,000. Together they contribute NT$3,000 a month to their family. Their father said, "It's natural that young women today should want some money for clothes and personal items. Their brother worked in a bakery before going into the army, and he didn't give that much to the family, so it isn't right to ask too much of his sisters. Still, we're on a tight budget and cannot save very much." When Mr. Chen injured his arm in a work-related accident, his wife went to work as a maid.

Liu Jin-ping is the youngest in her family and lives with her mother, an elder brother and his wife and their son. All her earnings are turned over to her mother, and she receives spending money from her mother when she needs it. "It's not convenient keeping all that money on myself; besides I don't have that many expenses. If I give my earnings to my mother she has some cash on hand and can use it to join a credit club.[3] We're not a rich family and this money helps to pay for everyday expenses."

Liu A-lan works in a knitting business in Ch'ipei and walks back to her home in Ch'inan. Her mother found the job for her, citing the proximity and high wages as the advantages.

Depending on the volume of business, Liu's earnings range between NT$3,000 and NT$3,300 a month, and she keeps NT$300 for herself. Thus far Liu is the only working daughter in her family and her younger siblings are still in school.

Two Liu sisters work in the Western Electronics satellite plant in Ch'ipei and both attend school, over their mother's objections. Each earns approximately NT$2,000 a month and each month half of that goes to their mother. With the cost of tuition rising (to almost NT$5,000 for the two of them) their mother's continued opposition is understandable. Mrs. Liu explained to us, "Education matters less for girls. As long as a woman can read, it's enough. Anyway, they're both in their twenties and will marry soon, so what's the point of going to school?" When the company began to lay off workers, however, both discontinued school on their own (even though they were not discharged), and later, after the plant shut down its operations they found comparable paying jobs elsewhere but neither returned to school. The elder daughter explained, "Tuition has become too high, and even after graduating one isn't assured of a better [white-collar] job."

Chen is the youngest in her family, and before leaving home (in Chiayi) she was the only child still living with her parents. When she was employed in a noodle factory in Tainan she gave NT$1,000 of her NT$1,200 monthly wage to her family. "This was possible because the company paid for all our meals. Here [at Western Electronics] the biggest expense is food, and altogether I spend about NT$1,000 a month on myself, with about NT$700 of that going for meals and the rest for personal things. It isn't much, but I send the remainder [approximately NT$900] home."

Chang is a high school graduate who came to Western Electronics only reluctantly, not having been able to find a better job. She too spends about NT$700 per month on meals and remits NT$800 to NT$1,000 home each month. "Besides food there aren't that many expenses, except that train tickets home are expensive." As for her roommates in the dormitory, "by sharing clothes and cosmetics they also manage to send home about NT$1,000 a month; besides, when they go out the boys pay for everything anyway."

Chen, a working-student, depends on annual bonuses to pay for her tuition "and if I don't send money home one month I can save enough for each term." Altogether she spends NT$1,100 each month on herself and sends NT$900 home. When she received her high school diploma she explained why she had no plans for continuing in school: I have a younger sister and a brother still at home and they have to go to school. My elder sister only finished elementary school, and so I'm already fortunate in having gone to high school."

Working-students agree that one must be very frugal in order to attend school and be able to send home sums as large as NT$800 to NT$1,000 a month. Cheng is more typical in that she sends money home (usually half her earnings) during the summer months, but during the school year she is only able to remit NT$200 to NT$300 per month.

Shih lives at home, and with one older sister in college, her parents supported her decision to attend school while working. From her earnings she pays her tuition, has a savings account, and keeps a smaller amount as spending money. "My parents wouldn't ask for a specific amount but leave that up to me. Since I live at home I do bring money home, about NT$300 or so each month."

Most of these cases are representative of families in which the earnings of daughters constitute an important portion of family income but where there is also some flexibility such that a daughter may be permitted to attend school and/or to live away from home. In instances where factory women contribute their total earnings regularly, family financial need is almost always more acute.

> Lim and Chen are both garment factory workers who live with a grandmother and grandparents, respectively, and while the latter derive other income from their sons, they are largely dependent upon the earnings of the grand-daughters. Neither Lim nor Chen progressed beyond elementary school nor did they ever attend school on a part-time basis.

> Yang Chiu-lan and Yang Su-ying are cousins who live next door to each other in Ch'inan. Both completed elementary school and are garment factory workers. Yang Chiu-lan's widowed mother is employed on a part-time basis as a construction laborer and their family's income is supplemented by the earnings of another daughter and a son. Yang Su-ying, on the other hand, is the only daughter remaining (an elder sister having married out) at home and her earnings help to support three younger brothers. For each woman spending money amounts to little more than NT$150 per month.

> Su's father's business involves constructing the paper houses and other accessories used in funeral rituals. She entered a fish-net factory in Sanhsia after elementary school, although she now has a younger brother in college and another in high school. "With my elder sister married I'm now the oldest in the family, and so my family relies on me." All her earnings are given to her mother "for helping the family," and in her spare time she works with her mother at home assembling plastic flowers and repairing fish nets.

Even in cases such as these, however, sums are not demanded from daughters. Rather, the understanding between parents and daughters is generally implicit and the precise arrangements are arrived at and accepted without much discussion. In the view of older women, what is significant is that women in factories today receive their wages directly, and "so how much they give their families is up to them." They add, however, that "the minimum a daughter should give is fifty to eighty percent of her earnings, and a daughter who turns over all her wages would be considered the most filial." Young women, on their part, claim that parents rarely set a fixed amount that they must bring home; instead, a daughter considers her own needs and gives the remainder to her family.

I would suggest, however, that although older women appear to allow daughters choice in the matter, they in fact expect to receive a sizable portion of a daughter's income. And while daughters appear to emphasize flexibility in such decisions, I will show that a sense of obligation and the belief that a daughter ought to contribute as much as she is able to are strongly felt. Chiu, a working-student, said "being laid off must be very hard to take, since one would just be spending one's family's money and not contributing anything. At our age one should at least see to one's own expenses." Lai summed up the matter this way:

For women like myself, when we take money home it's because we feel we ought to, it's the right thing to do, and not because our parents demand it. On what we make there isn't much left over after expenses [meals], but whatever remains, whether a lot or a little, should be taken home. After all when we were growing up at home we spent so much of our family's money. As for working students, they may not be able to send much home, but at least they're not spending their family's money.

Yang Chiu-lan explained her actions the same way: "our parents raised us for such a long time; if you don't give what you earn to your parents, who else would you give the money to?"

A sense of responsibility to one's family is reflected in comments such as Wang's, who at twenty-four has been working for nine years: "since I don't earn that much it isn't right to keep much for myself [she is given approximately NT$200 a month as spending money]. My family needs this help, and it's embarrassing to ask for more [spending money]." When layoffs and work slow-downs became increasingly common in late 1974 several women in the Sanhsia area took it upon themselves, without urging from their parents, to use their spare time to seek better paying jobs elsewhere, even though they had not been discharged yet. For similar reasons women in garment factories prefer not to go to the Western Electronics plant in Ch'ipei because of the cut in wages they would have to take, despite the suggestion of their parents who regard the factory's proximity as a positive factor.[4]

Beyond the general category of household consumption factory women do not have detailed knowledge about nor do they express interest in the specific expenditures toward which their earnings go. In a conversation with Chen, for instance, the subject had turned to credit clubs formed by workers at Western Electronics:

It's too risky to join one here; it'd be safer at home. [Has your mother started one for you?] I don't know; I really can't say where the money I send home goes. [She sends NT$900 home each month.] I know little about financial matters at home.

The following comes from a worker who lives at home: "a daughter doesn't interfere with how the money she brings home is spent; in any case there isn't much to discuss." Yang Su-ying (mentioned earlier) believes it "proper to give one's earnings to one's parents," and says she "has become accustomed to doing so; my mother's money is the same as my money."

Considering that Yang rarely spends more than NT$150 a month on herself, and that she thinks carefully before asking her mother for spending money ("it would have to be for something important, not clothes"), her refusal to differentiate between the contributions of various family members seems puzzling. But her attitude is by no means unusual or exceptional. Hwang, for instance, bought a used television with her earnings for her family, and when my assistant asked why she did not buy a new set, since the price difference would not have been great, she replied, "I can't take it with me when I leave [to marry] anyway, so why should I spend more?" A Su woman in Ch'inan had purchased an electric fan with her wages as a factory worker, and when she was about to be married, she had packed it along with her other belongings. Seeing this, her mother became very angry, and finding an old pair of her daughter's slippers, she threw them outside and said, "These are also yours, why not take them too?" In discussing this particular incident with us, another Ch'inan woman explained that "as far as most women are concerned, just because they paid for something [for the family] it doesn't mean that it's theirs to take with them when they leave."

It appears, therefore, that while daughters "belong to other people," their earnings (until they marry) do not, and the sole exception to this pattern I found underlines the structural ambiguity of daughters. Liu Su-fong is one of four daughters, all of whom began working after primary school. In a family known for its conservatism (in Ch'inan) it came as a surprise to discover that a portion of the earnings the four sisters turn over to their father is placed in savings accounts by their father, who, furthermore, encourages them to use part of their earnings to buy gold jewelry for their dowries (none is engaged yet). Liu's father maintains the opinion that "it isn't right to take a daughter's money because she belongs to other people." (He receives portions of and strictly controls the earnings of his married and unmarried sons.) Apparently this line of reasoning is logical only to Mr. Liu, and no other parent expressed this point of view.

When a daughter leaves her natal family to marry, she is entitled to a dowry, and we might ask how a worker's income figures in this. Clearly, the answer depends in large measure on the economic circumstances of a woman's family. Yang Su-ying's mother told us that "when Su-ying marries she won't have much in the way of a dowry because all the money she brings home is spent on household expenses." Although the situation could not be helped, Mrs. Yang was worried nonetheless: "The larger the dowry a woman has, the better; her life with her mother-in-law will be easier, and she can lift her head up. She can also get by with doing less around the house." Liu A-lan's mother, on the other hand, is preparing early for the large expenditure by placing NT$1,000 of her daughter's earnings each month into a credit club. "This way when she marries she will at least be assured of a dowry. The family can't spend all the money she earns." She then spoke of a Lim woman who had used up all the money her daughter had brought home: "when it came time for her daughter to marry, all she could give her was NT$3,000; even her own son criticized her. So this is why I set up the credit club for A-lan; later on there won't be any gossip."

This, however, is not a widespread arrangement. In families where daily expenses leave little for savings, money is not likely to be allotted for a daughter's dowry, and when the need arises funds may be drawn from what savings there are or obtained by starting a loan club. That is, although parents may not set aside sums on a regular basis expressly for a daughter's dowry, when one is required they (and often the woman's brothers) do take the responsibility of providing one. The same applies when sons marry. Families who must budget carefully from month to month are ill-equipped to meet the costs incurred by a son's wedding. Yang Chiu-lan's mother, for example, anticipated expenses amounting to NT$60,000 when her son, already of marriageable age, marries. For some time she had been nagging her son to set an engagement date, only to be told, "how can I get engaged when I have no money?" His mother's solution was to form two credit clubs from which she hoped to obtain NT$50,000; "it can be repaid slowly later on. In addition, [his] two sisters can help out with their earnings."

Reference has already been made to the contribution a working daughter makes toward the tuition of her siblings and particularly for brothers. This is one area that is frequently specifically designated as a daughter's responsibility, unlike food, housing, medical or other expenditures which are not singled out in this manner. Ong and her sister, for example, were explicitly told of their responsibility, and the fact that their brother is an only son made their grandmother's instructions more urgent: "You have only one brother, so you and your sisters should try your best to provide him with tuition fees." Although his marks in lower-middle school thus far have not been high, his grandmother expressed hope that he will do better in the future "so he will have an easier time finding a job."

Ong's grandmother's "request" is part of a broader assumption (one that scarcely needs to be verbalized) that a daughter's income belongs to the family rather than to the wage-earner herself. A filial daughter is one who spends almost no money on herself, but at a minimum, a daughter (adopted or natural) is *supposed* to give a portion of her earnings to her parents. When Liu Mei-ying's (an adopted daughter) father remarried, she was not treated well by her new step-mother, who favored her own children, and Liu subsequently went to live with her grandmother and her father's brother. Her step-mother saw the situation somewhat differently: "From the time she was small she never regarded us as parents. Although she worked outside for a long time, when she came home she would always go to her uncle's and would never come to see us. And she has never given us any money from her earnings; *it's as if we didn't have this daughter at all*" (emphasis added). Chen's mother expressed an almost identical sentiment, complaining that her daughter (a junior college graduate whose education was made possible through the earnings of an older sister who works as a prostitute) brought little money to her from her job as an office clerk. Mrs. Chen finally exclaimed, "What's the good of having a daughter if she doesn't bring any money home?"

A point that bears mention here is that neither Mrs. Liu or Mrs. Chen took steps, beyond protesting, to remedy the situation; other cases show the same pattern:

> Yang Chiu-lan has one older sister working and living in a San-chung factory. Their mother told us that when her elder daughter first went to work after primary school, she turned over all her earnings to her mother and would ask for spending money when she needed some. "But now things are different; after working outside for several years she seems more belligerent, and keeps NT$400 to NT$500 of her earnings [each month] for herself." After a brief illness Mrs. Yang returned to her job as a construction laborer despite the objections of her son and younger daughter. "It's hard work but I have no choice. [My elder daughter] is better at spending money and she takes less home. On one pay-day I had to send her brother to get some money from her, but he didn't come back with much."

> Liu Mei-ying's grandmother, in view of Mei-ying's relationship with her step-mother, did not oppose her living away from home. She was, however, angry at her adopted grand-daughter for not regularly bringing money home. "She just kept spending the money she earned on herself, on tuition, and books, even though I told her not to go to school. From time to time she'll bring NT$100 to me, but rarely to her uncle. [Her dowry was purchased with money her uncle gave her.] Other people who don't know assume she gives her earnings to her uncle."

> On one occasion, Yang Chiu-lan, known for her filial behavior in the neighborhood, decided to take part in a company-sponsored outing, something she was not in the habit of doing. After she left her mother complained to Liu Mei-ying's grandmother that Chiu-lan had insisted on going even though her mother had been against it, and the following exchange took place:
> *Mrs. Liu:* "You shouldn't scold her when she gets home. She brings all her earnings to you, and she's so obedient besides. You aren't earning money now [having been sick]; you should treat her a little better.
> *Mrs. Yang:* "It's not that I want to be so strict, but because I'm not working and business is poor at her factory, we're always short of money. And NT$100 for an outing doesn't make sense. And it's not just NT$100; I had to give her another NT$100 as spending money. Where's all that money going to come from? She's still young now; she has lots of chances to play later. Look at me, I never went south until last year [for a religious festival]."

These cases raise the question of what sanctions parents might apply after their dissatisfaction has been clearly communicated. A factory job was most crucial for Liu Mei-ying since it allowed her to be self-supporting and to leave an unhappy situation at home. At the same time there was little likelihood of any real interference from her step-mother, who was aware that Liu had the support of her grandmother. For Liu's step-mother to use the threat of ostracism from the family, therefore, would have been meaningless since Liu herself had in effect already severed ties to her family. (It is true that Liu's grandmother applied pressure on her to bring more money home to her uncle, although after tuition and living expenses it was improbable that Liu had much money left over. In the end, in the instance where compliance really counted, marriage, Liu acted according to her grandmother's wishes. See chapter 10.) In Chen's case, she saved a portion of her wages for her dowry (she was engaged the year before), and her mother's displeasure was alleviated by the knowledge that, when the time came to purchase the dowry, less money from the family's savings would be required. As for Yang Chiu-lan, her insistence on taking part in the company trip was a rare display of determination. As her mother told us on another occasion, in a less heated state, Chiu-lan seldom requests any spending money. While Mrs. Yang could not say this of her elder daughter, the fact remains that the latter continues to remit over half of her wages each month, and her weekly visits home indicate a desire to maintain close ties with her family.

It is undeniable, however, that in the case of Yang's sister, her mother's complaints have less impact because she lives away from home, unlike Chiu-lan who is subject to her mother's influence on a daily basis. Under the latter set of circumstances a word or a look from one's parents generally suffices to deter a daughter from pursuing an issue. Parents whose daughters live in dormitories can always insist that they return home, but as long as income is received regularly and a daughter's misconduct is not extreme, there is not much to be gained in resorting to such a step. But above all, daughters are socialized to place family interest above their own, and they recognize that they work in order to help their families. Their interests may not always coincide with those of their families, but family obligation in the form of economic assistance takes precedence, and risking the alienation of one's family's affection just so one can attend school or buy more clothes seems too high a price to pay.

The notion that "daughters should be treated better" because they make an economic contribution to their families is taken by parents (mothers) to mean that they should be somewhat easier on their daughters or more lenient with them. This is customarily manifested in allowing a daughter more freedom to choose her own clothes (although not how much is spent) or in saving better food for her when she returns from work. Working daughters are also exempted from some household chores.

Grandmothers often voice their concerns about the fate of their grand-daughters when they marry because being in the factory all day, "they won't know how to do housework." Because of work schedules and frequent overtime, mothers of working women do expect less of their daughters in this regard. Factory women who attend school, in particular, have little time to prepare meals, and may do little more than their own laundry. Chuang, who lives at home, said, "I do my laundry usually on my days off; otherwise my mother does it. I really don't have much choice because I'm so rushed in the mornings. I used to help with the meals before the company changed our working hours. Now when I get home, dinner is already prepared. I do help on weekends; after all, I'm the oldest and besides, there isn't much else to do at home." Where there are sisters-in-law present, a working woman may have her breakfasts cooked and her clothes washed for her. This was the case for two Chen sisters in Ch'inan until their sister-in-law joined them at the factory;

shortly thereafter, their father sustained an injury at work, their mother went to work, and the three younger women shared the household chores after work. But Yang Su-ying, who is an only daughter, prepares dinner and carries out household chores regularly, and spends most of her days off performing other tasks at home.

Division of labor at home, then, is flexible and is determined by the working hours of daughters and family composition. In no case did we detect that a working daughter felt, by reason of her contribution, that she was *entitled* to be exempted from housework.

It has already been noted that for women who live at home, keeping NT$200 to NT$300 of their earnings for personal expenses each month is not considered unreasonable by their parents. Although such sums do not permit major purchases, they do enable women to join friends in leisure activities from time to time. This does not mean, however, that women always make use of the opportunity. Yang Su-ying, for instance, admitted that she would like to be able to go out and play more, but said, "When I think of how much it costs I'd rather not go. Earning money isn't that easy, and so it's better to be thrifty." When her company sponsored a trip south she calculated that expenses would come to nearly NT$700 and on that basis, decided against going. For the same reason, her cousin Yang Chiu-lan says she rarely goes to movies, as much as she enjoys them, since "they are too expensive."

For women living away from home, the freedom to use their income in ways they choose comes more easily, and the most important consequence— the ability to continue school—can improve factory women's future options. Kao's case has already been described (chapter 5); knowing that her parents were opposed to her studying, Kao came north to Western Electronics on the pretext that better jobs could be had there, and informed her parents that she was attending high school only after she had already paid tuition. She is in other respects a filial daughter, spending little money on herself.

Female workers speak in disapproving tones about the speed with which a woman can learn bad ways, and add that even if parents wanted to supervise their daughters more strictly, it is virtually impossible short of demanding that they return home. On the subject of leaving home, a worker from the south said, "it's good to come out and see more. Before, at home, if you wanted to go out, you'd have to ask your mother for money and let her know where you're going." Similarly, another woman who sends one-third of her earnings home each month, said, "At home you have to ask your parents for money, but if you come out and work, you earn it and you spend it yourself; what could be better!"

The point is, however, that women do *not* spend all that they earn; a majority send at least half their wages home, and those who spend the largest amount on themselves are likely to be working-students. For the remainder, beyond recreational and clothing expenses that seldom exceed NT$400 a month, their comments (about the lack of control parents have) may be interpreted as no more than displays of bravado, and actual behavior conforms to the consensus of what constitutes proper conduct (e.g., regular remittances home) for young working women. Women recognize the obvious fact that parents cannot supervise the activities of a daughter far from home, but this does not mean that all of them take advantage of this opportunity.

The ability to earn an income, therefore, has permitted some women to allocate part of their earnings for education or for small purchases, and it has freed them from some of the duties at home for which they might otherwise be responsible. But these privileges do not mean that daughters have been granted a larger say in affairs that concern the entire family. The sums of money women are able to control are not large enough to significantly affect the family budget. (Going to school is often ruled out by parents precisely because tuition involves substantially more than the NT$200 or NT$300 a month women have for spending money. Here we see another way in which parents are able to limit the opportunities made available by wage-earning.) The notion of assuming a more permanent role in decision-making at home still strikes most women as presumptuous. Spending a portion of what one earns in a manner one chooses is quite a different matter from telling members of one's family how the household income should be utilized. For women living in dormitories this is not feasible in any case. When asked about the possibility of exercising a larger voice in family affairs, women responded in similar ways:

> It's all the same [regardless of who earns the money]. The most important thing is that my family needs this help, and so I work. No, this could never happen, especially where girls are concerned. We only give our earnings to our families and wouldn't interfere. One wouldn't even think about such things, or about where every dollar goes. In any event, the money belongs to the whole family; it's all the same.

I came across only one case where daughters openly voiced their opinions about how their income ought to be spent, and it involves a family that is virtually dependent on the earnings of its three daughters for its livelihood. The father is in poor health and has not had a job for some time, and neighbors praise the frugal habits of the daughters. When their younger brother was about to graduate from lower-middle school, their mother had said that if he should pass his entrance exams, his sisters should "try their best to make it possible for him to go on." The eldest daughter, however, protested: "He doesn't like school and his grades are poor. If he wants to continue, he'll have to put himself through school by working." But more typically, when a family considers a large expenditure, the subject may be floated and discussed in passing, but it is unlikely and probably inconceivable that a daughter would be consulted or that her opinion would be solicited. In several cases in Ch'inan, for example, when a major household item, such as a television set or a refrigerator, was purchased, the reaction of the young women involved was summed up in the statement, "it's up to the head of the family to decide." None took part in the selection of a particular brand-name, style, or model, nor did any of them offer an opinion as to acceptable cost or how to go about making the best buy.

Several studies on Chinese working women indicate that they enjoy a greater say in family affairs and control of their incomes. Writing about factory women in pre-1949 China, Lang (1946) states that even though parents may disapprove of a daughter's decision as to whether or not to send money home and how to dress, the girl who earns an income cannot be stopped. Lang continues, "Thus the first battle against parental authority which the girls have waged unwittingly, without understanding its implications, has been almost won: the family has had to recognize, in fact, if not in theory, their daughter's right to dispose of her own money" (1946:265). My data on Taiwan hardly bear out this conclusion, for while daughters can now use their spending money with greater freedom, the amount of spending money they control is still determined by someone other than themselves. Fei's (1939) remarks are somewhat more applicable to the Taiwanese case; he calls attention to the fact that in factories wages are paid to the woman herself, and notes that at least during that moment she is able to spend a part of her earnings in accordance with her own wishes. Fei adds, "if a girl spends a reasonable amount, it will be accepted without interference. But she is not allowed to spend all her wage" (1939:234). As is the case in Taiwan, however, what is deemed a reasonable amount and what expenses are judged frivolous are usually determined by a girl's parents.

If a woman does not expect to be shown more respect or to be given complete control of her earnings, it is because she regards wage-earning as part of the obligations a daughter owes to her parents. First, a daughter has a debt to repay, one incurred by the upbringing her parents gave her. Other obligations may take more specific form, such as the duty to help her siblings attain an education, or it can be the general notion that at this age, even if she cannot add substantially to the family income, a daughter should not be a further drain on her family's resources.

Education (when one is already employed) is one area where some women do see decision-making as a definite concern of their own; day-to-day activities after work-hours, and the type of friends one chooses also belong in this category but these affect the family budget to a lesser degree. (In some cases going to school does constitute an act of defiance, but it might appear less objectionable because employment may still allow a regular remittance, albeit a smaller one, and at a minimum, the working-student is self-supporting.) By and large, however, family decision-making is an activity that takes place in the background of family life; choices are made in loosely defined fashion, and the way in which family plans are formulated is not thought to be a concern of the working daughter.

Any attempt to explain this passivity on the part of daughters must take into account at least two considerations—the potency of psychological sanctions and the lack of alternatives available to unmarried females in Taiwan. I indicated earlier that a word or a look of disapproval may be sufficient to discourage a daughter from certain actions, and that in the past (prior to the availability of regular employment for women), there were virtually no situations that would have occasioned defiance and that would have warranted applying sanctions. It is relevant to recall that when jobs outside the home became available to young men in northern Taiwan in the 1930s, sons began to refuse the *simpua* matches (minor marriage) arranged for them. We need to remember here that parents probably backed down once their authority was challenged, since they were dependent on their sons and would not have wished them to move away. Thus, the issue was probably never forced.

This leads us to consider why daughters are less likely to challenge their parents' authority. As M. Wolf makes evident in her writing on Taiwanese women, even though daughters are less valued than sons in the family, that unit nonetheless constitutes the only form of warmth that a young girl knows. The prospect of marrying into a household of strangers is anxiety-provoking, and if it is hard for an outsider to comprehend the genuine attachment of daughters to their natal families, one needs to bear in mind that for the woman herself, she has known no other form of security.

Factory women have not come to regard their occupations as a viable or desirable alternative to marriage; they may speak of themselves as self-supporting but this view does not extend very far into the future. Resistance to family wishes, therefore, would only be self-defeating, and remove a daughter from a source of affection and concern not to be found elsewhere, at least prior to marriage. It is true that people never tire of repeating that "daughters belong to other people," but the obedience and the filial piety (now expressed in the form of an economic contribution) expected from a daughter also reflects a high degree of incorporation into the family for as long as a daughter remains with her natal family.[5]

Finally, even if daughters were given some control over the disposal of their earnings, it remains to be seen whether channels for reinvestment exist. Customarily, older Taiwanese women are able to invest their money in loan associations, or they can become money lenders or buy livestock, but these are not activities young women take up. Education, in contrast, *is* perceived as a means to upward mobility, although not all women are permitted to use their wages for this purpose. (One might add here that several women knew well enough to discontinue school during the recession without any prompting from their mothers.)

10

Dating and Marriage

Most factory women say that because of the increased social opportunities that come with dormitory living, the dating period is prolonged and marriage is delayed. One Ch'inan woman who had returned from a dormitory to help at home would disagree: "in a dormitory a person has more opportunities to meet people, and so will tend to marry at an earlier age." Older women tend to support her opinion. One grandmother, for instance, was surprised that my assistant was still unmarried, since she had so many opportunities to be outside.

Regardless of whether women marry "earlier" or "later" as a result of working outside, it is in the area of marriage and dating that personal autonomy has increased the most for women. Women are not always satisfied with the opportunities they have, but factory employment does mean that a woman encounters and is in regular contact with a larger number and variety of people than, say, a woman who is an agricultural worker. Female workers have more opportunities to meet men and do not need to rely on go-betweens or family members for introductions, and women consequently have the freedom to choose among the men with whom they become acquainted. Even if dating remains infrequent for girls under eighteen, they are nonetheless made highly conscious of dating practices by the activities of older coworkers. This chapter deals with dating patterns, qualities considered desirable in one's spouse, age at marriage, notions about the quality of married life and residence after marriage.

Going out to play requires that one has sufficient time (or control over one's time), spending money, and companions, and all three may be difficult to come by. On the whole, women living away from home, especially in major urban areas, come by them more easily. There is little in the way of entertainment or recreation in Ch'ipei, where there is a Western Electronics plant, but the main plant is situated in Taoyuan, a city that offers coffee shops, theaters, a bowling alley, an indoor swimming pool, dance-halls and so on. Most of these activities are new to women coming to work for the first time, and as one socially active dormitory resident said, "without much to do in the dorms, it's just a matter of one girl taking another along to these places, and so you have more people initiating others." The extent to which factory workers take part in such activities has increased but should not be exaggerated. The complex atmosphere of dance-halls and skating rinks keeps a good number of women from ever joining their coworkers in such recreation.

The ease with which factory women can meet men varies with the type of firm in which they work. First, by and large, in the factories that hire women at all, workers are predominantly female, leaving a disproportionately small number of men with whom women might become acquainted. Second, many women have reservations about the character of male workers who hold assembler-level positions in factories. To take two extremes I quote from the comments of a woman who works in a family knitting business in Ch'inan and of a woman at Western Electronics:

> I met my husband here in this very room [where both of them still work], as did my husband's brother and his wife. There's another married couple here as well. In a place like this, people are closer together [referring to what are rather cramped quarters] and are together for long hours, and our days off depend on how many work orders we have, and so they usually don't coincide with the holidays of other people. When we go out it's usually with each other. This way, there're more opportunities to get together; otherwise one would have to rely on go-betweens [matchmakers]. If a person depended on herself to meet people, her opportunities wouldn't be many.

From the Western Electronics employee:

> One bad thing about this company [of over 4,500 employees] is that there're too many women and not enough men. There're few organized activities such as outings or dances. If you figure that there's one man for every ten women, that means that nine of them are bound to be disappointed. This isn't good for a woman, as it will lead her to lower her expectations. But men can afford to be choosy, and it's the woman who ends up not having much self-confidence.

A smaller number of women at Western Electronics do find that the factory expands their chances for meeting male workers. While one new worker on the second shift complained about the rowdiness of some of the male workers on the third shift, her coworker viewed the situation quite differently: "between shifts there is time to talk and get to know them, and when outings are arranged, they invite us to go along." One garment worker described a recent outing in which most of the participants became acquainted through their jobs: "most of the boys work in the packing section, and some girls who bring the finished garments down to them meet them first, and then one acquaintance leads to another." But these speakers are more fortunate than most of their coworkers, who, if they had hope of meeting interesting persons in the factory, are likely to be disappointed. According to one study of Kaohsiung factory workers, this is evidently not a pattern unique to Western Electronics (see Tables 18, 19, and 20).

Table 18. Making Friends of the Opposite Sex

"If You Have a Friend of the Opposite Sex, How Did You
Become Acquainted?"
(Huang 1977:181)

	Electronics	Textile	Other
Friends Introduce	26	11	3
Factory	5	4	2
Supervisors Introduce	4	0	0
Family Relatives Introduce	8	5	2
Pen Pal	3	4	0
Acquainted Outside	56	2	2
Other	7	3	3

Table 19. Making Friends of the Opposite Sex
(Continued)

"Is It Easy to Meet and Make Friends of The Opposite Sex
in the Factory?"
(Huang 1977:182)

No Response	46	15	8
Yes	28	12	3
No	259	56	22

Table 20. The Kind of Marriage Partner Desired (Asked of
Female Workers)
(Huang 1977:184)

	Elementary	Junior High	Senior High
No Response	150	52	18
Male Staff in Factory	4	3	1
Male Worker	1	6	0
Male Outside Factory	194	143	74
Other	38	37	17

Ideas about qualities deemed desirable in a boyfriend/husband and notions about the best way of selecting a marriage partner, insofar as they differ from traditional conceptions, are attributable not so much to wage-earning but to the influence of peers.[1] The following comes from a twenty-two year old Ch'inan woman working in the Western Electronics satellite plant:

If a woman has the opportunities she should start to get to know boys early, otherwise she'd feel rushed and anxious when she's older. If two people are acquainted early, it doesn't mean that they must marry, but then they have more time to understand one another, so that if they do marry, the marriage will be better. My father's sister [29] was engaged several months ago; her mother [the speaker's grandmother] asked many people to act as go-between. Doing things this way isn't right at all, and so she ended up with a truck-driver, which is hardly desirable since so many of them are coarse and gamble. Her mother was the one who made the decision about the engagement, even though her daughter was reluctant. Now she regrets having consented and although it's already been several months since the engagement, she's still not willing to go through with the wedding. And she keeps telling me that I should take the opportunity to know boys when I'm young so I won't end up like her, forced to let others make a decision for her. Her father is dead and her mother lives with her second son and his wife, so there's really no one to take care of her. It's a very sad situation.

The desirability of meeting a person on one's own rather than through a go-between, the importance of being acquainted with several men and of knowing a potential mate for a "long" time are becoming widespread ideas among factory workers. "Meeting someone on one's own" usually refers to acquaintances established through the introduction of friends. Friends are judged reliable whereas go-betweens are less trustworthy because they "place too much emphasis on a person's background and give too little information about a person's character."

There's nothing wrong with knowing and going out with several boys. It's not as if you have to marry one. If you know more men, then you are better able to choose when it comes time to marry.

My sister-in-law married at seventeen and met my brother through a go-between; that's how things were done then. Nowadays, especially for those of us who have gone to school, women prefer to meet men on their own. One shouldn't rush into anything.

In addition to determining whether a potential mate shares one's interests or is a compatible companion, some women have a further rationale for wanting to prolong the courtship period. "In the beginning you only see the good side of a man, and only later discover what he kept hidden from you: for example he may not smoke or drink in your presence but does so after you are married. By then it's too late and you can't take back your feelings." Virtually all women agree on the desirability of having the opportunity to "understand" one's future spouse prior to marriage, but the sentiments and values they express do not always dictate the actions of these women. There are those who give verbal support to such notions (e.g., "twenty-four or twenty-five is about the right age for a woman to marry") only to marry after a brief acquaintanceship. Su, for instance, was nineteen when she married a twenty-one year old man, the brother of her coworker in a garment factory. After one month and two dates they became engaged and were married several weeks later.

Although Su's case is not identical to the experiences of other young women in the Sanhsia area, it is more representative of the Sanhsia sample than of informants at Western Electronics. The age at which girls begin to go out with boys, in groups, or as a couple, is markedly earlier in the Western Electronics group. Unlike the seventeen or eighteen year olds in Ch'inan who profess that they haven't the nerve to have anything to do with boys (which is accurate, judging from their behavior) some of their counterparts in the Western Electronics dormitories date and do not think it unusual. We can contrast this with one woman in Ch'ipei who went out regularly with her fiance only after their engagement: "If a couple goes out often before becoming engaged, people will talk. But afterwards, it's all right." Her sister-in-law added, "After she becomes engaged a woman is already thought of as belonging to the man's side, and the woman's side can't control her too much or not let her go out with him." Another Ch'inan woman (twenty years old) was cautious to the point of refusing to accept the invitations of a man introduced by a relative, fearing that if nothing came of this (that is, marriage), she would be gossiped about.

The earlier social maturity of many women living away from home is not difficult to explain; roommates and coworkers initiate one another to new activities and parents are not there to object. But wage-earning and factory employment have not altered all facets of workers' lives or their outlook. The direction of change in terms of attitudes about dating and marriage is clear (the ability to exercise choice is stressed), but patterns prevailing before factory employment became available persist as well, and both tendencies are reflected in the findings of surveys. Unfortunately neither Huang's or Hsieh's figures are broken down according to residence at home or in company housing (see Tables 21 and 22).

Since most women do not have as many opportunities for meeting desirable types of men as they might like, the preferences they state must be recognized as simply an expression of their values. Aside from personal traits such as dependability, with good behavior heading the list, educational level is sometimes a consideration. The latter is mentioned most frequently by women who are high school graduates or attending high school, the idea being that the educational level of one's husband should at least be equal to one's own. As one Ch'inan woman said, "it's not important that he have lots of money or be highly educated, although those who are well educated tend to be better behaved and more considerate." But in view of their own (low) educational background, most women's expectations are modest. Lim, after making some remarks about education and occupation, finished with, "but one has to think about her own qualifications; I haven't had much schooling and I don't have the ability to earn high wages, so as long as he's suitable, it's all right."

There is the belief among many working students that a high-school diploma will improve their marriage prospects ("others are also choosy"; see below). This is not, however, a view their parents hold. Even if a daughter could make a more desirable match by reason of her educational background, her

Table 21.   Preferred Manner in Which to Get to Know Mate
(Asked of Single Female Workers)
(Huang 1977:185)

	Electronics	Textile	Others
No Response	22	3	4
Free Love-Match	170	41	14
Family Head Decide	99	29	13
Other	55	13	2

Table 22.   Frequency and Percentage Distribution of Choosing
Marriage Partner
(Respondents are Single Industrial Workers)
(Hsieh 1972:88)

	Male		Female	
	%	Number	%	Number
By Parents	10.7	16	19.7	29
Children by Themselves	14.0	21	0.0	0
Children Make Decision Then Request Parents' Permission	75.3	113	80.3	118

parents generally do not anticipate that they will be able to draw upon the resources of the man's family.

I have already mentioned that factory women prefer to marry northerners and/or non-farmers. Older women are not unsympathetic to this view; Chen's grandmother (in Ch'inan) did not look favorably on her grand-daughter's friendship with a man living in a more isolated community some distance from Sanhsia. Her grandmother told us, "a woman who marries a man living there will have a bitter life, what with tea-picking and all. People say that the two of them can move out, but it's not easily accomplished, and even then, if she returns [to his home] she must work just the same."

The location of a man's home matters less than how he makes his living. Men who are factory workers (excluding foremen and other staff members) fall short of the ideal (see Table 20). One woman said, "Factory girls don't often marry men who work in factories because their wages are so low; it's probably not enough to support a family." Moreover, many of these men, not having completed their military duty, are too young to be seriously considered by women as potential mates. But more than age alone women say that such jobs do not require any marketable skills. Referring to a coworker's fiance, Yang noted that "he hasn't even fulfilled his military requirement yet. Besides, he works in the packing department in the factory; it's work that anyone can do.

There's no future there, and even when he gets out of the army, finding a job will still be a problem because he hasn't learned any skills."

The degree of choice a woman can exercise in determining the age at which she marries and whom she marries is affected by factory employment in various ways. First, the greater amount of time she spends away from home expands her opportunities to meet men (even though they may not be "suitable" types). Second, the age of marriage is sometimes delayed, although this should not be construed as a sign of new freedom, because postponing marriage is often a decision made by a girl's parents in order that she may continue to fulfill family obligations for a longer time. At the same time, the influence of peers and an evaluation of the costs and disadvantages of marriage lead some women to choose to delay marriage, although very few are so determined that they would reject marriage if the opportunity for a match appears. (This contrasts with a case described by Salaff, where a female worker in Hong Kong broke up her relationship with her boyfriend when his mother applied pressure on them to marry immediately [1975:109].) In any case, should a woman wish to postpone marriage, her inclination no longer necessarily diverges from the interests of her family, since her income represents an alternative her family welcomes. On this basis one would expect that women now have greater freedom to refuse matches arranged for them by their families.

Even though marriage is the one event in their future which women can be sure will take place, questions about marriage invariably elicit giggles from women who then reply that they are too young to think about such matters. They are knowledgeable enough, on the other hand, to point to coworkers who marry at eighteen or nineteen and say that "it's too young; at that age, a girl doesn't know anything." It does not take long to find that "the right age" is twenty-four or twenty-five, and women say matter-of-factly that a single woman of twenty-six is no longer categorized as a spinster these days (although a woman who is single at thirty "will probably never marry").

Women should not marry too early. Once married she has less freedom, she can't do as she pleases, such as going out. And all she ends up with is housework and taking care of children—work that's never done. So a girl ought to live it up while she's single. But a person shouldn't wait too long; then childbirth becomes more difficult, and when you're old, your children will still be very young.

One Liu woman told us that her engagement was her mother's idea, and the latter said to us, "it's a big relief to see her engaged. She's twenty-five this year, and if she doesn't marry now, later on people will be choosier. It won't be long before she's thirty, and once a woman is twenty-six or so, it's much harder to find a mate."

Factory women were quick in pointing to a woman's hard life after marriage in explaining why delaying marriage is desirable; two other factors they cite as leading to later marriage are education and increased experience outside. One working student said,

> It's not good to marry too soon; that'd be like stepping from the classroom into the kitchen. The more educated a woman the later she will marry. A woman picks and chooses, but other people also evaluate you. And so if a woman has had little education and if she meets someone who is all right she'll just marry him.

A high-school graduate expressed a similar rationale:

> The higher a girl's educational level the later she will marry because it's not as easy to find a mate. A man's qualifications should be better than a woman's. But it's different for those less well educated; they can't be too selective, and if two people are compatible, they just marry. So there are more possibilities open to them.

Workers who have some experience of the independence that living away from home allows them are in a better position than workers who remain at home to contrast the carefree days of a single girl with the restrictions that housework and child-care impose on a married woman. Women are always ready with anecdotes or descriptions about the hardships that follow upon marriage for a sister, classmate, or coworker. One Chen woman was fortunate in having married a man in a community not too far from Ch'inan and could therefore return home for visits; her sister described her new circumstances:

> Before she married, when she went to her husband's house it was only to play, but now she must help with the chores because it is her own house. Before, at home our mother did most of the chores when we went to work, but a woman can't do this after she marries or else people will talk.

To this, their mother added: "She must have done quite a bit of housework in the beginning, because when she came back her fingers were red and calloused." All this did not go unnoticed by neighbors, who gossiped about eyes red from crying, and who predicted that the frequent visits home would soon be curtailed by the husband's family. "It's all right now but they won't be so polite about it later. You can't get around the fact that a daughter-in-law has to work hard; she belongs to someone else now and can't stay at her mother's all the time."

The picture that such accounts impress upon young women sometimes leads them to exaggerate the amount of autonomy they in fact enjoy.

> It isn't good to marry too early; it means giving up the 'spring of one's youth' which is the best time. A woman should make use of these years and enjoy herself since they are so short.

Sincere as these statement are, much of a factory woman's time is in fact spent inside a noisy plant doing monotonous work. Women may genuinely believe that marriage can mean the beginning of a "bitter" life, but the awareness that there is no place for an unmarried woman is even more firmly held, and the age at which women in the Sanhsia and Western Electronics samples *actually* married renders their statements about desirability of marrying late somewhat empty. (Of the twenty or so women in my assistant's elementary school class, all of whom were approximately twenty-four years old in 1974, only three were unmarried and two of these were engaged.) Tao, an eighteen year old worker in Western Electronics, had gone on at some length about the bitter life in store for women after marriage. When I asked if there were any positive aspects of marriage, there was no hesitation in her reply: "Well, it means security; a person doesn't have to worry anymore." Wang, a twenty-four year old worker living in Ch'inan, ended on a similar note: "marriage is the beginning of a hard life for women, but not marrying is not the answer either; later on there'd be no one to take care of you."

The inevitability of marriage and the lack of viable or attractive alternatives to it, combined with notions about personal freedom before marriage and the absence of it afterwards, understandably produce in many women ambivalence and anxiety about marriage. It is the recognition that security comes only with marriage that leads women to stress the importance of safe-guarding any opportunities that come along. As illustrations, several workers explained that "some women in their mid-twenties may have broken off a relationship or an engagement earlier and now at their age they tend to regret their decisions, especially when they see girls younger than they announcing engagements." The feeling is that "if two people are destined to meet, then a girl should protect this opportunity and not let the chance slip by."

One pattern lending support to the statement above is the relatively high rate of women who are pregnant when they marry. One report on population growth in Taiwan states that an island-wide survey of women between the ages of eighteen and twenty-nine in 1972 showed that thirty percent of the married women in the sample admitted that they were pregnant before marriage (Sun 1976:50). (Unfortunately, there is no breakdown by occupation.) Women caution each other about the perils of "boarding the bus and paying for the ticket afterwards," but we should note that a sizable number of women who are aware of the lower value and reduced bargaining power of a pregnant bride nevertheless end up in precisely this position. (But from another perspective, a mother with a son of marriageable age is liable to see this situation as giving her and her son a decided advantage. Yang Su-ying's mother bemoaned the high costs of a wedding for her son and said that it would be best if her son's girlfriend came to visit and became pregnant in the process, because that would mean a simpler and less expensive wedding.)

The discrepancy between what women say and do underlines the importance of distinguishing between the ability to articulate strategies to achieve generalized goals and actual values held. Women recognize that delaying marriage postpones the responsibilities that marriage imposes. But as their actions show (e.g., marrying well before twenty-five), women do not always act on these strategies and instead, they opt for marriage (and the security it brings) when the opportunity comes. (The same discrepancy, between verbalized attitudes and actual values, also applies to the idea of independence.)

Factory women are far more unequivocal about their preferences with respect to residence after marriage. Unfortunately, this arrangement is something over which they exercise little control. The growing number of young men who migrate to towns and cities for jobs and the movement of women to industrial centers make neolocal residence more feasible. From the point of view of one elderly woman in Ch'inan, women have less to lose now by marrying early because the likelihood of their living away from their in-laws has increased.

Factory women clearly opt for neolocal residence, and although the cost would be high and a couple would have to bear this extra burden (e.g., rent) themselves, no one mentioned this fact as an advantage of residing with one's in-laws. (Nor did anyone point out that continued employment in a factory could ease the financial strain.) One would think that the greater autonomy enjoyed by women living away from their husbands' families would be apparent to everyone, but not all women hold such a view. I came across a number of female workers who take for granted the presence of in-laws and who say that the question of residence after marriage is one that is for the latter to settle. Certainly the rural setting from which these women come, their continued ties to the countryside, and the marriage and residence patterns they witness around them at home shape their orientation (even if they are a bit naive in their appraisal of relations within large households). During a conversation wth several roommates in the Western Electronics dormitories one woman referred to the increasing number of young couples moving out on their own and the advantage of this. Her roommate, however, countered with: "That's not necessarily so, even though many young people are leaving the south one still needs the consent of one's parents-in-law before moving out." This was followed by a third speaker: "It's not right to leave one's father-in-law and mother-in-law by themselves, nor is it right to expect one's mother-in-law to do housework all her life."

In an earlier section I mentioned the grandmother of a woman who was opposed to her granddaughter's friendship with a particular man because his family lives in a more isolated village in the mountains. Her reservations were based on the reasoning that "although many people would like to move outside, it's something few accomplish; it's not that easily achieved." Experience provides Chen's grandmother with a realistic perspective that younger women often lack; one factory worker, soon to be married, said, "we can't move out right now because it will look bad, and people will criticize the new daughter-in-law. But I think we can move out not long after." From what we know about the position of a new daughter-in-law in her husband's family (M. Wolf 1972), it seems far-fetched to suppose (as some factory women do) that a young wife could be successful in arranging for her and her husband to move out; such a decision is not for a young wife to make.

If these expectations appear overly optimistic we find another curiously naive set of ideas (and a double standard) given by a number of women who claim that patrilocal residence would not be completely undesirable. Tseng, a working-student and a youngest child, said,

> I wouldn't mind living with my mother-in-law at all. [You're not worried about not getting along?] Well, if you don't do anything wrong, the mother-in-law won't do anything to you. Having a mother-in-law at home would be more convenient; she can help with the housework, baby-sit, and if you and your husband go out, she can watch the house. My three sisters-in-law at home have things pretty nice; they take turns cooking, since one can't expect my mother, who's in her fifties, to do everything. [Does any of them work?] No, none has a job; even if they wanted to, our family probably wouldn't allow it because after all, they each have their own families, and they ought to look after them. [Later in the conversation she said,] After I'm married I hope I can find an office job, and my mother-in-law can do the housework and take care of the children.

Chen, another working-student, also wishes to continue working after she marries; I asked whether this would change after she has children. "My parents-in-law will be there, and my mother-in-law can watch the children during the day." Such a remark illustrates a combination of traditional expectations (that residence will be patrilocal) and new desires (to keep one's job). Clearly, Tseng and others who share this opinion are projecting into the future on the basis of the relative ease of their present circumstances. In other contexts they echo the notion that life becomes hard for a woman after marriage, but evidently they do not sufficiently appreciate the concrete factors that differentiate the mother-daughter relationshp from the mother-in-law/daughter-in-law relationship. As the next chapter will show, type of residence is one determinant of whether a woman is able to continue working after marriage. Managing a household for two is quite a different matter than helping to maintain a household of ten people, and if a woman is expected to clean, cook for hired laborers and family members, and to raise pigs, etc., the wiser choice would be to remain in a factory. As we will see, however, some mothers-in-law scoff at the arrangement Tseng suggests, and thereby leave a woman without many options with regard to residence or working outside.

If a causal connection can be established between the experience of factory work and ideas about desirable number and sex of children, it would probably be a tenuous one at best, for as long as factory employment does not improve a woman's future options or guarantee her greater security, there is no reason to believe that the experience of wage-earning in itself will produce substantial changes in women's notions about fertility. The future security of these women will rest on their husbands and on having children.

Women foresee conflict between outside employment and raising a family (see chapter 11), and the pressure to produce children remains strong in Taiwanese families. This is confirmed by the findings of Speare et al. (1973) on the relation between employment, education, and fertility in Taiwan. The authors state that few of the working women in their study hold jobs that can be considered appealing alternatives to childbearing. Only fifty-five percent expressed satisfaction with their jobs (unfortunately the authors do not specify the kinds of jobs these women had) and for most women their work experience took place between school and marriage (1973:334). In addition, they found that most women began their married lives in the homes of their husbands' parents, a pattern that reinforces the traditional concept of the wife/mother role.

Work experience, however, had little effect on fertility attitudes, and instead the most important factor affecting the number of children desired is level of education (the urban-rural difference is not a significant variable). As Speare et al. rightly point out, it is possible that some of the measured effects of education are actually due to the effects of socio-economic background rather than to education per se (1973:333). In another study education is the only variable showing a strong consistent relationship to the use of contraceptives among women in the twenty to twenty-four age group (D. Freedman 1975:111). One difficulty in correlating factors such as education and employment experience with fertility attitudes is that the latter are also shaped by family influence, and the composition of a woman's household (e.g., whether a mother-in-law is present) and decision-making patterns in the household must be taken into account. Moreover, while Speare et al. investigated the impact educational level had on fertility, they do not touch upon the content of the education dispensed in Taiwan's schools or the ideology of the larger society.[2] As will be elaborated in a subsequent section, ideas communicated through mass media in Taiwan seem to promote the view that, for women, employment outside the home is not in the best interest of children.

It is conceivable that a factory job can be sufficiently attractive so as to motivate women to plan their families with employment in mind (especially if the alternative is to remain home and serve a large household), but most female workers assert that it is not always feasible to hold a job and take care of children. Considering the costs of child-care relative to factory wages, working may in fact prove to be impractical. It is true that mothers-in-law do assume child-care roles where daughters-in-law must work for economic reasons, but it does not follow that preferences about the number and sex of children desired will necessarily change as well.

In most respects ideas on this subject have not been substantially revised. Wang told us that her cousin had just given birth to her third daughter: "there're already two girls and with no son it's a worrisome problem. [Aren't girls just the same as boys nowadays?] But if all three daughters marry and there's no one coming in, then there will be no one left." Chang, a high school graduate, considered such a situation: "If a person has no sons and just daughters, a uxorilocal match should be arranged for at least one daughter so there'd be some continuity." As the following exchange between a sixteen year old worker and her seventeen year old friend shows, women may claim that it matters little whether one has sons or daughters, but different expectations of sons and daughters linger on.

> Chen: There's less difference now between sons and daughters.
> Lee: No, some people still insist on having at least one son.
> Chen: At any rate, it's best if the first child is a girl, because girls are better at doing things around the house, and they can look after their younger brothers and sisters.

These are facile statements for young women to make, for marriage is still some years away. Women of marriageable age, on the other hand, tend to see the implications more clearly, and some (including high-school graduates) readily admit that they anticipate changes in their thinking after marriage.

> Now I don't feel that it makes any difference, but I can't say what I'll feel after I'm married. My sister and her coworkers all say the same thing—that there's no difference. But after marriage there is no doubt that women hope for a son, and a first-born who is a daughter is likely to be a disappointment. There's a feeling that a woman is 'safer' if the first is a boy. But an important factor is one's parents-in-law, because they won't treat a daughter-in-law as well if she has a daughter. A son is important because he means the continuity of the family.

It is worth noting that the speaker (who has attended high school part-time) made a further distinction: "as for how one treats a son and a daughter, it really depends on one's economic position. If you're well off, you can afford to treat them equally and let both, for instance, go to school." An awareness of the costs of having children has sharpened, and it is this consideration rather than the anticipation of continued employment that leads some workers to say that they prefer small families. This tendency, predictably enough, is most notable in working-students, who have had to bear the costs of their own education. Women with many siblings, in particular, are conspicuous in pointing out the advantages of a small family. "Having a large family nowadays isn't good; tuition alone for each child would be a heavy responsibility." This worker went on to talk about her previous job, explaining that because she is the second eldest and old enough to work, she felt that she could not ask her parents to pay for her tuition. Another worker gave a broader assessment: "Nowadays two children are enough, even if both are girls. Before, with most people being farmers, having lots of children was all right, but people can't afford to now because children today enjoy so much more, what with school, better clothes, and playing. It would be too costly." Yet another worker stated, "With family planning [only three informants mentioned the availability of family planning programs, and all are high school graduates], one doesn't have to have too many children. If there are too many it's hard on everyone; if there are fewer and each comes later, then each can enjoy the best that the parents can provide." This came from an eighteen year old worker at Western Electronics, the oldest in her family, who had entered a factory at fifteen and had earned a high school diploma during her years at Western Electronics. She had originally hoped for a nursing career but explained that family needs, specifically the education of younger siblings, had interfered with those plans.

This section takes up the role that parents play in the marriages of their daughters, and the data come primarily from information gathered in the Sanhsia area. None of my informants at Western Electronics married during my stay there, and the families of married workers at the factory, being in different parts of Taiwan, were not always accessible. The number of cases I am able to present, therefore, is not as large as one would wish for, and the small size of the sample cautions against over-generalizing.

One would expect that the new wage-earning ability of daughters might prompt parents to postpone the age at which young women marry, thereby prolonging the time during which daughters are able to continue contributing to the family income. As far as I could ascertain, however, this happens only in cases where the earnings of the daughter constitute a substantial and indispensable portion of total household income. The mothers of two cousins in Ch'inan both expressed such intentions, and their circumstances are similar. (Yang Chiu-lan's mother is a widow and works at a construction site as a laborer; there is another unmarried daughter employed in a factory as well as one son who is working; a younger son is still in school.) Mrs. Yang spoke about the high costs of a wedding for her son: "These days it'd take over NT$60,000 for a man to marry, which makes things very difficult. But if a daughter marries her family can make some money [from the bride-price]. [If you married off your daughter then you could get a daughter-in-law.] No, I can't do that: if I let my daughters marry now, that means losing their earnings. I wouldn't let them marry so early [at twenty-one and eighteen]." As for the cousin, Yang Su-ying's income from her job in a garment factory helps to support her family, including three younger brothers, all of whom are still in school. A neighbor has expressed interest in Yang Su-ying as a wife for her son, but Yang Su-ying's mother explained, "our family still needs her to earn money. I would have to wait at least three more years [she was nineteen then] before allowing her to marry." Under these circumstances a daughter herself is well aware of the importance of her income, and takes seriously her financial responsibility to her family.

Even where the loss of a daughter's income would not impose a severe financial strain, there is another arrangement that mitigates that loss. When Chen Su-ming married at nineteen, her family made it clear to the man's family that they intended to keep the bride-price and would not "return" it in the form of a dowry commensurate in value. Her grandmother told us, "there are still two younger brothers at home, both in school, and they're too young to go out and earn money. Before, there were both Su-ming and her sister working; now only her sister's income is left."

It might be presumed that a desire to accumulate sufficient savings for a respectable dowry would lead parents (and daughters) to delay marriage. One grandmother said, for example, that a woman cannot go over to the man's house empty-handed "with nothing except herself," and the size of a woman's dowry is still thought to affect the kind of treatment she will receive from her mother-in-law. Knowledge of this cannot be reassuring to young women. Referring to a family across the street, Hwang said, "it's the larger dowry of the second daughter-in-law and the small one of the first that account for the difference in the way their mother-in-law treats them. But how can one save several thousand on what we earn?" Even in situations where a woman is permitted to retain some of her earnings, the amount falls short of the sum needed for a "proper" dowry. Liu Jin-ping went to her husband's family with a dowry (valued at approximately NT$100,000) made possible largely through the generosity of her brothers. On the day that her dowry was transferred to her husband's house, Liu told us, "it's embarrassing to talk about the amount of the bride-price, but it only came to NT$46,000; that's barely enough to pay for two or three things here [pointing to some furniture and appliances]."[3]

Whether more families will follow the agreement that Chen Su-ming's family and her husband's family reached remains to be seen, although Mrs. Yang's remark about being able to "earn" money from marrying off a daughter suggests that at least a portion of the bride-price need not be returned in the form of a dowry.

Because the marriages I recorded were not many, I do not have sufficiently detailed information about what happens in situations where a woman herself is reluctant to accept a match arranged for her.[4] Speaking only in terms of the cases for which I have data, these women have in common special circumstances that place each of them in a more vulnerable position than might be true normally. But what is striking about these cases is that none of the women perceived factory employment as offering an alternative that would enable her to reject a particular match, nor is there any indication that bargaining or negotiations, based on the income that a factory job brings, took place between parent and daughter.

Chen, an adopted daughter, worked to support her aged grandparents. Although her grandmother realized the difficulty of locating men willing to enter a uxorilocal match she apparently regarded this as the only solution: "since she is the only one left we can't let her marry out." Marriage was not a subject her grand-daughter was willing to discuss, even in the most general terms, saying only that "I'll let my grandparents decide." Another adopted daughter, Liu Mei-ying met her husband through a mutual friend but had second thoughts about going through with the engagement, and her situation has already been described (see chapter 9). Her grandmother said to us, "I really had to talk some sense into her; I told her that if a person has money and decides not to marry, I wouldn't mind it a bit. But Mei-ying has no savings; who's going to support her? She can't rely on her uncle forever, and I'm getting old. So if she doesn't find a husband willing to support her, how is she going to manage? After that, her thinking cleared up." Mention has already been made of another factory worker in Ch'ipei, who, unmarried at twenty-nine and with no one to "take care" of her, felt she had no choice but to consent to a match arranged by her mother. In another case, Yen, at twenty, married a man of her mother's choosing. Her mother, a widow, had no sons, and despite her opposition her elder daughter (adopted) had married a mainlander who refused a uxorilocal match. For her younger daughter, therefore, the fact that her husband completed only elementary school and was far older was outweighed by the financial security his family offered. Although Yen acknowledges that her husband is generous and treats her well, she admits that theirs was a match where affection developed only after the wedding.

It is difficult to imagine why, under usual circumstances, parents would be eager to press a match on a daughter now that daughters have become economic assets. One might also add that the distance separating many parents from their daughters who live in dormitories makes it harder for parents to exert their influence in such matters. Women of marriageable age in the dormitories, for example, tell of letters from home asking them to return because a well-meaning friend or relative has arranged an introduction. Typically, the reaction of women to such requests is: "I just write back and say I'm not interested." Women living at home also dodge such inquiries, but those in dormitories are naturally in a better position to circumvent any introductions their families may be planning. Women's wage-earning ability has made such delaying tactics more acceptable to their parents, but there are limits to such postponements; daughters, after all, belong to other people.

11

Factory Employment After Marriage

In earlier chapters it became evident that unmarried women have no trouble in finding factory jobs but that they are not given complete control over their earnings. In this chapter I will show that although married women *are* in a position to enjoy the benefits an income brings, they are not always *free* to continue working after marriage, nor do they always *desire* to do so.

Before discussing the feasibility and desirability of continued factory employment after marriage, a word should be said about company policies on the hiring of married women for production-related positions. Although company practices vary, the demand for industrial workers has made it necessary for some firms to hire "even grandmothers," as young women say. Some companies claim that married women with children are less suitable because of a supposedly higher rate of absenteeism. Western Electronics provides a female worker with a week's paid vacation when she marries, and women are entitled to fifty-six days' maternity leave. Advance Electronics (near Ch'inan) gives a similar marriage bonus but the worker is then discharged and married women are not hired. As Advance's personnel manager explained to us, "we feel that a woman's husband and family should come first." Such policies are not always verbalized or stated formally, but as a worker in one Japanese-owned factory stated, "women who get married tend to feel embarrassed about staying on," and in the small serum plant in Ch'inan women say that everyone "knows" and leaves after marrying. Hence, although married women do not face overwhelming obstacles in locating a factory job, the belief that it is more difficult for married women to find work has wide currency and it influences women's thinking about their future.

The reasons women enumerate in explaining why they would prefer not to work after marriage are summed up in the remarks of Liu Su-fong (unmarried), who has worked for nine years:

If the husband earns enough money, it's best if the wife does not work. This is especially so if a woman has children, because if she has a job, she will have little time for them, the home will not be like a home, and her husband will miss the warmth of a home. The wages for *factory* jobs like this are not high; it's usually because of economic circumstances that people do such work; otherwise, there's not much reason to be doing this sort of work. The family should come first; if a woman goes out to work just to make a little more money and neglects her children, it's not worthwhile.

A high-school graduate, living in a dormitory, stated that she would in fact prefer to live at home "because at home parents are there to look after you, and after marriage one can rely on one's husband. [Would you like to work after you're married?] I'd rather not; I feel that if a person has the interest later on, then she can return to work. But taking care of the family and home is what a woman should be doing." The risks a working mother takes are serious. Chang, a high-school graduate, gave the following argument:

Once a woman has children it's very important for her to devote all her attention to her family. One sees too many kids whose parents didn't bring up properly, and it's really a shame. Then they pick up bad habits, often because their parents do not give enough time to them, and to get the attention they crave, they end up in gangs.

The workers mentioned above also emphasized the burden that a factory job and housework together impose on a married woman, but there are other factory women (predominantly those living in dormitories) who point to the monotony of staying at home and doing housework. They express a desire to continue work after marriage, and some, as I indicated earlier, naively assume that a mother-in-law will be on hand, willingly to see to household chores. Their disdain for housework is predictable in view of the fact that they, living in dormitories, have been exempted from any housework for long periods. Yang, for example, said that she would like to continue working not so much for the money "because it doesn't amount to much but for the chance to be with friends and the chance to get out. Besides, since my sister-in-law does the housework, I've never been interested in housework." Hsu, having been away from home for five years, claimed that she "couldn't bear the thought of staying at home, with nothing but housework to do." Now accustomed to life outside, these women see domestic life as too confining. Generalizing about women today, Chiu said,

Staying at home would be boring, especially for someone who's been outside and exposed to more. Although factory work is "bitter" it's still better than staying at home . . . And a woman who works may not have as many problems with her mother-in-law. If a woman has to be with her mother-in-law day in and day out, there will be more conflict and friction.

Where the husband's household is large and where the workload is correspondingly heavy and relations more complex, the escape a factory job offers becomes even more appealing.

The economic gains of a job are naturally not lost on women, but the number who cite this as an incentive to work after marriage is unexpectedly small. Less surprising is that these women are either already married or workers who live away from home—precisely those who have the opportunity to exercise a degree of economic independence and who are therefore able to appreciate the prerogatives their income offers them. In all these cases the advantage of working is expressed in terms of "not having to ask one's husband for money." One woman who had been away from home for several years elaborated:

> It's the woman who gets shortchanged after marriage. A man will go out even after he's married and will leave his wife at home, but it doesn't work the other way round. Once married, he feels you belong to him. That's why it's better if you have a job; he makes money but you earn money too, and don't have to ask for handouts. The best time for girls is before they marry; at that time a man will do whatever you say, but you can be sure it won't be that way after marriage. He'll expect you to stay home and do everything just because he gives you some money.

The comments of married women confirm the gist of the comments above:[1]

> [Lok became a hairdresser at the shop located in the factory complex at Western Electronics after she married.] It's good to be able to earn some money, then one need not rely on one's husband for everything. He still sends some money home from his earnings. It's a good thing I'm working; there's more money to spend and more freedom; but then where would I find the time to spend it? Before I married I used to go shopping or to movies, but now there's no time.

> [Lee has been employed at Western Electronics for three years, and has three children ranging from the seventh grade to third grade.] I save most of what I earn for myself and the children [in credit clubs]. My husband gives me very little money for clothes, so almost all my clothes were bought with my earnings. When I'm tired I'm tempted to quit, but then I think about the money and that's enough reason to stay on. As the children get older they'll need more money for tuition.

The economic autonomy described by these workers would seem sufficiently appealing to lure married women away from home into the factory, yet in fact, whatever preference a woman may voice, these are frequently appended with an afterthought: "but one can never tell what the situation will be like in the future." This section examines some of the considerations that determine whether women will be allowed to work after marriage, be required to work, or be free not to do so.

The occupation of a woman is an important factor in her decision. Secretaries at Western Electronics frequently point out that one advantage of their work is that it is suitable for married women and mothers. Although they may, conceivably, offset some of the costs of child-care by their higher salaries, it is the nature of their work, which is viewed as more enjoyable and lighter, and makes their dual roles possible. Many working-students who quickly dismiss the idea of remaining in a factory, react with considerably more enthusiasm to the prospect of an office job. One of them said, "It's best not to have to work [after marriage] unless it's a very good job, light work that interests you, because a factory job is not good work."

Within a factory, women in quality-control, tester, or group-leader positions are more inclined to have reservations about leaving their relatively light jobs. Garment factories, known for their long hours, are less likely to be considered by a woman who is responsible for a family. Yet a job in an electronics factory generally means lower wages, and makes the cost of hiring a babysitter prohibitively high. Family-operated knitting businesses, with their more informal working atmosphere, often allow women to bring their young children with them to work. The fact that these jobs may be only a few steps away from home allows greater flexibility in managing minor household tasks. One study carried out in Taiwan in 1969 reports that among the married women in the sample who were employed, over sixty percent helped on the family farm or in a family business located near home, and that nine percent earned money from handicrafts and other home industries, all of which could be easily combined with childcare; only eight percent had jobs outside agriculture, and outside their own homes and businesses (Mueller and Cohn 1977:328).

Degree of economic need has also been noted as a determinant of whether a married woman works. The frequently heard remark that it would be ideal if a woman did not have to work after marriage expresses a hope for improved economic status, and at the same time, an underlying recognition that there is always the possibility that one may be obliged to work for financial reasons. Ong replied to questions about work after marriage as if the answer were obvious: "Of course it's best if one doesn't need to work after marriage: it's best not having to worry about meeting expenses." Liu's first thought was directed to the economic circumstances of the man's family: "whether or not a woman works will depend on his family's financial situation. But a person must consider her own [economic] background, and she may have few opportunities to meet someone who is really well-off."

One eighteen year-old worker at Western Electronics said, "the cost of living keeps going up, and if a husband alone worked, things might be tight, so it would depend on the economic position of the family. If finances are such that the wife must work, then we can only try to get an ordinary job, such as in a factory. So it depends on what the husband says." Where the need for an additional income is urgent, there is not likely to be any argument about a woman going outside to work, nor is there apt to be any disagreement in cases where the husband's economic position is secure. Yen continued to work for a month or so after marrying but left at the request of her husband, whose family's business supported them comfortably. Similarly, Liu Mei-ying gave up her job at the urging of her husband: "his intentions are good, and I don't mind. Besides, he gives me spending money each month." In contrast, two women from the Liu settlement in Ch'inan cannot be said to have married into affluent families, but their husbands were opposed to their working after marriage, raising the objection that "with a wife outside all the time a home really isn't a home."

All except two of the married women who were employed in factories worked because their families needed the additional income. Mrs. Hsieh, for instance, was employed at the Western Electronics plant in Ch'ipei for five months before she left. During that time, her two younger daughters (under five years old) were sent to her parents-in-law, and the eldest was left at home. She said, "hiring a babysitter was too costly, but with no one to look after him, he began to get into trouble, and so I had to quit." Mrs. Chen takes her infant daughter with her when she goes to work as a kitchen helper in a factory. Two older children are in primary school, and a third son (two years old) is watched by neighbors. A relative of hers also worked in the Ch'ipei plant for half a year, leaving her (adopted) younger infant daughter with her mother-in-law (who is in her seventies) and sending her elder daughter (also adopted) to kindergarten. She left her job when the second child became too active for her elderly mother-in-law to manage.

One of the exceptions has already been mentioned; Lok, a hairdresser now but formerly a factory worker at Western Electronics, has one young daughter who lives with her husband's parents in southern Taiwan. Asked if her mother-in-law had raised any objections to this arrangement, she replied, "no, why should she? I'm bringing in more money, and now my husband sends them more money. As for my daughter, they're not taking care of her to make things easier for me but for the sake of my husband, who used to become very agitated by her crying." The second woman whose decision to keep her job was not based simply on financial need was one of three female trouble-shooters at Western Electronics, and her lighter work and high wages made her dilemma difficult to solve. At twenty-five Wu has one daughter (age two) who is cared for by a babysitter, since her husband's family lives in the south. When I spoke with her, she was pregnant with a second child, and I asked about her plans after the birth of this baby:

> My husband wants me to stay home this time and not work anymore. It's probably the best thing to do, or else other people will say, 'What kind of mother is she?' But having worked for five years, I wonder if I can bear to stay at home with two children and housework. My husband attends evening school and doesn't get home till ten, so it'd be dull at home. Besides, one's mood is better if one has a job; a person can talk with friends at work . . . Well, maybe being at home won't be that bad; there you're your own boss, whereas at work there's always someone telling you what to do.

Although Wu originally intended to take advantage of a paid maternity leave, she subsequently gave notice and left the factory shortly before giving birth (to a second daughter).

If the alternative to a factory job is the drudgery of housework (perhaps under the supervision of a watchful mother-in-law), it is easy to understand why women are ambivalent. But for Liu Jin-ping, twenty-four and engaged, the question had more immediacy. Although she claimed to be undecided, her anxieties stemmed from the work load at home that she anticipated. Marrying into a family with a father-in-law but no mother-in-law and two younger sisters still living at home (who commute to factories), Liu was well aware of the chores that would fall to her:

> If I work I'd have to get up very early to prepare breakfast for everyone and their lunches as well, plus all the other housework. I don't know if I can manage that physically. But if I didn't work I'd be alone at home and it would be dull. [What about going to a factory closer to home?] Once you're married companies are less eager to hire you.

After marrying she left her job as a group-leader in a television factory (even though her wages at the time were higher than the monthly earnings of her husband), and in this case the absence of a mother-in-law was the deciding factor.

Working-students have an additional consideration; Chen, a group-leader at Western Electronics, began by saying that she would prefer not to work if her husband earned enough, but that it had occurred to her that since working and going to school was so hard and "bitter," it would be a shame not to make use of that education. She then continued, "Nowadays many people hire babysitters, and then one can always ask one's parents-in-law because they will be there anyway."

Let us look further at Chen's assumption and evaluate it in the light of what older women say on this subject. Chen's expectation of assistance from her in-laws may not be entirely realistic, but for the most part, as far as the possibility of continuing to work is concerned, the turning point comes when a woman has children. The woman who had earlier said that staying at home would be especially boring for a woman who had been outside, later added, "life really becomes hard for a woman after she has children because she can't go out to work." As for coworkers who return to the factory after the wedding, women remark that "it's all right because there are no children yet." The importance placed on a mother's presence at home so that she can bring up her children properly has already been noted. A more concrete justification is an economic one: after child-care costs very little remains from a factory worker's wages. Hsu, still single, spoke about women she knew: "most will work until they're pregnant, because then there is the problem of who will take care of the child. To hire a babysitter on what we earn is not worthwhile. More and more couples are living on their own now, which is a good thing, but the one advantage to having your parents-in-law around is that they can watch the children."

Even a mother-in-law, of course, expects to be compensated for assuming childcare responsibilities. One grandmother stated, "it's the mother-in-law who takes care of the house and the children while the wife works. If it weren't for the mother-in-law, the daughter-in-law wouldn't be able to work." It is noteworthy that women foresee that this money will come from their wages rather than from their husband's earnings. This was the view one woman expressed:

> A mother-in-law is not like your own mother and she wouldn't be as close to a daughter-in-law as a mother is to her daughter. So if a woman works after marriage she would not turn over all her wages to her mother-in-law but would only give a small sum as a token.

Another woman stated, "many mothers-in-law think that any sum you give them is too small, and so a woman may as well stay home rather than work; she may have less money but there will be fewer problems as well." Although it should be obvious to women that they could continue to work for a longer period after marriage by delaying the birth of their first child, data on the effects of family planning programs in Taiwan indicate that they have had little impact on the fertility of women between twenty and twenty-nine (Cheng, Kuang, and Tai 1972:317). Among the married women in my Sanhsia sample, all had become pregnant within the first year after marriage.

When Yang Chiu-lan says that she would like to continue working after marriage *provided* her mother-in-law helps with the housework, she is at least conscious of the possibility that older women may not be so willing to assume additional duties in order to free a daughter-in-law to return to the factory. In conversations with older women, there is general agreement that unless there is a pressing economic need for a daughter-in-law's income, older women prefer not to have a daughter-in-law working outside because that would leave them with the burden of housework. This is especially true if there are very young children to be looked after.[2] One Liu woman told us,

> I don't like living with my second daughter-in-law because when she goes out to work, all the housework and feeding the ducks and chickens are left for me to do. It's not that she's unfilial, but I'm already so old, and shouldn't have to do such hard work. So I prefer to stay here; with my [third] daughter-in-law at home, she does all those things.

A Chen woman who lives with her youngest and remaining daughter in Ch'inan declined to go live with her daughter-in-law:

> She didn't want me to raise pigs anymore but to help her take care of the children, but I didn't want to. I can only get NT$1,000 doing that, and I would have no freedom of movement. And if something goes wrong all the blame is sure to fall on me. That would be harder work than raising pigs [which she sells]. So I told her to find someone else or to go to her own family.

Returning to one's natal family, however, is not always feasible, as the following remarks from a Su grandmother indicate:

[Mrs. Su cares for the two children of her elder (adopted) daughter, a prostitute, and the children of her son. Her younger daughter, recently married and pregnant, had asked her mother to take care of her child as well.] I can barely manage the way things are now with all the work I have to do. Besides, I only get several hundred dollars a month from my elder daughter and sometimes she even criticizes me for not taking care of the children the right way. I cannot refuse to take care of my son's children—they're 'insiders'—but it's different with a daughter's children—they belong to outsiders. I never thought it would come to this; here I am so old but I'm still working for my children. It should be the other way around; they should make it possible for me to rest.

Other mothers-in-law and grandmothers say that if they must do housework and babysit, they may as well go outside to work for other families since they could earn more than a daughter-in-law would give them.

A woman who desires to keep her factory job after marriage, therefore, (a) must find a company willing to employ married women, (b) would have to be childless or find low-cost childcare[3] or a willing mother-in-law to assist in childcare, and (c) must be prepared to deal with the objections a husband might raise.

In her writing M. Wolf (1972, 1974) outlines some of the ways in which women, through non-institutionalized and informal processes, obtain the things they want. Although these strategies are not available to unmarried daughters, married women do utilize them and a woman's influence at home might be further increased if she stays in the labor force after marriage and after bearing children. M. Freedman, for instance, points to the increased opportunities for independent action among married women who earn their own livelihood (1971:63–64).

In his book Cohen (1976) gives a detailed analysis of the private fund of money women acquire (through wedding gifts and the dowry) when they marry.[4] In a complex household, a woman with her "private money" may save, invest, or use her cash for other purposes without being subject to the control of the financial manager of the household or of her husband (Cohen 1976:178–79). An unmarried daughter is a jural minor, and a daughter-in-law is entitled only to funds of support from her husband's family. But in a complex household, within the *husband-wife unit*, a woman may allocate her private fund in ways she chooses. Women use their "private money" for personal needs when requests for funds have been denied by the financial manager of the household; they purchase clothing for their children or finance their children's education, and they invest in grain and loan associations (Cohen 1976:179–80).

M. Wolf also mentions women's "private money" (1972:138), but she observes that this fund "is not likely among peasant women to survive past the first year of marriage" (1975:135). In the agricultural community Cohen studied, women add to their private fund by selling vegetables and piglets raised in their spare time. In this context the implications of factory employment for married women are obvious. If a wife's "private money" were augmented by regular wages, her ability to invest and acquire larger sums and to exercise some leverage in decision-making would be substantially increased.[5]

As the preceding pages show, some women are aware that having their own income will reduce their dependency on their husbands and regard wage-earning to be a means of acquiring greater autonomy. But once again we see that women are not always able to act on strategies they perceive. At present women are handicapped by a lack of child-care facilities outside the extended family and the high cost of child-care relative to a factory worker's wages. In addition, a woman's mother-in-law may refuse her request to assume child-care responsibilities. Their predicament underlines the fact that some opportunities made available to unmarried women by factory work cannot be equally utilized by married women.

Although a follow-up study would be necessary to see whether those women who express a desire to work after marriage are actually able to do so (and why or why not), their stated preferences at this time indicate a consciousness of new options.[6] While not all of those in dormitories have developed an inclination to continue working, we may note that *those who do all live away from home.* Even these workers, however, qualify their hopes with certain conditions. P'an, a Western Electronics employee who had lived away from home for four years, concluded, "nowadays a woman can stay outside after she has a family but only if her mother-in-law is there; hiring a babysitter isn't worth the cost." Since Taiwanese young women are evidently not delaying the birth of the first child and since child-care may not be available, the work "careers" of many married women are apt to be brief.

Conversely, those women who see the husband's (or mother-in-law's) opinion or his economic circumstances as decisive factors (in determining whether or not a woman works outside) are *workers who have lived with their families* for the greater part of their working years. Unlike their peers in the Western Electronics dormitories who have been managing on their own for several years, Sanhsia women tend to be compliant. It cannot be said of them that they are determined to continue working after marriage.

12

Self-Perceptions: "A Frog in a Well"

It is undeniable that significant changes following factory employment have occurred: the amount of time a woman spends at home with family members has decreased; exposure to more complex organizations, familiarity with a youth sub-culture, and interaction with peers have increased. Despite these changes Taiwanese female workers do not affirm or articulate any new-found "improvement in status." In this chapter[1] I present some factors that may help to explain this puzzle: why do women who now contribute substantially to family income, in ways not possible until a decade ago, and who are now vital to their country's further development, fail either to assert increased authority in family matters or to assert that their social standing has been elevated?

In this section I am chiefly concerned with factory women's perceptions, with how they measure status and define the sources from which high status is derived, and with specifying the contexts in which they feel they have acquired greater independence. I suggest that there are three sets of related factors that combine to limit the emergence of an unambiguous sense of elevated status among factory women.

The first has to do with the pervasive emphasis on education among Chinese youth in Taiwan. Educational level is important as an indicator of status for both men and women, but while educational level is closely correlated with occupation with respect to men, for women the correlation is more ambiguous. Manual workers in factories include not only elementary school graduates, but women with lower-middle school and high school diplomas. Their titles (group-leader, inspector, etc.) may differ (and even these promotions are not based on educational level), but are all classified as "workers." Because manual labor does not confer prestige, it is easy to understand why no positive worker identity has emerged among women (I return to this in chapter 13). Instead, better-educated women lay stress on their educational level, and these distinctions, drawn along educational lines, often lead to divisiveness in relationships among women. At the same time, women are sensitive to the superior educational backgrounds of office employees, and vertical relations are also characterized by distance and distrust.

The second set of factors concerns how women preceive the relationship between their present circumstances and their prospects. Third, women are ambivalent about being self-reliant. I shall argue that together, these factors make it possible to understand statements from factory workers that express not so much a sense of improved status as one of dissatisfaction and of resignation.

I have already noted that high educational level and the white-collar positions it makes possible are the ways in which prestige is acquired, rather than by the mere fact of wage-earning or high salary. Because a college diploma qualifies a woman for an office job, it might be supposed that parents would be willing to support their daughters' wish to continue in school since a white-collar job might bring a higher salary. For Taiwanese women this is not the case because, first, the wages an experienced garment worker earns are not appreciably lower than the salary a clerical worker earns. Second and more important, when a woman completes college, she is of marriageable age, and this means that her family does not stand to reap the benefits deriving from her education. But a daughter who enters a factory after lower-middle school can expect to work and bring money home for at least five years before she marries.

As indicated earlier, contributing to family income is conceived of as a natural and legitimate obligation by women. Simultaneously, however, there is an awareness that there are other women of their age group who are able to continue in school, and for whom the question of a job at this age never arises. This contrast with a factory worker's own situation brings forth references to one's poor "fate" or "bitter lot." One informant who, at twenty-three, had been working for close to ten years described a relative of hers: "Her fate is very good; at sixteen she is still going to school, whereas factory girls like myself were already on our own at that age, and had to do everything for ourselves."

The extension of compulsory education through lower-middle school has brought a high school diploma within closer reach; young women are now three rather than six years away from completing high school. For a majority, however, being able to attend school on a full-time basis unencumbered by a job continues to be the ideal. One woman who was working and attending school said, "If financial circumstances permit, the ideal would be to be in school; it's still the happiest time, and I envy those who can do this." Another worker said:

> I have a younger sister, fifteen, who will be finishing lower-middle school soon, and I don't wish to have her come up here [to this factory] because I've known how 'bitter' it is—going to school and working at the same time. I'd be willing to help pay her school fees.

The advantages that a high school diploma confers are evident to everyone. One woman said,

Since I only finished primary school, what other job could I obtain except manual work? And the small amount of money a person earns in such jobs does not really count for anything. It's true that those who go to school have to spend a good deal of money, but it's an investment, and they receive large returns later.

Status is measured by occupation, by how one earns an income rather than the mere fact of earning an income, and completion of lower-middle school does not qualify a woman for the clerical and office positions to which prestige is attached. In response to the question why so many women are willing to devote a substantial portion of their earnings to tuition, women typically point out that "nowadays, a person who has had more education is more highly regarded, enjoys greater prestige." It is not unusual to hear about women who tell others that they are high school (or lower-middle school) graduates, when in fact "everyone knows that they only finished lower-middle school [or primary school]." Some women add that although a person may not actually have graduated from high school, to have attended high school still "sounds better."

Women who work the day shift attend classes from approximately six to ten o'clock in the evenings, and depending on the distance between factory and school (and, in some cases, home), they generally take only a few minutes for a quick meal or snack before rushing to catch a bus. Other women who attend school during the day are up before seven to be on time for classes that usually begin at eight and last till three in the afternoon, rushing back to the factory for the four p.m. to midnight evening shift.

One Cantonese woman described her situation: "My family wasn't very well off when I finished primary school, so I came out to work. If my fate were better, at my age I would be in college now." She then went on to recount the hardship of working and attending school, which she did for a year. She subsequently gave up school only to have made another attempt in the following year, and is presently in her final year in lower-middle school. The realization that such a schedule is taxing, however, does not diminish the motivation to continue one's education. One woman recalled that after lower-middle school, she felt that since "everyone" goes on to high school, if she did not she would be left behind and would not be able to catch up with other people. At Western Electronics the first group of workers to graduate from high school numbered approximately one hundred and fifty; the number of those who are presently attending school has increased to well over one thousand. (I should point out that the proportion of students at Western Electronics is probably higher than that in many factories because there is a relatively large number of high schools nearby, and being an electronics factory, working hours at Western Electronics are generally shorter and more regular than is the case in garment/textile factories.)

Even workers not attending school are aware of the demands such a regimen makes on one's time and energy. One high school graduate said,

Although I haven't been through it [working and attending school], I did know working-students when I was in school. It seemed obvious that they weren't getting enough sleep or rest, but I suppose it's a question of getting used to it. And they really have no choice since they do this in order to attain more education.

Another high school graduate sympathized with working students:

It's understandable that they are willing to put themselves through this because education is so important; for a girl it sounds so much better if one is a high school graduate than if one only completed lower-middle school, and it's a factor that men [boyfriends] will take into account too.

In comparing themselves with full-time students, working students claim that the former appear younger and "livelier" and have more opportunities to play. As one of them said, "with our schedule there really isn't any time left to enjoy ourselves in the way young people our age should, and it seems a pity because these are our best years." The following passage sums up sentiments that many working students share. The speaker was one of several women who asked me about workers in American factories. Her puzzlement arose from her understanding that in America, everyone has the opportunity to attend high school, and she therefore could not see how anyone would be left who would be willing to do factory work. As she put it,

I often feel that my life right now, studying and working, is a bitter one. [She was in her second year of high school.] Other people realize this too, and say that it isn't easy to keep up this pace for three years. Whenever I run into former classmates who are now in college, I feel too embarrassed to even greet them. Well, perhaps my own feelings of inferiority are too strong, but this is work where you don't need to think or to use your mind, but only to move your hands. Such work is so monotonous that no one would ever choose to do it, and you can't apply what you learn in school at all. I'm just trying to bear with this until I graduate, and then I can leave this factory.

The prospect of being able to leave the factory is a welcome one among working students, and the expectation is that all of them will take this step. At the same time, spiralling qualification requirements for white-collar jobs have lowered expectations, and more and more find that they have no choice but to remain in the factory after graduation. The following comments come from a woman who had just completed three years of vocational training while employed at Western Electronics:

Before there was no need to worry about the job market; I just went to school after work. Now all sorts of matters come up and require decisions. Most companies want men for the good positions; that much is obvious from the newspaper ads. A friend of mine inquired into a possible opening for me but found out they wanted a man for the job.

Since a high school diploma is in actuality not easily achieved, it is comprehensible why most high school graduates are disdainful of factory work. One woman with a high school education who is employed as a bookkeeper in a Taipei boutique claimed,

> I would rather go without work than be a factory girl. If two women have the same educational level and one works in a factory and the other in an office, a man would be more interested in the latter, without first trying to find out what each person is really like. Therefore, this kind of status is very important.

Another woman who holds a clerical position in Taipei had this to say about factory work: "It is work even elementary school graduates can do. If I took such a job, even if it paid more than my present job, it would mean many years of school wasted." She had expressed some dissatisfaction with her own job and was inquiring into other openings, but ruled out factory work: "It isn't easy to find a job these days, and I'm not qualified for really desirable positions. Some factory girls earn more than I do but their work is very 'bitter.' Besides, factory work sounds bad, because then a person is classified as a manual worker."

If pressed, women concede that work tasks in themselves are not physically arduous; the "bitter" quality of factory work derives from a combination of working conditions and the attitudes they encounter in the course of their work: they earn money through labor; their hands may become coarse and rough; the plant can at times be hot; inadequate ventiliation leaves fumes or lint in the air; and many cannot leave the assembly line or walk around. All these factors stand in sharp contrast to the working environment that office women enjoy, a contrast that factory women consider unjust, and resentment, although misdirected, is often expressed toward office personnel.

Attitudes toward factory work and stereotypes of factory women held by the wider public do not enhance job satisfaction or a sense of self-worth. One high school graduate who planned to work only during the summer months explained her situation to me, and said: "This kind of factory work is a job where you cannot hold your head high; it is a low status occupation and does not give a person any face." There is a consensus among workers that as far as most people "in society" are concerned, factory work carries no status or prestige whatsoever. One worker said, "when others hear that you work as an assembler, they just 'shake their heads.'" Workers in many firms know, of course, that the goods they help to produce are destined for export, but there is little consciousness of the fact that they form one important base from which Taiwan's prosperity grew. Rather, the situation is perceived within a more limited perspective: a firm has the capital to hire them, they perform the tasks assigned, and are paid for their labor.

The media, too, contribute to these images: storylines in television programs frequently depict a young woman who must take up factory work to help support her family, and is generally portrayed as an innocent figure who arrives in the city only to be exploited or duped by unscrupulous persons. She is a character who evokes pity since in most cases she is without the resources to improve her own position. In the latter part of 1974 when layoffs of factory workers became commonplace, some women were offended by the tone newspapers used in describing them; one working student complained that journalists wrote about them as if "all of us factory girls are poorly educated, young and immature, and as if we have no mind of our own but just do what we are told by the companies." The author of an article on factory women in the Kaohsiung export processing zone reports that during interviews, women expressed their resentment of a public who regard their lives as disorderly and who hold them in low regard (C.C. Yang 1976:64).

Factory women uniformly express frustration in response to the condescension and snobbishness they encounter in office workers. As indicated in chapter 8, their interaction with the latter group is in fact limited, yet factory workers feel ill-at-ease in offices because "the positions of office employees are higher than ours." Two testers (a position higher than that of an assembler) who had been in the factory for over four years commented heatedly on this subject:

> The women in the offices really think themselves very special, and this can be seen in the superior airs they assume, even in the way they walk and act. This must intimidate those workers just out of school. Even the restrooms are divided, separate ones for them and for us workers. Actually, their wages are not that much higher than ours [as testers], but they certainly carry themselves as if they were way above us. It's best not to go into the offices unless you have to.

During my stay in the factory the company sponsored an art contest, and when I asked one group of workers, merely in passing, why they did not submit entries, one of them expressed skepticism about the whole affair: "These contests are always 'fixed' in favor of office personnel. That's how it always turns out." My pointing out that winners were to be chosen by balloting did not dissuade them from this view. Another added, "there is a very clear distinction and a wide gap between workers and office women; they may be nice to each other, but that certainly isn't the way they treat us."

Although white-collar and blue-collar status discriminations generate the greatest frustration among factory women ("We use our labor in our work, unlike the office women, but that doesn't give them reason to make us feel inferior."), factory women at Western Electronics complain more generally that "there are far too many levels in this company." (The most conspicuous signs of status distinctions, aside from titles of address, are in dress, as plant employees must wear uniforms, with different colors for group-leaders, assemblers, quality control workers, foremen, and superintendents. Dining rooms are not segregated, although the higher cost of meals in one section of the cafeteria serves to keep most factory workers in the other area.)

Some women, of course, allow that such a multitude of levels is inevitable in a firm as large as Western Electronics, and that such organizational requisites make certain patterns of interaction virtually impossible. "In a smaller factory, from the managers on down to the workers, people know each other better; people would greet each other. But in a larger company a person can only know those in her immediate work area." "In a small factory workers and managers have more opportunities to know each other; contacts are more frequent, and this way *kan-ching* [feelings] develops. But this would not happen in a large company." This knowledge may give women reason to lower their expectations, but it does not modify the environment in which they must work. Status distinctions that put distance between employees, the heterogeneity and large size of the work force, combined with sometimes conflicting job demands do not always produce an atmosphere conducive to the type of warm relations that workers value.

The preoccupation with educational background and job rank creates divisions in friendship networks. One working student explained why she returned to school two years after lower-middle school:

> There's very little one can learn from a job like this, and finding someone with whom one can really talk isn't easy. The situation here at work is more complex than at school because there're all kinds of people here, of many different backgrounds. For example, people differ in their educational levels; those with more schooling not only know more in the academic sense but tend to be more mature, and will think things through; with differences such as these people may not necessarily get along well.

In terms of the prestige value it carries, then, educational level becomes a double standard in evaluating others. Workers as a group resent being looked down upon by office employees, but at the same time, these same workers make fine distinctions among themselves according to educational achievement. (We might recall here, for instance, that workers with limited schooling are perceived as being more susceptible or prone to acquiring improper habits.)

Women claim that a person cannot really "grow up" at home, and they consider that knowledge gained from observing people is one aspect of gaining maturity. Yet in the course of learning about interpersonal relations, women discover that many people are opportunistic and that individuals are often superficial and manipulative in their dealings with one another. It is within this framework that many workers consider their present life situations to be "bitter" ones: in addition to being on their own without family members to look after them, they occupy the lowest positions in any of a series of hierarchies, and are placed in the midst of relationships often characterized by this opportunism. As one group-leader said, "it isn't only superiors who treat us this way, but relations among women themselves are also frequently opportunistic."

Saying that human feelings run "shallow and thin" in the factory has become a cliché, and while newer workers may merely be repeating what they hear, experienced workers are able to draw upon more specific cases.

It's less complex at school; at work people do things with ulterior motives. Work can disrupt relationships and make things more complicated. For example, if two girls are assemblers and there is a chance for a promotion for one, each will hope inside that the other will not get it, and suspect the other of thinking the same thing. This puts distance between two people who might have gotten along well in the past.

If you just watch people at work—assemblers, group-leaders, foremen—conflicts are bound to arise due to the nature of their work. You can see how people put up fronts to get what they want, and you can see people being sarcastic and insincere.

Opportunism and self-interest are the traits factory women most frequently attribute to people beyond the home and school.

A person can be nice to you one day when it's to his advantage to be, but he can change his manner the very next day. Many people are this way nowadays, and this applies not only to the way managers and foremen are with the workers, but it is true of the girls themselves as well. One day someone will think of a way to be nice to you because she wants something from you (e.g., a group-leader who needs to rush to meet a deadline), but the next day she may only think of herself and not consider other people. It's not just this company; I hear the same thing from classmates at school who work in other factories.

It would not be accurate to imply that all factory women are equally disturbed by the quality of relations they find at work, but there is the belief that it is not easy to know people well. In any case, an awareness of opportunism in work relations instills in some women a cautious or wary attitude (that occasionally borders on cynicism) toward interpersonal ties.

A person who comes out to work must be "round and slippery" in order to maintain smooth relations with everyone; but then, if you think about it, this is hardly a good trait to have.

Before turning to women's views of their future prospects, I wish to examine why interaction is marked by distrust and why social relations are believed to be difficult, a pattern that closely approximates findings of other studies.

By the time girls enter factories they have already been subjected for many years to a socialization process in which obedience and cooperation are emphasized above all else. The very term "obedient," which literally means "to listen to talk," reflects the pattern of passivity expected from children (cf. Solomon 1971:52). Children are also taught that the family is the source of their security and relatives the only people who can be depended on. The threat of isolation from family approval, therefore, is one of the most powerful sanctions that can be imposed (M. Wolf 1972:45, Solomon 1971:53). One of Grichting's findings from his survey in Taiwan is that high authoritarianism in the Chinese family and fear of the outside world (one that is largely perceived as hostile) are the main mechanisms for controlling personal conflict (1970:214).[2] But where daughters are concerned, the probability of conflict arising in the family is in any case not high since children are made to feel that they lack sufficient experience in society to offer opinions and instead should listen to their parents. It is little wonder then that girls leaving home for the first time invariably announce that they "don't know anything." This is not merely a culturally expected or polite statement; it accurately reflects a new worker's state of mind.

If the family is remembered as a source of security, the years a woman spent in school are also viewed in a positive light. In that setting, where group unity is encouraged (cf. Wilson 1970), girls begin to appreciate the security that the constant companionship of friends can provide. (Here we might recall workers resigning when their friends leave a company, a pattern that personnel managers find so distressing.)

School and home are orderly places that women later contrast with the disorder of the wider society. To an outsider it may appear strange that women should idealize in wistful terms environments that are in fact characterized by fairly strict discipline. But evidently factory women are not alone in this tendency. Silin writes that among managers in Taiwanese factories childhood and youth are "associated with a simplicity that is later distorted by age and cultivation" (1976:48), and the statements from his informants would find wide agreement among factory women, "'Children do not understand self-interest relationships (*li-hai kuan-hsi*) but only mutual attraction relationships (*kanching*)'" (Silin 1976:48); "'in school it is all mutual attraction... You don't ask a friend who his father is. It is only when you grow older... that you start to think of self-interest'" (Silin 1976:49).

It is from these homogeneous settings where the behavior of others is fairly predictable and where persons hold roughly the same sorts of values that women enter factories. The factory is the setting where their lives and the wider socio-economic system intersect, and extrapolating from their observations in the factory, women come to see relations at work as reflective of those in the society outside. Although women do not regard themselves as part of an "urban industrial class," it is in the factory that they begin to discern restrictions on their options in the future and where they experience the inequities and frustrations of being a lowly manual worker. It would be inaccurate to credit these women with a clear grasp of the relationship between the factories that employ them and the wider socio-economic environment; rather, the factory is their point of entry into the larger society and it mediates their orientations to the latter. Even though women may express disappointment in what they find, they nonetheless acquire a perspective of their society and its rules that differs from that held by their mothers, by their classmates who continue to be full-time students, or by women who remain on the farm.

Women's reaction to the factory is succintly summed up in Leacock's characterization of commodity production in urban centers:

> [R]elations within the group [were transformed] from direct, personal and basically cooperative to impersonal and highly competitive, ruled by "mysterious forces" that eluded understanding and control. With industrial capitalism came the metamorphosis of human relations into commodity relations, relations among things to be used (1975: 56–57).

In factories the content of relations is narrow in scope and involves only that aspect of the woman's identity that is pertinent to the work setting, whereas in school and at home a woman's personality was not segmented in such a fashion. Nor are relations in factory dormitories marked by warmth or an easy friendliness; women often say they don't know persons across the hall or next door, and this is consistent with one study that specifically examined company housing in a Taiwan factory. The data from that survey suggest that for single persons, dormitories "do not function as a substitute for the absence of family ties, nor do they provide a locale for meaningful social relationships; family-type relations were not found to have developed in dormitories and the conclusion was that persons are affiliated for restricted and special purposes only" (Schwartzbaum and Tsai n.d.:11–12). As one social worker who has devoted some years to the problems of workers in Taiwan told me, "If room and floor leaders are ever to be created in the dormitories, women would first need to develop the ability to exert authority, a willingness to take initiatives, and to develop trust in one another—qualities that are almost the exact opposite of what women are like now."

Placed in the context of research on similar subjects, the absence of a sense of community among workers is not surprising. Grichting, for example, asserts that while the emphasis on family solidarity provides a basis for stability, it hinders the development of community based on supra-family relations (1970:384). Silin cites Weber who made the same point, namely, that a strong commitment to one's family results in general distrust among non-kin, a claim that Silin admits is difficult to assess (1976:46). While we lack sufficient basis for attributing the impersonal quality of relations among dormitory residents to their strong commitment to their families, the desire to avoid potentially conflictive situations is genuine. Wilson refers to the adage "only sweep the snow in front of your own door" as an example of the belief that if one does not become involved in a situation one need not fear the consequences (1970:140).

In any event, as much as young women need and desire the companionship of peers, they find that friends are not easily made in the plant or in the dormitory. A high turnover rate works against the formation of bonds that endure for more than a few weeks, but more is involved than job mobility. As Moore has observed, it is frequently assumed "that informal patterns of interaction established in the work context result in genuine social groups that share various interests and activities both at the work place and outside it" (1965:50). He goes on to say, however, that the evidence on this point is virtually nonexistent. Much has already been said about the opportunism, ulterior motives, and self-interest that factory women detect in interpersonal relations in the company. But women themselves often perpetuate the divisive gradations based on education and occupational position that impose barriers to building friendships.

Women's opinions about the quality of interpersonal relations in the larger society may not be too far from the truth, and they fit in remarkably well with the picture of social relations that Solomon and Silin draw.[3] On the basis of his research among managers, Silin states that Taiwanese "assume that adult behavior is unpredictable and that individuals are likely to act in self-seeking and arbitrary ways. One is expected to remain wary in dealing with others, even associates. The majority of the population are felt to lack the *education* that would allow them to behave in other than a base manner" (1976:45–46, emphasis added). There is, moreover, an element of tension because there is an emphasis on avoiding both conflict and emotional expressiveness; "the ideal person masks his feelings" (Silin 1976:41). Yet by so doing a person makes himself/herself liable to accusations of being insincere or putting up a front, and factory women charge that people often present what is only a facade. In Solomon's analysis of Chinese political culture he also refers to distrust of outsiders. He adds that with such a view of social relations it is not suprising to find that childhood appears safe, and he includes this statement from one respondent:

> Youth is a relatively happy period of life because you have no responsibility. In those times society was relatively simple, not so complicated as today. Now if people seek to make friends they have some [ulterior] motive. Relations between friends usually have some political or economic flavor (1971:103).

Solomon notes that the terms "complications" and "confusions" are used repeatedly to describe the uncertainties in interpersonal relations. This is true of factory women as well, who characterize home and school as "simple" places while the world outside is "complex," "disorderly," and unpredictable. In Solomon's view, "complications" suggest emotional tension and imply that conflict is a likely possibility just behind the face of social custom (1971:103–104). Once again this brings to mind the remarks of factory women who contrast
superficial appearances with actual hostility and competitiveness lying just underneath.

Like the female workers in this study, Solomon claims that the respondents whom he interviewed sought idealized non-hierarchical friendships with peers even though they maintained, at the same time, more realistic expectations about the difficulty of establishing close relationships. Solomon traces this tendency in part to the upbringing Chinese children receive, noting that from the time children begin to have contact with non-family peers, they are led to acquire a distrust of other people's motives and doubts about their own ability to deal effectively with interpersonal disputes: "respondents frequently respond about how important it was that parents choose 'proper' friends for their children to play with, for 'bad' friends could lead a child astray into indulgence" (1971:125). Among factory women this belief finds expression in the emphasis they place on selecting one's friends with care, lest one pick up bad habits, and on how easily a girl far from home can learn bad ways.

A factory job can bring relatively greater freedom of movement, control over time, and greater familiarity with the outside society. But dissatisfaction with one's lot and with the work environment emerges as the novelty wears off. As one woman in Sanhsia who lived at home and who, at twenty-four, had been working for nine years said,

> When I think that at my age I'm still a factory worker, it's very depressing. When I was younger I even felt that working in a factory could be fun, could be a chance to play, but now when I see that the other workers are so young in comparison to me, it makes me feel even worse. Being in that factory is like being "a frog in a well."

The factory that once represented a wider world, or at least one means of entry into the larger society, appears progressively more confining as one's stay lengthens. Like a frog in a well, a worker inside a factory is able to see only a very small portion of the sky—the world outside. During conversations with the workers it was difficult to elicit comments or generate discussion about the future or about their goals (with the exception of working-students). The terms with which young women describe their present lives as factory workers (and the same terms recur), however, are striking and revealing:

> Many workers at the factory say that our working here amounts to wasting away our time, "burying our youth," because each day by the time we get off work, it's already very late. There's hardly any time or opportunity to meet with friends. In the factory, where one has no freedom, it is as if we've sold our lives to the company.

Another woman, twenty-one years old and living at home, shared the same sentiments:

> My life is so dull and unvaried: I get off work, go home and have dinner. There's no place to go after I'm home and nothing that's interesting to do. I don't even know how I get through each day; I'm not the only person who says this; many girls at the factory feel the same way, that being shut up in the factory all day is the same as wasting away the "spring of our youth." In the mornings we go off to work and often at night there is overtime. We have no

opportunity to come into contact with other people, people outside the factory. Anybody who wants to see us won't have an easy time of it. Everyone feels that we're just biding our time here, but there is no objective ahead.

These statements illustrate another source of the frustration many factory women feel: one's teen years and those of early adulthood before marriage are viewed as the most pleasurable and carefree period in a woman's lifetime. These years, the "spring of one's youth," however, are brief, and there is a widespread conviction that a woman should make the most of them, and take advantage of every opportunity to enjoy these years before she is burdened with the responsibilities marriage brings. Herein lies what many women see as their plight, for it is precisely these years they "waste away" inside a factory. When women say that the "spring of their youth" has been sold to a company or that it has been "buried," they are referring not only to the actual amount of time they spend in a factory, but also to a situation where one's interaction with others is limited to a handful of coworkers. In addition, there exist few occasions that allow them to become acquainted with a wider circle of individuals inside as well as outside the factory.

It is true that some women attempt to escape these feelings of entrapment by frequent job changes. In the opinion of some workers, however, these individuals earn a poor reputation by "running around so much," although they sympathize with the motivations underlying this. "For some women, perhaps, the stimulation and excitement from seeing new things and people are more important, and they do not mind having to adjust to new situations constantly. It's hard to blame them; being shut up in a factory all day, we see so little of the world, just like 'a frog in a well.'" But a larger number of women do not regard a change in companies to be a satisfying solution, since "a factory girl will always be a factory girl," or because "all factory jobs are the same."

At this point I wish to summarize how women view the independence that wage-employment can bring. Factory women, it is true, often refer to themselves as "girls of the present generation" or preface their remarks with "girls nowadays prefer to...," indicating that at least some recognize themselves as a group with a new set of attitudes distinguishing them from women in the past. Lest such terms be interpreted as harbingers of more concrete changes, it bears repeating that these sentiments are in large part a reflection of what one hears from friends rather than a mirror of actual behavior. It is conceivable, for example, that some women couch their leaving home and coming outside to work in terms of "playing" in order to de-emphasize the economic circumstances that necessitated such a move or to facilitate adjustment to a low-status occupation. One study of dormitory residents in a large factory in Taiwan reports that a majority of respondents indicated that if given the opportunity of having a job with equal pay, they would prefer to move back home (Schwartzbaum and Tsai n.d.:8).

Whether or not a factory worker considers herself self-supporting should affect her perceptions of future options. In strict monetary terms Taiwanese factory women claim that it is possible for a woman to support herself on her wages. This is not, however, a realistic or desirable prospect for them and it does not alter their expectations for the future. In this regard E. Johnson's findings about Hakka women in the New Territories of Hong Kong are relevant. Where once these women were employed outside the home they now derive income from the rental of houses, and Johnson writes:

> Their work is much more confined to the domestic sphere than it was in the past. Yet I detected no feeling of anomie among the women. From their point of view, the loss of apparently meaningful and productive work in agriculture has been more than compensated for by the relative ease of their lives, particularly the absence of hard physical labor (1975:219).

If nothing else, this passage shows that what might appear to be "meaningful and productive" work may not be seen that way at all by the women actually doing the work, and that their own perceptions must be taken into account. Women realize that while a factory wage allows them to be self-sufficient, it will not bring them the standard of living they desire, and that achieving the latter will depend upon pooling their resources with men who have skilled jobs and who receive higher wages.

In the conclusion to her study on the Chinese family in the 1940s Olga Lang states:

> Factory [women] have often been powerful in the family in spite of themselves... the attitudes and ideas are the same as those of women in olden times; they do not believe in woman's equality. Many women with modern education have been, in theory, ardent supporters of woman's complete emancipation and equality but have been unable to put any of their dreams into practice, and in their families they enjoy fewer rights than factory workers (1946:339).

With regard to present-day Taiwan a persuasive argument can be made for the notion that factory women living away from home are indeed more self-reliant than, say, women their age in college, and like the factory women Lang describes, those in Taiwan do not espouse ideas about female equality. Nonetheless, they are not powerful within their families or elsewhere, and instead would gladly trade their "independence" for the security of the college student who has a family to look after her needs. Projecting into the future, factory women prefer the leisurely life of the non-employed middle-class housewife over the "right" to perform her duties in a factory and at home. The life of the middle-class housewife in Taiwan's cities may be characterized by social isolation, as Diamond (1975) claims, but this is not an image many factory workers hold.

Men in Taiwan often say that women are inept in dealing with the world outside (M. Wolf 1974) but factory women are gaining, through their jobs, exposure to that world, and in some cases their knowledge of its workings surpasses that of men in the countryside. In their families' eyes women may have been transformed into economic assets, but when they describe their own situation, women attribute any changes they see more to the fact of being outside than to the fact of wage-earning.

A small number of women explicitly place themselves within broader changes they perceive occurring in society, and the excerpts below show how two workers articulate this. (Both, not coincidentally, are high school graduates.)

[Chuang pointed to the worker across from her and told me:] She's still very young, only seventeen, I think. Before, girls around seventeen would already be married. It was a very different life for girls then; most belonged to farm families and girls had no or very few worries about the future. The pattern of their lives and activities were pretty much set. They didn't have much to do except to stay home. It wasn't considered good for girls to leave home and work outside. Even today in the more isolated rural areas, there are families that still think this way. In the past the most important criterion about a man for the girl's family was whether his family owned land. Nowadays the girl herself feels that if the man has land, he is less desirable, and she prefers someone who has a job outside. This society is changing from an agricultural one to an industrial one. [Why should this create more worries for girls?] Today girls all come out to the cities, see much more and experience the many forms of life and behavior found in cities, and are no longer willing to return to a farming way of life. So there are more matters to be considered. I feel women are better off now; before, women and men were very unequal. Take the case of my mother: her mother favored sons and all my uncles had the opportunity to go to school, but my mother received no education at all. My [maternal] grandmother still favors my brothers over my sister and me. [What about your mother?] Sometimes she's like that; when I wanted to go to high school, for example, she was opposed to it in the beginning, saying that girls don't need much education because after marriage it will all be forgotten.

[Chang is a twenty-one year old worker.] Nowadays when a woman marries she will also have had wide experiences in the society outside; it won't be a case where her husband would know a lot more. There is no longer a meaningful distinction between outside and inside. [Wives are sometimes referred to as the person "inside."] Their knowledge of society, and their positions relative to each other, therefore, are now more equal. [The same speaker, however, on another occasion, expressed the belief that a woman's duty as wife/mother is to remain home and fulfill her responsibilities to her family.]

Note that in neither case did the speaker point to women's wage-earning ability as the decisive factor. Women do not stress their stronger economic position because for a majority their economic power has *not* in fact increased substantially.

Women's day-to-day experiences outside are more concrete, and they are acquiring knowledge that cannot be attained from textbooks. At the same time, this store of information (about how to seek employment, how to manage in a dormitory, and about interpersonal relations at work) is not always useful at home. Working daughters do run errands for their parents and accompany their mothers into cities when such a trip is required, but beyond this they are rarely consulted when family matters are discussed. (An exception is when jobs and schools for younger siblings are brought up, and on these subjects a working daughter's familiarity with the outside is recognized as making her more knowledgeable.)

Factory work has allowed some women to continue their education, and a larger group appreciate not having to go to their parents for even very small sums of money. Insofar as these privileges are made possible by wage-earning, women perceive that wage-earning has granted them more control over their lives; but the freedom to work as a sought-after prerogative (e.g., after marriage) or as an abstract right are not concepts these women hold.

Women are ambivalent about their limited independence, and most of them are independent, to the degree that they are, more by default than choice. (Women have the responsibility *not* to be a burden on their families.) Decision-making confers responsibility as well as freedom, and having to manage some aspects of their lives makes women responsible in ways to which they are not accustomed.

At this point I have arrived at three conclusions: first, a keen sensitivity to the low prestige accorded to factory work, and an awareness of the generally low educational level of factory workers generate a sense of inferiority among factory wage-earners. Second, although women give positive value to being self-reliant in the world outside and acquiring knowledge of that world, they find that learning to become independent can be a "bitter" process. They also discover that the world outside has its less attractive sides. Third, frustration stemming from the dead-end quality of factory jobs further contributes to the conditions that preclude any sense of increased self-esteem.

I now consider how factory women regard their economic role in the family, contrast their views with those of older women, and attempt to account for this difference.

Older women in Sanhsia say that a woman who contributes income to her family enjoys a higher standing in the family. In explaining the "low standing" of women in the past, old women described to me how daughters were in many instances adopted out. They talk at length about how times have changed: women now eat better food; they are able to buy more clothes, and they have more opportunities to play. But many of these improvements can be attributed to general betterment in standards of living over recent years. As for less tangible benefits such as "rights" and participation in decision-making in the family, it is remarkable that older women are unable to furnish concrete instances of how daughters now exercise greater authority or decision-making rights at home.

In contrast, working daughters do not assert that their status at home is elevated as a result of their wage-earning. There is, to be sure, agreement among young women that they enjoy more comfortable lives than did women twenty or more years ago. Their knowledge of the contrasts between their lives and those their mothers and grandmothers led is understood in an abstract sense and is not meaningful in the context of their lives. These women by and large define and measure status not by the mere fact of an income but how that income is earned; thus, the relationship between wage-earning and an awareness of improved status among women is not a simple, straightforward one. What is relevant and holds more importance for them is the fact that they spend the "spring of their youth" in factories.

Older women view the situation differently, as the following excerpts show:

> [From a Liu grandmother]: To be able to earn money means to have position and power. In the past we never went outside to work, and one could say that girls had no position. Everything was up to one's parents to decide, and after marriage, everything was decided by one's husband. If there were factories around at that time, all of us would have wanted to go.

> [From another Liu woman]: Girls now have better fates. Factory work is light and simple. Before, women's work was arduous and rough: tea-picking, weeding, housework, and so on. When I married and returned home "to be a guest," I had to borrow the clothes I wore. Girls today enjoy more comfortable lives; they eat and dress better. A girl who works outside sees more new things and her way of thinking becomes more up to date.

> [From a Lim woman]: A girl who works has a higher position at home because she takes money home and her family relies on her. Therefore, they will treat her better. For instance, if there are good things to eat, they would save some for her, and she would be allowed to have better clothes. The manner of elders would not be so fierce.

It is not difficult for women of this generation to articulate the overall improvements in the lives of women today as compared with their own experiences in the past. In listing the benefits derived from wage-earning, they are essentially drawing from a wider view of society where money does confer power. But as noted earlier, working daughters are not given anywhere near complete control over their earnings, over their education, or the prerogative to choose between living in a dormitory or at home. Furthermore, even though older women are apt to regard delayed marriage as a symbol of women's improved standing, I have shown that this decision may rest with a factory girl's mother and not with the woman herself.

What we find here is an apparent discrepancy: older women claim that because daughters bring money home, their standing in the family has risen. But if one searches for actual manifestations of this claim, concrete instances are rarely found.

Placed in the proper perspective, it must be remembered that for older women, the teenage years for a woman marked the beginning of a period when a woman's life became grim, and yet today it is at this time that young women are able to go outside and earn money. I submit that the discrepancy between what older women reason *should* result from wage-earning and their *actual* expectations of their own daughters can be attributed to their tendency to speak from two perspectives. On the one hand they exaggerate the privileges a daughter acquires through wage-earning because they, as co-managers of a household, can well appreciate the advantages that direct access to income bestows. What they seem to overlook in their remarks, however, is that their *daughters* are not given control over their wages. On the other hand, as co-managers of their families, older women tend to stress utilitarian factors. They recognize, among other things, that daughters will leave, and that other matters have priority over a daughter's "rights." Older women are therefore forced to act according to family interests, and only where a daughter's intentions do not interfere with those plans are they able to give substance to the idea of increased power for working daughters.[4]

The points of reference of young women are very different from those of older women. The orientation of the former is toward the outside, whereas older women, in a vicarious fashion, look back to the pattern of women's lives in the past. From such a past-oriented view, older women are prone to glorify regular wage-employment outside the home and to conclude that the standing of young women has been elevated.[5] Such an inference, however, glosses over aspects of factory work and wage-earning to which young women attach greater relevance. Although women are wage-earners, they are not always able to transform their earnings into the status they desire.[6]

If factory women do not seem to be able to see far into the future or even beyond the next year or two, it is in part because their present position has not substantially altered their options. Women foresee that they will marry, but the factory does not always enhance their chances of meeting prospective mates. Salary increments are small, and promotions do not elevate women into offices. Working students look forward to the better jobs that their diplomas will bring them, but the nature of the job market is beginning to deflate their hopes. To speak of aspirations, therefore, is to attribute to most workers greater certainty about the future than in fact exists. Seeing themselves in dead-end jobs that do not significantly affect or improve their futures, women do not have particular goals or mapped out strategies to attain them. It is not that female workers are unable to take long-term perspectives, but rather that mulling over the course of the next two or three years is not apt to be productive. One personnel manager remarked that factory girls do not look far ahead and as a result, their job performance is unenthusiastic and they are unambitious. Such a judgment overlooks the fact that most factory women are not equipped with the education or familial support that would allow them to develop ambitions in any direction.

13

Worker Consciousness

Factory work fills the interim between school and marriage; it is not an occupation to which women aspire nor does it generate goals toward which they could realistically strive. Nonetheless, factories are the setting into which women come in contact with persons and activities previously unknown to them. What they experience there sets them apart from women employed in restaurants, shops, or banks. On the basis of women's common experience in the factory, then, it seems reasonable to ask whether new forms of consciousness or identity about themselves as workers, as one occupational group with shared interests, have emerged.

At one time in recent Chinese history this kind of awareness among industrial workers did arise. Writing about the labor movement between 1919 and 1927 Chesneaux claims:

> [The working class constituted] a new kind of class, already alien to China's former mental universe and capable of behaving very differently from other social classes, especially the peasantry, from which it had so recently emerged. Despite the long hours of work and the low wages, new interest and new traditions gradually began to replace the customs of former days... Little by little a new calendar of traditional working-class festivals became established (1968:109).

Labor Day, for instance, was one of the first breaks with tradition, and workers also began to celebrate days commemorating victories achieved or martyrs since 1919. As these practices took on national and international character, divisive regional loyalties gradually disappeared (Chesneaux 1968:394). A qualitative change had taken place: the common experience of industrial work "had welded its composite elements together to form a new social force that was quite alien to older Chinese traditions" and that was differentiated from the social classes from which workers had been recruited (Chesneaux 1968:142).

In Shanghai female workers formed associations and participated in work stoppages, and were encouraged to take part in union activities, even to the extent of becoming committee members. The following case is given by Chesneaux:

> In 1920, during a rice crisis in Shanghai, women strikers from the Chapei silk-reeling factories entered a plant in Hongkew, persuaded nearly seven hundred women employed there to cease work and set about cutting the thread on the reeling machines (1968:158).

In addition, women protested working conditions by means of pamphlets and street demonstrations. Other observers writing during this period also make reference to such activities; Adelaide Anderson describes a meeting she attended in 1924 where a deputation of women silk workers demanded more reasonable hours of work, kinder treatment for children, and supervision by forewomen (1928:176). Ching and Bagwell mention female labor leaders urging the enforcement of government regulations concerning working conditions (1931:15). (These, however, were by no means uniform developments, and Chesneaux, in underlining the variation of worker movements from one region to another, notes that in Shanghai the growth of true industrial unionism was for a long time hampered by the large proportion of female and child labor [1968:389, 396].)

Chesneaux takes care not to attribute the emergence of class consciousness among workers simply to industrialism, and instead, he examines its development in a concrete historical context. In this respect he is in agreement with Edward Thompson, who argues that "we cannot understand class unless we see it as a social and cultural formation, arising from processes which can only be studied as they work themselves out over a considerable historical period" (1963:11). Furthermore, both Thompson and Chesneaux stress that the creation of the working class is a product of political and cultural, as much as of economic, historical factors. Chesneaux, for instance, states that the class consciousness of the Chinese proletariat developed within a historical context in which the two basic problems to be faced were the dominance of large foreign interests and the militarists (1968:232). Thus, demands presented in labor movements went beyond the basic economic ones.

This point is repeated in a description of a merchants' and workers' strike in Shanghai; according to Chow, the significance of this strike lay not in its economic consequences, but in its nature: it was the first political and patriotic strike in Chinese history, where the aim of the workers was not to increase their wages or better their treatment, but to protest against the Chinese and Japanese governments (1967:157).

Another writer who stresses the historical relativity of class consciousness is John Foster, whose study is focused on the class struggle in early industrial England. He states, "the particular levels of material and cultural consumption around which groups define their identity are not arbitrary but *historically determined and concrete*" (Foster 1974:212, emphasis in original). In the Chinese case, reference has already been made to the particular historical forces in the 1920s that produced an internal situation favorable to the rise of the labor movement (i.e., anti-warlord and anti-imperialist political activities and the leadership of the Chinese Communist Party).

Moving closer to present-day Taiwan we can take labor relations in Hong Kong as a comparative case. While differing in their political structures Taiwan and Hong Kong have in common an export sector heavily reliant on the labor of factory women. England and Rear's study presents the following features of labor in Hong Kong: first, they note that the predominant expression of industrial conflict has been labor turnover, which is an individual rather than collective form of action and which cannot be defined as confronting managerial authority (1975:278). From the point of view of the worker, simply to leave is a safer course than to attempt collective action when he wishes to get away from an unpleasant environment. In this respect the industrial workers in Hong Kong are not different from factory women in Taiwan who also demonstrate their dissatisfactions with their job through individual decisions to quit (and who, moreover, rarely give their supervisors their true reasons for leaving).

Second, England and Rear find that a high proportion of factory employees in Hong Kong feel that they have lowly evaluated occupations (1975:68). Third, based on comparison with other studies, England and Rear conclude that Hong Kong people define their work in a largely instrumental manner, and that insofar as work is merely a means to economic ends, they do not tend to become involved in social ties based on the workplace beyond those necessary for keeping their jobs (1975:69–70). Citing one study in particular, England and Rear indicate that compared with Southeast Asian workers, Hong Kong and Taipei workers are the least socially involved with their fellow workers.

From findings such as these England and Rear state that by and large Hong Kong workers cannot be said to hold strong feelings of occupational community. In their report, however, one does find instances of job action involving women; in 1970, for example, about 170 female workers in a Hong Kong wig factory were barred from entering the factory one morning after a request for a wage increase, and eight factory women in another wig factory claimed that they were held prisoners in the elevator for fifteen minutes after they had removed several dismissal notices the day before (1975:259–60). Although these are also examples of how firms resist collective action, these initiatives nonetheless represent alternatives unimaginable to most factory women in Taiwan.

Discussing the factors inhibiting organized protests against working conditions, England points to the following characteristics of the labor force: the large number of casual and part-time employees, the high proportion of young workers, the high percentage of immigrants from China who wish to avoid political involvement, the growing proportion of women (in 1968 they constituted forty-seven percent of the manufacturing sector), the relative ease with which a worker can change jobs,[1] and the fact that individual piece rates are not conducive to collective-mindedness (1971:235). These obstacles to effective unionism apply with equal force to Taiwan, but they diminish in importance in view of the fact that strikes are forbidden in Taiwan. This is because Taiwan is still technically in a state of mobilization against Communist attack.[2]

England and Rear attribute the increasing frequency of overt labor-management conflict in Hong Kong in recent years to a greater awareness of labor of its rights and of what its rights ought to be (1975:286). Other than knowing that the legal working age is fourteen—since their families might have attempted to get them into factories earlier—Taiwanese women's consciousness of these rights is negligible. One manager in the personnel department at Western Electronics told me that the government tends to watch foreign firms more closely to be sure that they are following regulations so as to avoid charges of allowing foreign exploitation of Taiwan's workers. On a visit to a Chinese-owned factory this manager discovered that most women were staying beyond the legal number of working hours, and as he glanced over the time cards, the guard stationed at the entrance remarked, "No need to look at those; I'm the one who punches them at the 'proper' time."

When one considers that most women realize that they are union members only after seeing the deduction for dues on their pay-slips, it is highly doubtful that they would be well informed about matters pertaining to hours and so on. As for available channels for expressing grievances, it is difficult to generalize without any systematic survey of large and small, foreign and Chinese-owned factories. Based on the data gathered from workers at Western Electronics and informants employed in the Sanhsia area, however, it seems safe to say that women either choose to leave or "talk out" the problem among themselves and let it go at that.

Most Taiwanese women, when asked, will state that the purpose of a union is to promote the welfare of workers, although if pressed they are hard put to cite examples of benefits they have received as a result of union activity (beyond the gifts they receive on Labor Day, e.g., a mug or towel). Those who do have opinions on the subject are cynical about the motivations of persons who serve on union committees, charging, for instance, that some pocket union funds for themselves. Without an understanding of *how* a union presents its "demands," and what determines whether action is taken (information that is not introduced during orientation sessions at Western Electronics), women are ill-equipped to take action about grievances.

It is true that women commonly enter and leave a factory because their closest friend(s) decide(s) to do so; this pattern, however, should not be construed as a sign of collective-mindedness on the part of women vis-à-vis management. Peers are a source of security but not in the context of dealing with superiors at work. Given the notion that confrontation with one's supervisors and more generally, that any kind of conflict, should be avoided at all costs, it is readily understandable why women are not predisposed, individually or as a group, to voice their grievances and prefer, instead, to simply leave and find a job elsewhere. So long as jobs are plentiful, this is a rational choice.[3]

In measuring job satisfaction or loyalty, the crucial question seems to be, at this point in the worker's life (considering her age, sex, and education), what are her expectations for personal mobility and future prospects? Without a strong commitment to paid employment (beyond the next two or three years) it makes little sense to expect that factory women will develop notions about the possible benefits collective action may bring. (It seems likely that this will remain the case so long as single women view the main purpose of their jobs as supplementing family income, and so long as married women regard themselves not so much as workers but as housewives trying to bring some extra money home.) Women do exchange information about fringe benefits and wages offered by different firms (although arriving at accurate comparisons of wages is made difficult by varying systems of calculating piece rates, bonuses, and so on), but discontent with one's present position leads to a change of jobs and not to thoughts about attempting to effect changes in policy.

To digress a bit, it should be noted that some firms do try to commit their labor force and establish greater stability.[4] It is difficult to assess how much weight women give to differing fringe benefits and inducements offered at various factories when choosing one firm over another. Decisions are made according to a combination of considerations—distance from home, quality of dormitories, hours (for working-students in particular), wages, presence of friends, and so on. At any rate, one study that examined management practices in Taiwan concludes that motivational techniques are mainly monetary in nature, although subsidiaries of American firms have somewhat more developed and sophisticated compensation and management policies (Negandhi 1971:49–51).

In this respect Taiwan provides a striking contrast to the situation that has been described as characteristic of Japanese factories. Ballon, for instance, claims that in Japan it is not the occupation that counts but the place of work; the Japanese employee is said to be highly motivated by the realization that his main stake is in the enterprise of which he is a member (1969:75). Kobayashi (1969), writing about his part in motivational management at Sony, makes statements that lend support to Dore's remark that Japanese supervisory relations are based on an assumption of original virtue rather than original sin (which Dore found to be a more fitting characterization of British factories [1973:234]). Kobayashi not only emphasizes the merits of trusting employees, but he is a firm believer in making each worker feel that he is vital to the company's operation. He advocates communicating to all workers (at regular meetings) information concerning the general activities of the plant:

> Thanks to the information, people can grasp in a wider realistic perspective the meaning of their individual work, its target . . . Even the cleaning men perceive that their work is an

indispensable part of transistor development and production. The frank supply of full information also gives everybody a vivid impression that he is among the trusted people of the plant (1969:48–49). Each worker's job may look like a repetition of simple operations. But each worker takes part in working out the entire production plan. With this awareness of participation, he recognizes his responsibility in every move of his hands and finds the job pleasing and rewarding (1969:53).

As Cole and Tominaga (1976) have pointed out, however, the notion that occupation is unimportant and that what is really important to employees is enterprise loyalty is an ideology held and promulgated by *management,* and one must examine the reasons why this is accepted by workers. Cole and Tominaga suggest that an emphasis on loyalty to the firm and a concomitant implicit rejection of the notion of employee organization by occupation has been the basis of managerial strength in Japanese enterprises (1976:88). But in the case of Taiwanese factory women, it is not even necessary for their employers to adopt such an ideology or to pursue such a strategy; whereas in Japan management in large firms controls job training, in Taiwan women require little formal training to perform their jobs. Similarly, one would expect that enterprise loyalty would not be so carefully instilled in factory *women* in Japan, who are also expected to work only until marriage or the birth of children (Patrick 1976:11). Moreover, there are limits beyond which management in Taiwan's firms cannot afford to go in the way of providing various non-monetary incentives if wage-rates are to remain competitive.

Female workers in Taiwan view the worker-management relationship in instrumental terms ("they pay us and use our labor to make money"), which might lead us to ask why an identification with worker interests focused on issues such as wages and hours has not emerged. Women in factories certainly share sufficiently similar experiences to allow worker-consciousness to grow, but rather than class awareness we find women directing their resentments to group-leaders, supervisors, coworkers, or the office staff. Women at Western Electronics can without difficulty point to the symbols that distinguish the status of workers from the statuses of other personnel in the company (uniforms, wages versus salaries, separate restrooms, and so on), but any tendency to see a correspondence between the ranks and divisions within the company and class distinctions in the larger society is deflected in part by the belief that position and prestige (in the company and in society) rightly and legitimately accrue to those who have the requisite education.[5] Women are more preoccupied with coping with opportunism in social relations and fine gradations in status and rank (which undermine worker solidarity) than with trying to learn more about the union and how it actually serves workers (or how it may be pressured into doing so).

Pointing to the age and sex of these workers as a way of accounting for the passivity of women and the absence of class consciousness is not a satisfactory explanation. Women in Shanghai in the 1920s were not deterred by their age and sex from participating in labor movements, activities that Chesneaux ties closely to the political context existing at the time and to particular historical circumstances. Similarly, any attempt to undersand why class consciousness has been supplanted or superseded by a particular kind of false consciousness (e.g., resentment of other women) requires us to return to the larger political and economic environment in which Taiwan's factories are located.

Based on his study of industrial firms in Taiwan, Silin writes that in general, in the day-to-day operation of the firm, there are few appeals directed to employees based on the need to contribute to Taiwan's social and economic progress. But training manuals contain a "well-developed argument in which workers and lower-level managers are reminded of Taiwan's need to industrialize" (Silin 1976:170). The effect these entreaties have on factory women is difficult to ascertain; in any case, it appears that women are asked to reconcile or make sense of two conflicting messages—on the one hand, that their labor is essential to their nation's growth, and on the other hand, the knowledge that their occupation is rewarded neither with high wages nor respect.

As for why their wages are low, female workers invariably point to the obvious fact that theirs is a job anyone can do. They recognize that small firms, even though they might not be financially secure, will offer high wages in the hope of attracting women willing to work long hours; but beyond this women have little conception of the limits within which their wages may be raised or of the determinants of the overall wage-scale of workers. During the 1974 recession one Western Electronics worker told me: "I never did believe that Americans could buy *all* those television sets year after year!" Women, however, are less cognizant of how dependent Taiwan's economy is or that international capital can easily move to other areas.

In Taiwan unions do not exert significant pressure on the wage structure, nor is government regulation an important determinant of wages. According to one source, the only form of government regulations is a minimum wage law, under which wages were set at NT$600 per month in 1972, an amount that was twenty-eight percent of the average wage level in manufacturing industries in 1970 (W. Galenson 1972:40). Population increase has produced an abundant labor supply that has kept wage rates relatively low. In addition, the gap between labor productivity and real wages in the manufacturing sector has widened since the late 1950s, and this has further strengthened the competitive position of Taiwan's exports (Liang 1972:248–49). If rapid export expansion is to continue in Taiwan, therefore, the ability to produce goods at prevailing world prices is a necessary condition, and as one economist forecasts, "any comparative advantage which [Taiwan] may attain in manufacturing for export to developed countries, apart from strongly resource-based industries, is . . . likely to be industries which are intensive in the use of unskilled and semi-skilled labor (Liang 1972:254).

A number of consequences for the position of women in the labor market follow from these conditions. So long as there exists a situation where "the less education a woman has received, the greater chance she has to be employed," and where the largest number among unemployed women are those who have senior high school diplomas (Tsui, Loh, and Chang 1972:353–54), women will remain at an economic disadvantage. One writer proposes the following scheme to induce more students in Taiwan to enter vocational and technical schools and thereby reduce the disjuncture between the nation's manpower needs and its educational system:

> [I]f the salary scale of different occupations can be devised on the basis of their importance measured by the high-priority needs of the economy, and salary differentials can be established significantly in favor of shortage professions, it certainly would give added incentives to students to enter them (C.S. Shih 1972:230).

But if factory women were to be paid at a level commensurate with their importance to the economy or at least at a level commensurate with their productivity, they would in effect be pricing themselves out of the international export market.

The question of how female workers will become conscious of such constraints on their development as a working class and of the connection between occupations and the larger political and economic systems cannot be answered at this stage. At present factory women in Taiwan identify with the values of those who employ and supervise them, and their aspirations do not represent a separate category of labor interests. As Thompson has warned, we ought not assume any automatic or direct correspondence between the dynamics of economic growth and the dynamics of social and cultural life, but rather, we should pay attention to political and cultural continuities. He adds, "[We should not] think of an external force—the 'industrial revolution'—working upon some nondescript undifferentiated raw material of humanity, and turning it out at the other end as a 'fresh race of beings'" (1963:194).

Factory women do not reject the values of those higher in the occupational hierarchy than they, and similarities in cultural attitudes are not difficult to find. One writer, for instance, noting the higher premium Chinese in Taiwan set on a "regular" curriculum as opposed to vocational training, believes that public appeals will not be effective in shifting people away from a bias favoring white-collar jobs, and instead, he suggests that more direct economic incentives are needed to counteract these biases (Wan 1972:199). It has already been made clear, however, that women make distinctions not solely in terms of income, and another writer acknowledges that "considering the Chinese traditional view that education should be regarded as an end in itself rather than as an instrument of economic development, it is understandable that [an] approach with a strong economic orientation would not be very popular in Taiwan" (C.S. Shih 1972:224).

Another point made by Shih, whose subject is manpower and education in Taiwan, reveals in a striking way the prejudices facing women in Taiwan, although this is probably done inadvertently. Citing the high proportion of women in Taiwan's colleges and universities (in 1971 women constituted 37.29% of total enrollment), Shih first remarks that this is a pattern not usually associated with developing countries. He goes on to say:

> [H]owever, as in almost all societies, women's main role is played in home-making. Then the problem of profitability would naturally arise: would it be worthwhile to provide higher education for women whose main duties are in the home (1972:212)?

In response to this, Shih quotes one writer who argues that,

> it is precisely in homemaking that attitudes are fixed, ways of life established, and traditions continued. The profound change in patterns of behavior and expectations which is necessary if the concept of economic progress is to be introduced into traditional societies must depend in great part upon the attitude of the homemaker (1972:212).

Marsh, in his survey of Taiwanese men in Taipei, includes attitudes about class conflict and expressions of class consciousness. He finds that these are articulated more in the "commonsense" context of employers' treatment of employees than in the abstract context of "class interests" (Marsh 1968:582). Forty-nine percent of those interviewed believe employers in general "sometimes take advantage" of their workers, and thirty-eight percent of white and blue-collar employees believe that their own employer has "sometimes taken advantage" of them (Marsh 1968:582). Marsh adds that despite the fact that between one-third and one-half of the Taiwanese think employers sometimes take advantage of workers, they do *not* draw from this the conclusion that "the interests of workers and capitalists are completely at variance, and therefore they should always be in conflict with one another" (1968:583). Only three percent of the sample subscribe to this view, in contrast to the eighty-seven percent who felt that "'worker's interests coincide with capitalists' interests and they should therefore cooperate'" (Marsh 1968:583).

If this provides us with a glimpse of the class attitudes of adult men who probably have a stronger and longer-term commitment to their jobs, then it seems absurd to suppose that factory women could develop notions about conflicting class interests or occupational solidarity in the course of a few years' employment. Occupational consciousness is one thing (women are well aware that they occupy low-status jobs) but common identification centered around changes that are felt to be necessary in the existing system is quite a different matter.

As for the future prospects of factory women, it is frequently remarked that Taiwan is undergoing a transition from a condition of labor surplus to one of labor scarcity, and that because of this real wages will rise faster in the next ten years than they have in the past (J. Fei 1972:53). There is the prediction that Taiwan like Japan and Hong Kong will have to give way in the production of labor-intensive goods to other areas where large reservoirs of under-employed labor still exist, turning to capital-intensive manufactures instead (W. Galenson 1972:40–41). This trend appears to have been the assumption in one report on manpower planning, whose authors write:

> In the course of economic development...technical manpower is the most precious asset. Unskilled labor, on the other hand, not only contributes very little to economic growth, but is also a potential source of social unrest if a majority of these individuals fail to find employment (Cheng, Kuan and Tai 1972:314).

Such an assessment underestimates the importance for sustaining Taiwan's economic growth of its pattern of low-wage trade with other countries. Presumably, of course, more women will enter vocational schools and will be qualified to take up positions in capital-intensive sectors as they are established. But one report on women workers in Taiwan, anticipating employment problems arising in the next decade from a larger labor force,[6] predicts that female employment opportunities in the manufacturing sector will not be as great as in the past, and that "female employment will more likely be centered in the service industry" (Tsui, Loh and Chang 1972:357). One cannot say with any certainty that this is a prospect factory women (or young women in general) would welcome, and it would leave them in no higher a position in the social and occupational hierarchy than before.

14

Wage-Earning, Family Structure, and Women

Chapters 9 to 13 show that the effects of wage-earning on factory women must be studied in the context of a particular type of family organization and of the labor market in Taiwan. I will examine the larger socio-cultural context in chapter 15; in this chapter I consider the relationship between wage-earning, family structure, and women, and analyze the Taiwan case in light of similar developments elsewhere.

Whereas earlier research on economic development tended to point to positive changes such as greater personal freedom and emancipation of women, a number of more recent works have called attention to the possibility that modernization can have an adverse effect on women. Tinker, for example, argues that in subsistence economies the process of development has tended to narrow the economic independence of women as their traditional jobs are challenged by new technologies (1976:33). Boserup (1970) shows in her survey how in the course of development women may be relegated to jobs in the backward sectors of the economy.

A review of the changes and continuities in the lives of Taiwan's factory women reveals that wage-earning has not generated substantial improvement in any clear-cut direction nor has factory employment proved to be detrimental to their positions. More general remarks concerning development theories and approaches to social change will be presented in chapter 16. Here I wish to examine hypotheses that lead one to expect certain changes with respect to women as a consequence of employment. In showing why these changes have not occurred, I will suggest why some of these notions are misconceived and where they require revision. I then take up the argument set forth in Michael Anderson's *Family Structure in Nineteenth-Century Lancashire,* a work that deals with the impact of industrial wage-labor on family relations, and indicate why its conclusions cannot be applied to the Taiwan case.

William Goode submits that two important ways in which industrialization affects family organization are: (1) industrialization calls for the physical movement of persons from one locality to another, thereby decreasing the frequency and intimacy of contact among members of a kin group, and (2) industrialization creates a value structure that recognizes qualities achieved rather than acquired by birth (1970:369). One consequence of this is that family members have less to offer an individual in exchange for his submission to the family, and Goode claims that without rewards, control is not possible (1970:370). In Taiwan, clearly, women are not dependent on their parents for an introduction to factories yet parental authority does not appear to have been attenuated. Behind Goode's propositions is the notion that exchanges and role-bargaining take place between parents and children, and this is an assumption to which I will return in discussing Anderson's work.

Goode notes that the modern industrial world is the first system to permit women to take independent jobs.[1] As a result,

> they have become independent of . . . their family. They obtain their work by themselves, and also control the money they earn . . . At the same time, it has changed the bargaining position of women within the family system . . . Once women begin to take these positions in the larger society, then they are better able to assert their own rights and wishes within the family (Goode 1970:372).

The data from Taiwan do not bear out such expectations. On the contrary, the Taiwanese family functions in much the same way as it did before the advent of factory employment for women: the family continues to be an economic unit and control of pooled family income remains intact in the hands of parents.

Another set of assumptions is that there will be incompatibility between industrialism and a worker's traditional culture, and that this will be reflected in conflicts between the individual's job and his other roles in non-industrial groups (Slotkin 1960:73). For Goode, if such conflicts are to be reduced and women's work roles are to be accepted, much of the change must come from the ideological sector. Goode points to ideological changes as the necessary, although not sufficient, condition of the improvement of women's position in Western societies (1972:22):

> [T]he gradual, logical, philosophical extension to women of originally Protestant notions about the rights and responsibilities of the individual undermined the traditional idea of "woman's proper place" (1970:56).

Although Taiwanese parents were, at one time, reluctant to permit daughters to work in factories, their acceptance of factory employment came quickly, developing into a concern that daughters be placed in *good* jobs. Moreover, to justify their daughter's outside employment there was no need for Taiwanese parents to develop the sort of individualistic ideology Goode suggests; instead, parents retain pre-existing expectations with respect to the wages of their daughters. They continue to believe that daughters are "lost" to other people, that they ought to repay the cost expended in raising them, and that family interests take precedence over the interests of individual family members. While it was unacceptable for middle- and upper-class Chinese women to work outside, lower-class families (particularly in southeastern China) did not have to alter their thinking to permit their wives and the daughters to work.

Writing about female labor in Europe in the nineteenth century, Scott and Tilly (1975) are also critical of models of social change that assume a one-to-one connection between cultural values and social change. They deny that change in one sphere leads directly and necessarily to changes in other spheres, a notion that is detectable in Goode's work and which represents a vestige of functionalist thinking. Data on Taiwanese workers, for instance, unequivocally undermine functionalist predictions and point instead to the need to recognize that people may act in new ways while retaining a commitment to old values. People respond to new opportunities on the basis of ideas they already hold; it is not always necessary to postulate new values to account for new patterns of behavior. As the preceding chapters indicate, the actions of Taiwanese women are comprehensible only when viewed within the context of a pre-existing set of familial values. This is another way of saying that it is not sufficient to examine only new opportunity situations, because decisions are shaped by particular social and economic forces that affected women's position *before* factory employment became available.

The ability of the "traditional" Chinese family structure to accommodate new production roles without important changes in organization has been demonstrated. Writing about the British working-class family during the Industrial Revolution, Smelser states that when children were separated from their parents during the work-day, (unlike an earlier period when a skilled spinner was allowed to hire his wife, children, and relatives), a need was felt to reconstitute the family, broken up in the factory, in the home. "The labor legislation of the 1850s, establishing the ten-hour days [reduced from twelve hours] completed the differentiation of the working-class family, involving a clearer split between home and factory, a split between the economic and other aspects of the parent-child relationship" (1968:88).

The differentiation of occupational roles within the family is not new to Chinese society, and in Taiwanese families today the productive roles of family members may be separated geographically and structurally from their familial roles. This has not, however, reduced the integration of the family as an economic unit, and Taiwanese parents, like the Hakka household heads described by Cohen (1976), continue to regulate the work and occupational careers of individual family members as part of a collective unit. Participation in production may no longer be situated at home but the activities of individual family members continue to be subject to family decisions and supervision. Employment outside the home can, without difficulty, be incorporated into the pre-existing system of family work, and the fact that daughters are occupationally differentiated from their families need not foster individualistic values.

Moreover, in the case of Taiwan it is factory women (especially those who leave home and join large enterprises) who are exposed to much more that is modern than are their fathers or elder brothers who remain in the countryside. First, this difference in experience underlines the fact that families do not always undergo changes in response to economic development as whole units. Second, the varying experience of different members have not threatened the stability of the Taiwanese family. Indeed, the retention of traditional ideas on the part of Taiwanese parents has allowed a particular type of family organization to persist, even as their daughters take up industrial jobs.

Factory women, on their part, feel no less comfortable at home because their work roles situate them in complex settings replete with modern technology. It is not only a confusion between societal and personal levels of change that must be discarded; allowance must also be made for the possibility that individuals can compartmentalize different facets of their lives and that they are able to balance a variety of traditional and modern attitudes and experiences. This is overlooked by linear models of change and functionalist approaches in which change in one sector is assumed to generate "compatible" changes in other sectors.[2]

Another line of thinking regarding the effects of industrial wage-employment on the family develops a point made by Engels, namely, that when children can earn more than the cost of their keep, they become emancipated, regarding their parents' house merely as a place to live and leaving when they choose (1973:161). Scott and Tilly assert that a major transformation in family organization occurs when familial values are replaced by individualistic ones (1975:61). The formation of such notions is facilitated by migration, when long distance weakens family ties. Scott and Tilly argue that the pressures of low wages, permanent urban living, and the forced independence of young girls "clearly fostered calculating, self-seeking attitudes among them" (1975:62). Women subsequently began to look upon their jobs as avenues of occupational and social mobility for themselves rather than as temporary means to earn some money for their families. This gradual transformation can without doubt be found in Taiwanese women who have been away from home and working for some years; I am reluctant, however, to apply without substantial qualifications an approach that rests on concepts such as role-negotiation and role-bargaining in analyzing the Taiwanese material or to suggest that Taiwanese women operate and make decisions with such concepts in mind.

One writer characterizes families in traditional societies as units in which relationships are perceived as exchanges of a variety of obligations, and where family members are valued for their respective economic contribution. In this context children are not just emotional extensions of their parents but are viewed as investments for security and future old-age support (Hareven 1976:202–203). This is not an inaccurate description of the Chinese family, and it forms the basis of analysis such as that developed by Anderson. It is an appealing argument, and where the Taiwanese data depart from his findings, the differences must be accounted for.

Anderson's framework includes questions such as: (a) how much psychic profit does this exchange offer me now compared with that; that is, by how much does what I get out exceed what I put in, and could I get more elsewhere? (b) when do I get the reciprocation? Is the return immediate or only in the long run? (c) how certain am I that I will receive the reciprocation an any relationship I enter? (1971:9). With these considerations in mind Anderson examines the behavior of children in working-class families in nineteenth-century Lancashire as they began to enter the industrial labor force. He writes that although there were ongoing kinship relations, these functioned in a context of calculation and instrumentality.

The presence of nearby towns, offering the possibility of greater individual freedom, injected a note of uncertainty into family relationships. Once workers arrived in towns peers provided further support to individuals who had begun to reject their familial obligations. The wage-earning ability of young people, of course, was the crucial factor in initiating any change in family structure:

> [T]he high individual wages paid to young people allowed them to buy all the means of subsistence, and thus made possible, at least in the short run, the termination of all relationships with parents and kin (Anderson 1971:103).

Moreover, children now had an alternative to family employment, which leads Anderson to believe that,

> as a result, parental power must inevitably, it would seem, be subject to some counter-bargaining on the part of the children. In particular, individual children must be kept content with what they, as individuals, receive, instead of their interest being largely automatically subordinated at the decision of the father to the interests of the family as a whole (1971:114).[3]

The high incomes of young people made it possible for them to leave home when disagreements with their parents arose. Anderson concludes that many young persons adopted an instrumental orientation to their families, reasoning that if they earned more than the amount of what it cost for them to remain at home (including what they had to contribute), they would be better off living elsewhere on their own (1971:128). Anderson quotes one contemporary source on the subject: "'The children [who] frequent factories make almost the purse of the family, and by making the purse of the family they share in the ruling of it and are in a great state of insubordination to their parents'" (1971:131). Where a bargain was favorable to both parent and child in the short-run, then the relationship would be continued, although the degree of commitment to such a relationship would be low, and if more attractive alternatives appeared, the child would take it.

To some degree, the bargaining Anderson describes seems to have occurred in Chinese families. The refusal of female silk workers in Kwangtung to marry (cf. Topley 1975) appears to be one side of a bargain struck with parents in return for continuing to remit money home, but even this option was limited by the fact that there had to be other daughters in the family before the family accepted this vow of celibacy. Similarly, the ability of some Taiwanese women to continue school is possible only because of their wage-earning, although in this instance it is difficult to imagine that a woman would leave home and sever her ties to her family if parental objections were raised.

This is precisely the point: while there is much in Anderson's argument that is persuasive and that conforms to common-sense expectations, it is not an accurate depiction of the position of Taiwanese factory women. Wage-earning does not cause them to adopt a bargaining mentality vis-à-vis their parents, nor do peer relationships outside often lead to a rejection of family obligations. Anderson himself mentions two factors that are particularly pertinent to the Taiwanese material, and these point to where we might look in explaining why the behavior of factory women in Taiwan has not followed the pattern Anderson outlines.

First, Anderson notes that the family is a power center where, so long as its power is maintained, it can inhibit or channel social change in some directions rather than others. This is because the family controls socialization and often has much economic influence as well. Anderson declares therefore that the ability of different family systems to maintain the commitment of their members is variable and must be taken into account (1971:7). The Taiwanese family is a clear instance of the type that has maintained its power and determined the direction of change.

Second, Anderson states that values cannot be ignored because bargaining does not take place in a vacuum (1971:9); however, it is not always clear in Anderson's study whether roles *and* values are both subject to re-negotiation. This point cannot be overemphasized in the Taiwanese case, because the instrumental orientation characteristic of Lancashire workers does not apply to factory women. This is not to imply that considering the values held by Taiwanese will provide, in itself, a satisfactory explanation; economic and social conditions also determine the adaptations of women to factory employment. Nonetheless, the process of deciding in favor of one course of action over another includes taking into account priorities and goals. Present choices are influenced by choices made in the past and expected choices in the future, and both are affected by material conditions and value systems. We would need to know the answers to questions such as: do daughters have an *acknowledged* right to economic independence; are the rewards of labor seen as *properly* accruing to the wage-earner (or to some other member of the family, for example, the head of the household)? Taiwanese do not believe so, and their views are related to their conceptions of the family, to how roles, statuses, and prerogatives are organized, and to how authority is to be allocated.

Even though Taiwanese women, speaking strictly in economic terms, are capable of supporting themselves at a standard that would not be appreciably lower than that at home, their bonds to their families have not been substantially weakened. In spite of the fact that they are able to secure their jobs without parental assistance, and that most jobs provide housing and welfare benefits, few women seriously consider terminating their familial relationships. For the Lancashire workers Anderson describes, continued ties with family members depended upon reciprocation for their contribution in the very short run, and even where this was forthcoming Anderson suggests that the level of loyalty was low. The same cannot be said of Taiwan's female workers: for them the notion of a debt to one's parents and the sense of obligations stemming from filial piety constitute a large part of their understanding of why they work. Predictably, women who have spent years living in dormitories become more distant emotionally from their families; this is not, however, necessarily accompanied by a reduction in their economic commitment to their families. As for women who live at home, an increase in the number of years they have worked and contributed to the family income does not bring with it a commensurate desire to play a greater role in family decisions or an expectation of more tangible returns.

Anderson writes that as far as lodging houses and neighborhood groups were concerned, no group was able to exercise strong normative control, and it is doubtful whether there would have been any great consensus over exactly what types of conduct toward the family were to be encouraged (1971:110). Factory women recognize, too, that once away from home it is easier to learn bad ways, but they do share roughly the same understanding of what their families expect from them and believe that those obligations are natural and proper.

Anderson claims that because third party ideological controls were weak, and because rejection of family obligations was sufficiently common for most to know of at least one case, "willingness to perform role obligations became for many something to be tested by trial and error, not something to be taken for granted" (1971:110). The decision of some Taiwanese factory women to invest a portion of their wages in their education may legitimately be regarded as a step where the influence of peers has been important. It does not signify to the women, however, a rejection of their responsibilities to their families, and many manage to send remittances home and are praised by their peers for doing so. Lest freer spending habits be interpreted as a rejection of familial obligations, it should be noted that in some cases the money that is spent on clothes and recreation and the like represents sums saved by eating less (or less well) and by being more frugal in other respects, *not* sums taken from wages that would have been sent home.

With respect to women who live with their families, the knowledge that others take their familial obligations more lightly does not lead them to reject the pattern of economic control they know at home. Many women are quite firm in stating that they are content to live at home and have no desire to move into dormitories, and their preference is *not* based on a calculation of short-run or long-run reciprocation. Norms defining the proper relationship between parent and child among the Taiwanese have not been weakened by the wage-employment of daughters. Anderson overlooks the crucial question of what confers the right to control one's income, and here we need to clarify whether it is a role or set of values that is being redefined.

Anderson devotes little attention in his argument to the role that *values* might play in family relations, and he glosses over the emotional security that a family provides and to which factory women give so much importance. The family as the only conceivable source of security (and here I refer not merely to economic security), affection, and concern is not a view that enters into Anderson's analysis, and his stress on *material* forms of assistance creates a one-dimensional characterization of young workers. If this were to be accepted, we should expect Taiwan's female workers to be highly independent and to enjoy a substantial degree of personal autonomy, and we would be hard put to account for the continuities we do find.

There remains one further paradox with respect to the position of factory women in their families, one that seems particularly puzzling since so much of the writing on the impact of industrialization on family organization dwells on the new options available and how these reduce the individual's dependence on and loyalty to the family. In the Taiwanese case we find continued attachment to the family from those who, one would suppose, are least likely to hold such sentiments. Daughters have heard that they "belong to other people," are aware that most of their lives will be spent in another household, and recognize that their brothers enjoy privileges denied them; yet many of these women retain a strong degree of loyalty (even if it is expressed only in the form of regular remittances) to their families. Clearly, whatever is at work here in maintaining a relatively close sense of identification with one's family, it cannot be reduced to economic considerations; Taiwanese factory women do not perceive themselves as being used by their parents and do not negotiate for more power. From their standpoint factory employment and wage-earning are incorporated, without much difficulty or introspection, into a preexisting body of ideas and expectations, and need not be set in opposition to the interests of the family.

Earlier, it was noted that exchanges of economic obligations are a central part of family relationships in traditional societies. In modern societies, family relationships have been said to be characterized also by their emotional content and by the degree of psychological satisfaction they offer their members (Hareven 1976:202). Anderson's study demonstrates how exchanges within the family diminished as alternatives became available, but we find no mention of the emotional support that the family provides. From the Taiwanese material the family emerges as a unit in which economic obligations are still central but where emotional and psychological security are not without importance for its members. If anything, the meaning attached to personal relations at home can increase because relations at work are not always characterized by trust or warmth, and the job itself brings little satisfaction.

15

Women in the Larger Context

The age and sex of factory workers and the Taiwanese family structure do not explain the present circumstances of Taiwan's factory women. As chapter 13 shows, we need also to take into account the social, ideological, economic and political context that allows the perpetuation of certain patterns in women's attitudes and behavior.

In response to a survey on the status of women conducted by the United Nations, Taiwan indicated that "various measures had been taken to create a climate of opinion favorable to the principle of equality of men and women in various fields;" Taiwan also expressed the view that "the fact that there were constitutional or other legal pronouncements in favor of equality also helped to create an atmosphere favorable to such equality" (United Nations Commission on the Status of Women 1970:82). To assess the accuracy of such a statement, one would have to investigate in detail prevailing definitions of sex roles, the content of messages about sex roles conveyed through the media,[1] and to determine the government's role in promoting such views. One would also need to evaluate the position of women relative to that of men in each social setting, to determine how knowledge about areas such as labor regulations and unions filters down to working-class women, and to ask whether such information is being disseminated in a systematic fashion.

Writing about urban middle-class housewives in Taiwan, Diamond warns that "if we choose to ignore the developing political and economic scene, we are reduced to explaining ongoing behaviors and values either as continuities from the traditional past, real or spurious, or as changes lumped under the catch-alls of 'acculturation' and 'modernization'" (1975:4). In this context I cannot give the broader political and economic determinants of women's position in Taiwan the full treatment they deserve, but I will ask in the light of these broader factors why it should make any difference that factory workers are female and why they tend to look upon their work in short-range terms.

From her study of women's emancipation in the People's Republic of China, Davin concludes, with reference to other societies as well, that if development were left to run its own course, there is little assurance that the position of women would be improved; there must in addition exist an ideology explicit in its recognition and promotion of women's equality. That is, although no conscious decision may be made to reduce women's participation in development, the "normal" course of development implies such a pattern (Davin 1976:2). In the absence of an egalitarian ideology that is systematically promulgated, then, the extent to which wage-earning and control over income can enhance a women's status remains in doubt. The reconciliation of a woman's family obligations with her productive labor outside the home does not appear to be a high priority in the government's view in Taiwan. Indeed, whether and how governmental agencies work toward allowing women to perform both to the detriment of neither remains an open question.

For young Taiwanese women the family and its ideology play a dominant role in shaping their outlook. Another institution that contributes in a central way to the formation of attitudes and values is, of course, the school. Althusser names schools as the major ideological state apparatus in mature capitalist systems, where children in the course of acquiring knowledge and techniques also learn rules of respect for the existing socio-technical division of labor (1971:132). Further information would be required to see just how submission to the rules of the established order is achieved in Taiwan's schools (cf. R. Wilson 1970), but one study does provide a glimpse of the values that receive emphasis in elementary schools. Additional data on this subject would permit more precise statements about those values inculcated in Taiwanese youth that make Taiwan's workers so attractive to investors.

From her analysis of elementary school text-books used in Taiwan Martin (1975) found the following features: the predominant characteristic stressed is filial piety; the individual's focus is the family, which is presented as a unit of warmth and security; texts deviate little from the traditional ideal of working with one's mind rather than with one's hands, and they give few examples of people engaged in manual work; and there is an emphasis on academic achievement that tends to encourage education as an end. As Martin correctly points out, the question that remains unanswered in a survey of this type is to what extent the picture presented in the textbooks corresponds to actual beliefs held in Taiwan (1975:260).

Even though this question must await further research, we do have some indication of how education and its purpose are conceived. The following appeared in *The China Post:* "girls' education has much to do with the future happiness of families and a healthy society. It has also direct bearing on a husband's career and the way children are brought up. Girls' education today has a special responsibility of fulfilling its destiny with ideals and substance" (2 May 1974). This view lends support to Diamond's statement that, in this respect, there has been ideological continuity in the Kuomingtang: since the inception of the New Life Movement the purpose of education for women is that they will thereby become better housewives, mothers, and better citizens (1975:37). But apparently there are limits to how far even this justification may be carried: one report on manpower, for instance, hints that while higher education will enable a woman to become a better homemaker, giving women these opportunities should not be allowed to interfere with *men's* ability to obtain higher education (C.S. Shih 1972).

There is also some consensus among writers that education is an important marker of status in Taiwan. Diamond states that education has become an end in itself as a symbol of elite status (1975:38), and Grichting concludes from his survey that Taiwan is becoming somewhat polarized in values, with the main differentiating feature being education (1970:266). When asked how they determine a person's class position, thirty-eight percent of Marsh's respondents chose occupation and another twenty-nine percent chose education as the indicator (1968:576). Here, one might bear in mind that in many cases occupation reflects level of educational attainment. In the case of rural Taiwanese women, therefore, it is no surprise that most occupations open to them would exclude them from middle-class status.

Another writer notes that at first glance women do seem to be employed everywhere in Taiwan: in banks, department stores, markets, fields, barbershops, restaurants and so on; she adds that men, therefore, are apt to question the need for a liberation movement since women are "already out of the kitchen" (Lu 1974). Upon closer examination, however, the author indicates most employed women are young (between fifteen and nineteen), most are laborers and are not in white-collar positions, few are found in higher supervisory positions, and as far as seeking employment is concerned, the lower her educational level, the easier it is for a woman to find a job (Lu 1974:58).

The claims made above are suggestive and point to a number of questions that deserve further inquiry. Since education as a means to upward mobility is by no means new in Chinese thinking, it should perhaps not be surprising that people in Taiwan are not making distinctions among themselves that are purely economic in nature. (For Taiwanese women, for instance, even though waitressing can bring twice the wages a worker can receive in an electronics plant, few prefer to do the former.) Hence, even though their parents draw a distinction between males and females with regard to the utility of education, many female workers share with men a high motivation to acquire an education.

This being the case, the exhortations of the government to young women (and men) to enter the industrial labor force (at an early age) seem to be working at cross-purpose with the hopes of women themselves. The government does take worker shortages seriously, going so far as to allow lower-middle school students to begin their summer vacation earlier in order to hasten their entry into factories. Future research must, therefore, ascertain whether there is, on the part of the government, any manipulation of educational values so as to encourage more young people to terminate their studies and join the labor force instead. (The interests of the government and the interests of women *may* coincide where women are able to remain in school by virtue of income derived from factory jobs; this is not, however, an option open to all women in all industries.)

There is no need to belabor the point that manual labor does not confer prestige on workers in Taiwan.[2] Yet conceivably women in Taiwan should be able to find consolation or greater satisfaction from the belief that their contributions, as housewives and mothers, are valued. If model women workers in construction and heavy industry are absent, model mothers in Taiwan are held up for emulation and are lavished with national attention each Mother's Day. That women should take responsibility for the happiness and well-being of their families and that this should be regarded as proper are consequences Zaretsky predicts from the division between the family and production in capitalist society. The split between the world of commodity production and the private labor of women in the home is accompanied by a split between people's personal lives and their place in production, and housewives and mothers are given the responsibility of maintaining the emotional and psychological well-being of family members. Zaretsky states, "for women within the family, 'work' and 'life' were not separated but were collapsed into one another. The combination of these forms has created the specific character of women's labor within the family in modern capitalist society" (1973,I:85). The essays written about women by several authors in Taiwan demonstrate precisely this. Uniformly, women are encouraged to take charge of the values the family is thought to nurture: love, personal happiness, etc., with the reminder that the husband's primary responsibility is to earn a wage. As Zaretsky notes, the division between personal feelings and economic production has been integrated with the sexual division of labor.

Thus far, the position of Taiwanese factory women has been examined in terms of the new opportunities made available by employment and how women have responded to these options. What has not been discussed yet are those conditions that determine which opportunities will be open to women and those factors that shape the nature of the labor force of which women are a part. It is indisputable that women make choices, but the alternatives available to them are the result of particular historical and economic forces over which they have very little control. The values and attitudes women hold may shed light on why factory women behave the way they do, but these values in turn require explanation.

In a paper on women in Hong Kong, A. Wong (1973) claims that political and ideological factors have played a minor role in raising the status of women, but that the increase in the industrial demand for female labor has raised the political and economic leverage of women. Such an assessment, however, is based on the simplistic assumption that change in one area of women's lives leads directly into commensurate changes in other areas as well. As we have seen in the case of Taiwanese women, factory work occupies only one portion of their lives and there are other forces at work (school, family) that influence their lives outside the factory. Factory women have not only failed to become an informed, self-conscious proletariat, but their work experiences are situated in a particular sector of Taiwan's labor market (i.e., in low-skill jobs that are vulnerable to shifts in international economic trends), the nature of which shapes their orientation to wage-earning.

If we wish to know the social and economic consequences following from wage-earning for women in Taiwan, we need to be aware of the factors that determine when and where women will be employed. Some general features of the job market to which factory women belong and the social environment beyond it have already been mentioned. Although marriage and access to production are not always mutually exclusive, there are a number of factories that will not hire married women. With a high school diploma a woman may be promoted to an office position, but vertical mobility for a woman within the plant rarely goes up to the foreman level. There is also the widespread assumption that women's earnings constitute incomes supplementary to those of other household members. This assumption leads to the supposition that women are willing to work for lower wages than men because their actual financial needs and the cost of their time are lower than that of men's, a notion that in turn shapes wage policy and promotion decisions. It is true that factory work in Taiwan has afforded many women a new-found mobility, but in the eyes of a large portion of society, constant movement is not judged to be proper behavior for young women. Here is an instance where the mere absence of sanctions is not sufficient to render certain choices socially acceptable, since these women are often stigmatized for exercising their freedom ("running around").

At present there cannot be said to exist a good fit between the curriculum offered in schools and the needs of industry, as far as young women are concerned. The education they receive is poorly integrated with their working situation and serves only to alienate them from their jobs, an alienation that is exacerbated by the escalation of qualification requirements for white-collar positions. In this respect Dore's comments on the effects of such a qualification spiral in developing nations are an accurate observation of conditions in Taiwan: in response to such a situation, the less educated redouble their efforts to enter secondary schools, and secondary school graduates make greater efforts to enter universities, with the result that the school system comes to generate frustration rather then confident achievement (1975:8).

As a largely unskilled, technologically ignorant labor force, factory women thus acquire some measure of economic independence *only as members of a class that is economically disadvantaged.* Access to strategic resources is reduced by reason of both their gender and their class. Women employed in factories often must work for economic reasons, but their job options are in fact few in number. Thus, while they may appear to enjoy greater sexual and social freedoms than middle- and upper-class women, female workers remain disadvantaged occupationally and economically. Moreover, inasmuch as educated women have not organized and allied themselves with working women, the position of factory women, as women, cannot be expected to improve substantially.

The importance of analyzing women's job options and the effects of production upon their status within a class context becomes all the more apparent when one remembers that measures designed to increase the participation of women in the labor force are not prompted so much by a desire to bring about a fundamental change in the status of women of a certain class, but rather by the recognition that overall economic growth requires full utilization of the potential labor force. Encouraging women to enter industry, then, is not always motivated by a desire to further the emancipation of women, but to achieve certain economic goals. Without specific programs implemented to increase women's social and political equality, it is highly questionable to assume that steps intended to expand overall development will lead automatically to greater social, economic, and political participation for women in a society. On the contrary, policies formulated to increase women's employment may only intensify exploitation if wages and working conditions are not improved.

At the same time, while women are becoming wage-earners, their place in the family and the definition of their familial responsibilities have not been substantially altered. Thus, on the one hand women are encouraged to take part in production, and on the other hand they find themselves subject, in practice, to discrimination. Many occupations, for instance, are coming to be defined as suitable for women, and Papanek suggests that while it is possible that these are based on physical differences, it is more likely that some socially produced behavioral traits of women (e.g., greater compliance—which factory managers in Taiwan mention) are used to "explain" the suitability of some jobs for women (1976:59). One therefore needs to bear in mind the possibility that new or traditional occupational definitions applying to women may only be methods for obtaining labor at low wages.

Writers who expect that wage-earning will significantly improve women's position in society, therefore, are predicting what might happen *if* there were more economic mobility in the society generally. But factory work does not lead to better occupations for women; in addition, firms in Taiwan wish to employ *young* women, and so their careers are necessarily quite limited.

A sizeable portion of the goods factory women manufacture ties Taiwan to a world-wide capitalist system. Any evaluation of the impact of industrial growth on women, therefore, cannot overlook external conditions such as international systems of investment, control of capital and production, and the fact that production in developing nations is frequently part of a world-wide system based on dependency.

The structure of dependence has been described as:

> a situation in which the economy of certain countries is conditioned by the development and expansion of another economy to which the former is subjected. The relation of interdependence between two or more economies, and between these and world trade, assumes the form of dependence when some countries can expand and can be self-sustaining, while other countries can do this only as a reflection of that expansion, which can have either a positive or negative effect on their immediate development (quoted in Dos Santos 1973:109).

In the negative sense this applies to cases where development is constrained by world relations that lead to the growth of only certain economic sectors, "to trade under unequal conditions, to domestic competition with internal capital under unequal conditions, and . . . to the exploitation of the domestic labor force" (Dos Santos 1973:116). Along similar lines another writer argues that women are underdeveloped in special ways that relate as much to their participation in economic systems dominated by Western capitalist nations as to any previous conditions of "backwardness"(Bossen 1975:599). For instance, if women are relegated to one kind of economic production they may become a vulnerable labor force that can be bought cheaply and easily recruited to produce that one item. The precariousness implied in such an arrangement was made clear to all Taiwanese women during the 1974 recession.

Taiwan's decision to adopt a course of economic growth that includes "selling" its "most valuable natural resource," labor, has joined its development in a particular way to an international economic system. Thus, internal conditions such as the female occupational structure and the social and economic consequences of female employment must be viewed in the context of the world economy. The political economy of women's work in Taiwan is a subject for another study; here it is possible only to point to some of the factors, originating in the industrial structure and its relation to an international economy, that impinge on women.

Because a sizeable portion of Taiwan's manufacturing sector is export-oriented, it is vulnerable to the external market, and resulting fluctuations in production and employment are to be expected (when, for example, consumer tastes change or new import restrictions are imposed). To compete successfully against the products of the rest of the world, employers must keep wages relatively low, and wage-levels therefore are not dependent upon labor market forces. The fact that most of the manufacturing industries employing women are labor-intensive means that workers can easily move from one firm to another; the absence of a high demand for skilled workers in these sectors, together with high turnover, in turn discourage the organization of training programs for workers. (As Saxonhouse states in reference to Japanese women in the cotton-spinning industry, if the skills acquired by a worker were equally valuable at another mill or elsewhere, the individual mill owner would reap no direct benefit from his payment of training costs [1976:114].) It is little wonder then that factory women regard themselves as easily replaceable, quickly hired and quickly dismissed depending on need, and that they see their job security resting on the fortunes of their employer, which some of them at least recognize to be subject to the whims of foreign consumers.

More information is needed on the role of employers and the government in regulating the labor market in Taiwan. Data on this subject would permit more informed assessments of how economic roles are differentiated, of how wages are determined, and precisely how the low market valuation of women's labor is maintained. As Saxonhouse has noted for the Japanese case, the transient, female character of the pre-war manufacturing labor force has been studied too much from the decision-making perspective of the rural migrant and too little from the perspective of the manufacturing employer (1976:102). The same could be said of the present study, and clearly, future research must be directed to those forces that determine the opportunity situations and constraints that women face.[3]

Factory women view their occupation as one basis for social differentiation and stratification (they are a notch above maids and service workers but are well below office employees), and this identity has certain consequences for their self-image, behavior and expectations. What remains to be explained is why the positive valuation the government places on their labor has not filtered down to the women themselves and why it is not manifest in the overall occupational structure and status system. One thing that seems certain is that the professed ideology of the government concerning sexual equality cannot be confused with the actual conditions under which sex roles are defined. Relying in large part on a world-wide economic system that Taiwan is not able to control, female workers do assume a prominent part in that linkage, but they are crucial to Taiwan's economy only for so long as their market value remains competitively low.

16

Studying Social Change

This study has focused on how Taiwanese female workers have been affected by regular employment in factories. I began by exploring the options that became available to these women along with factory employment and their responses to these options. Subsequent sections have shown that such a perspective is incomplete, and that we in fact need to begin by examining broader political and economic processes and how these determine the opportunities open to women.

To do so, we must distinguish changes in behavior and attitudes that might be defined as modern from socio-economic changes on a large scale, and we must not assume that the latter automatically leads to the former. For example, the growing participation of women in the labor force may be an index of modernization but in itself it tells us nothing about whether subjective notions of equality between the sexes will develop. In this section micro-perspectives on social change will be considered first, followed by a review of macro-approaches to change. It will be seen that the issue in both instances—with respect to individuals and with respect to social systems—is to account for how persons and societies can accommodate change in one sector while maintaining continuity in other sectors, that is, how they allow the co-existence of the traditional and the modern.

One feature of modernization frequently mentioned is the wider range of choice among alternative courses of action that becomes available to individuals, along with a tendency for persons to base their decisions according to self-interest rather than group loyalty or group opinion (cf. Hall 1975:20–21, Dore 1967:4). It is understandable, therefore, why processes of decision-making have received much attention in studies of social change. As its proponents might say, the decision-making approach allows us to specify the factors involved in the selection of one alternative over another and adds the dimension of choice to our analysis. Moreover, as Bee notes, this approach explicitly emphasizes the relationship between individual behavior and the larger socio-cultural system (1974:221).

Barth (1962), for instance, examines how social forms are generated by investigating the behavioral alternatives on which such forms are based.

According to Barth this is a perspective that permits us to account for changes as well as continuities. Thus, we need not postulate new values to explain new forms of behavior, because persons may perceive and adopt new ways as a strategy for fulfilling what is traditionally valued. In this regard one also needs to bear in mind the distinction between a change in the opportunity to make individual choices and a change in the criteria by which decisions are made; that is, the former may represent a new pattern even while the latter does not change.

What is often taken for granted in the decision-making approach, however, is the notion that persons have sufficient and accurate information about the implications of their decisions. Taiwanese factory women, by and large, provide a good illustration of the possibility that individuals are not always certain about their objectives or well-informed about the consequences of their choices, and that we should not assume that individuals act according to well-defined strategies. Factory women often do not possess the necessary information about alternative courses of action to make "rational" choices, and some alternatives are never considered.

Robert Paine, in a critique of exchange and transaction models (on which works such as Barth's are based), stresses two factors, power and values, that are particularly salient in terms of understanding decision-making among Taiwan's factory women. Discussing the relation between power and the availability of choice, Paine points out that where the parties are not of equal status (e.g., Taiwanese daughters and their parents), exchanges between the parties are not themselves open to bargaining (or are so only in a limited sense). In fact, the exchanges themselves are likely to represent the asymmetrical relationship between the parties (Paine 1974:6).

Paine also argues that it is misleading to claim that the transactional process may generate relations of equality, and he underlines a distinction between exchange based on reciprocity and that based on complementarity (a distinction he derives from the work of A. Gouldner). In Gouldner's view, reciprocity is recognized as exchange where "'giving and receiving are mutually contingent . . . [and] *each* party has rights *and* duties'" (cited by Paine 1974:8, emphasis Paine's). This mutuality is missing in exchanges based solely on complementarity where "'one's rights are another's obligations, and vice versa'" (cited by Paine 1974:8). It is complementarity, of course, and not reciprocity that characterizes the relationship between Taiwanese parents and their working daughters, and as Paine declares, power differential in a relationship is inimicable to reciprocity (1974:14).

The way values impinge on choice-making has already been touched upon in an earlier critique of Anderson's analysis. Paine's comments on the issue of values follow a similar line of reasoning, as in his distinction between extrinsic values (means-to-ends) and intrinsic values (those that have moral value and that are never questioned, but accepted on faith). It is the latter that Anderson overlooks; while we need not go so far as to suggest that all actions follow from moral values, we get little sense of the place moral values have in the social and familial system Anderson describes. As another writer points out, "the restraining power of the traditional statuses lies not only in the ... customary nature of their requirements, which makes them easier to fulfill, but also in moral certifications implicit in the role images" (Tumin 1960:286). Hence, there are values that are not treated as resources to be exchanged, and conceivably, statuses that are not negotiable (e.g., the role definition of Taiwanese daughters). Moreover, "because extrinsic values are those of means, rather than ends, the sources from which they emanate can be immaterial to the beneficiaries;" in contrast, intrinsic values are usually not separable from the question of who bestows them (Paine 1974:11–12). That is, affection and expressions of concern from parents are important to factory women precisely because they come from parents and they constitute the security the family represents.

The advantage of an approach such as Barth's is that we are able to see how choices made by individuals generate social forms. If this perspective of social action is to be rendered more realistic, however, it must take into account the fact that choice is available only in certain situations (the question of power) and that even where it is available, the right to choose may not be exercised (the question of values). Recognizing this, we can then examine the ways in which people assimilate or reorganize certain aspects of their lives in a situation of change so that they are able to preserve a commitment to other sectors of the culture.

Discovering what determines where individual choices are possible demands expanding our perspective to include the larger ideological and economic context and the distribution of power in a society. To appreciate the historical determinants of decision-making, an analysis at the microlevel is inadequate. A macro-perspective on change, however, must give sufficient attention to the particulars of a historical-social context while at the same time avoid construction of a unique picture that has little utility for comparative purposes. No society replicates another merely by virtue of developing, and development theories that conceive of social systems as inevitably arising out of certain preconditions obviate the need to account for why one pattern occurs rather than another.

Foster's emphasis on historical relativity in his study of the British working class has already been mentioned: "In trying to analyze a particular social formation ... nothing can be more dangerous than to try to analyze it in terms derived from experience elsewhere ... What really rules out the possibility of any long-term regularity is the degree to which subgroup cultures are geared into particular sequences of historical change" (1974:212). It is undeniable that certain consequences are situated in specific contexts of transition that distinguish one society from another. Narrower questions such as whether industrial workers are separated from the land or retain their ties to land, and what the nature of family organization is should figure prominently in understanding why particular social forms result. Furthermore, concepts about stages and features characteristic of the modernizing process have frequently been based on the historical and causal sequence of Western modernization (e.g., the decline of kin ties and the emergence of nuclear families and greater individual freedom), and data on the effects of industrial capitalism on social life in many more local cases will be necessary to create a balanced picture.

Fuller information on specific instances of development will also refine the meanings of "traditional" and "modern." An approach based on a simple dichotomy between the traditional and the modern cannot, for example, reconcile the assertion that increasing sexual equality accompanies modernization and the knowledge that such equality has not been realized in many societies thought of as modern. On the one hand, "traditional" can refer to patterns found in the past, and on the other, to patterns prevailing in the present and coexisting with the modern. Moreover, just as the traditional can be altered by the modern, we also need to ask how the traditional has bearing on the modern: the belief that daughters "belong to other people" among Taiwanese, for instance, continues to influence the effects wage-earning in a modern context has on the lives of working women.

In a parallel fashion the term modernization is also employed in a variety of ways. Modernization is regarded as one type of social change, or as a cause of change, and as the result of change as well. This lack of specificity often results in confusion as to what is to be explained. Anthony Smith is one writer who distinguishes three types of usages of "modernization:" first, modernization can refer to processes of change or aspects of the social structure during such processes; second, it can refer to particular periods of time; and third, it can refer to a set of policies defined by the elites of developing nations (1973:61–73). It makes little sense, therefore, to confront tradition with modernity without reference to a specific tradition or a specific aspect of modernity.

An approach sensitive to context, then, will facilitate an appreciation of unevenness in processes of change; the benefits following from more advanced technology, for example, may accrue sooner to men than to women. As Smith points out, different sectors of a society may, for instance, respond at varying rates to the introduction of a new mode of production, and there is no reason to assume that accomodation will be simultaneous (1973:38). The aim of several earlier chapters has been to demonstrate precisely such a time lag; factory women conform to modern expectations of behavior at the workplace but do not necessarily discard their roles as filial daughters. The factory produces modern female workers but the Taiwanese family manages to remain faithful to its priorities as well. In an earlier section it was noted that Taiwanese families have not changed as an undifferentiated unit, because the experiences of sons, daughters, and parents have not been identical and their exposure to the modern has not proceeded at the same pace.

In addition, attitudes or behavior we might regard as contradictory apparently create little discomfort for the women themselves. They adapt to an industrial mode of production and all its accoutrements at the same time that they hold onto, for instance, traditional religious ideas without showing any conflict. Such apparent inconsistencies clearly call for models of the modernizing process that allow for diversity and complexity in people's adjustment to new occupations, new forms of communication, bureaucratic organizations, and so on. Before one can specify or suggest how particular variables are related to one another, one must be attuned to the myriad variations in the relationship between old and new forms and recognize the possibility that new forms merely increase the range of possible choices available to people.

The wage-earning ability of factory women and the economic independence this would theoretically confer on young women demonstrate convincingly that new and old forms need not be in conflict; wage-earning has simply provided Taiwanese daughters with a new way of repaying their debt and fulfilling obligations to parents. Factory employment is a new activity that permits the achievement of traditional goals, and filial piety continues to be a motivating force. As Bee has stated, rather than thinking of change and persistence as being in opposition, we would do better to view behavior as a series of adjustments between tendencies toward both change and persistence (1974:13).

One also needs to bear in mind that adjustments to change are not always balanced or integrated in a compatible fashion, which is often assumed in mechanical models of change. This notion can be traced to functionalist thinking which postulates that transformation in one sector of the social system or in one institution will lead, in a somewhat automatic yet not always specified manner, to corresponding modifications in other sectors or institutions. However, economic growth in Taiwan, for example, is not self-sustaining; its course is directed by government policy and dictated in part by circumstances external to Taiwan. There is no reason to expect that it will stimulate "compatible" changes in other spheres at the same rate.

Thus one of the central issues in the study of change is to explain continuities in a context of *new* circumstances, to delineate those antecedent structures (such as the family in Taiwan) that allow for coping with changing conditions, for retaining or even promoting fidelity to already existing values. Factory women in Taiwan are not cultural blanks, and discovering their subjective interpretation of objective events of economic and social change is a step that will render transformations and persistence more comprehensible. It will also clarify the relationship between material conditions and ideology.

Factory employment is one facet of a pattern of economic growth that is designed by individuals other than young women and influenced by forces beyond Taiwan, but which nevertheless structures the actions of working women. Therefore, the adjustments factory women make will only be intelligible when attention is directed beyond patterns of socialization and authority in the family to the linkages between internal conditions in Taiwan and external developments.

Notes

Introduction

1. See Davidson (1903) and Gordon (1970) for a general historical background of Taiwan.

2. Initially I believed that women at Western Electronics were using Mandarin for my convenience, but it later became apparent that the use of Mandarin is more widespread than might be expected, even though the majority of workers are Taiwanese. My impression is that facility in Mandarin serves as a marker of educational background.

3. "To speak about change, one needs to be able to specify the nature of the continuity between the situations discussed under the rubric of change" (Barth 1967:664).

4. If, in the People's Republic of China, women's position in the family has been raised, it is probably more a result of explicit ideological support for women's equality than of the part daughters play in production.

Chapter 1

1. Even in the People's Republic, however, where women have been encouraged to take an active part in production in virtually all areas and where there is explicit ideological support for this, the redefinition of sex roles with respect to housework has not been total, and working women are left with a major share of housework. The government's policies concerning the relationship of women to housework and to labor outside the home have fluctuated according to economic priorities and constraints (cf. Davin 1976). In addition, child care costs are usually viewed as the working mother's responsibility.

Chapter 2

1. For my purposes here the term "traditional" refers to the period before the appearance of factories and the availability of jobs in industry for women; in Taiwan this period goes up to the late 1950s.

2. I concentrate on rural women and exclude from discussion women from elite backgrounds, since the opportunities open to them (especially in terms of education) make possible lives very different from those of women I observed.

3. The minor form of marriage A. Wolf describes (1975), for example, was precisely a strategy designed in part to minimize the disruption caused by the entry of an outsider into a man's family.

4. If a daughter is the first-born she may be kept by her natural parents in the hope that she will lead in a baby brother, or because she will be needed to take care of her younger siblings as she grows older. A third- or fourth-born daughter, however, is not so essential, and may be given out in adoption.

5. This practice ended in the 1930s in northern Taiwan.

6. We obtain some sense of the rationale behind segregation of the sexes (among those who could afford it) in the following commentary: "Strict seclusion of women is in agreement with their roles. Since a woman's status is ascribed to her by that of her father, her husband, or her son, there is no need for her to be socially active. What might be termed social life according to modern standards may cause women become less obedient" (Hui-chen Wang Liu 1959:96).

7. Ahern points out that it may be certain events that are polluting rather than women per se (1975:213).

8. I might add here that factory girls, in reference to reprimands from superiors, often indicate that displeasure is conveyed by a look or "having to look at his expression."

9. Short essays written by factory women that appear in company newsletters often take as their themes the sadness of leaving home and one's mother, and the uniqueness of a mother's love. The following, for instance, are titles taken from *Zenith Taiwan News* 3 (20 December 1973); 3 (5 January 1974): "Longing for Mother," "My Mother and I," "Being On One's Own is Like Being Tossed About on the Open Sea."

Chapter 3

1. For example, in Kwangtung province, south Kiansi and south Fukien (double rice-cropping areas), women performed twenty-nine percent of the labor, nineteen percent in the Yangtze rice-wheat area, fourteen percent in the spring wheat area further north, and only five percent in the winter wheat-millet area (Davin 1976:118).

2. As an example of how the contract-labor system affected workers, Chesneaux describes women who were housed on factory premises where they were under constant surveillance by the servants of the manager. "For three years they were thus entirely cut off from the outside world, with no means of communication with their families" (1968:57).

3. Marion Levy, for instance, states that in working with machines, a woman in industry "learns to think in empirical terms and to think critically about empirical phenomena" (1968:311). This not only suggests that women did not need to or were not able to think in empirical terms before but it also precludes the possibility that people are able to compartmentalize diverse attitudes and ideas.

4. See Topley's (1975) data concerning sisterhoods formed by workers in Kwangtung whose purpose was to resist marriage and/or consummation in marriage.

5. In spite of an "apprenticeship system" in some large factories, few firms seemed to have organized training for their workers in order to raise the level of their skill; technical training was provided only where it was indispensable to a particular task (Chesneaux 1968:83).

6. Workers' lack of faith in doctors and clinics referred to them by the factory is paralleled by a similar distrust among women in Taiwan. Ching and Bagwell report that women "do not believe the clinic to be good and so do not attend in large numbers" (1929:17). And Shih finds that "some [workers] accuse the doctor of being rude to them because he does not show them the same smiling face he shows to office workers" (1944:105).

7.   T'ien writes that some women left because their parents were against their coming in the first place and were forced to return home (1944:190), a pattern that is also true of some workers in Taiwan today.

8.   I examine the implications of this movement, described by Topley (1975), in a later chapter. Here it is essential to point out that one very salient factor in the movement's success was the belief that only unmarried women should work with cocoons, due to notions of ritual pollution associated with married women.

Chapter 4

1.   Benjamin Cohen, in his study of multinational firms in Asia, raises the question of why the governments of South Korea and Taiwan would encourage foreign firms to establish subsidiaries to produce and export items which local firms are already exporting. Cohen suggests that one possible answer is that government officials expected, at the time the decision was made, that foreign companies would bring in large amounts of cheap capital or superior technology, and Cohen notes that these officials may not have foreseen how small the economic benefits would be (1975:134). But Cohen argues that the main reason for attracting foreign firms may in large part be of a political nature rather than merely economically motivated. From interviews with South Korean officials Cohen indicates that they believe that (1) the United States government is less likely to impose restrictions on imports from South Korea if there are substantial numbers of United States firms exporting from Korea, and (2) the United States government is more likely to protect South Korea from military invasion if there are a large number of United States firms there; and Cohen goes on to suggest that officials in Taiwan seem to hold similar ideas (1975:134). Here he cites a report from the *New York Times* stating that "'aside from purely business considerations, the Nationalists clearly hope that heightened economic ties will contribute to inducing the United States to preserve diplomatic relations with Taiwan'" (1975:134).

2.   The wage rates I obtained during 1974 are higher than the figures given here; my informants in the electronics industry earned between NT$1,700 and NT$2,200 per month, while women in the textile/garment factories could earn as much as NT$3,000 to NT$3,500 each month. In 1974 US$1 = NT$39.70.

3.   With respect to these figures, one should bear in mind that many factory workers, male and female, continue school on a part-time or full-time basis while they work.

Chapter 5

1.   Stavis, in his study of agricultural development in Taiwan, writes:

> Farm labor is hard and uncomfortable. It requires working in the hot sun. This is doubly hot for women, because in Taiwan a dark sun-tan is considered unattractive so women in the field wear long-sleeved shirts which cover the hands, long trousers, a large hat, and a towel around the face to protect them from the sun. It is also physically very hard work (1974:22).

2.   The result of such attitudes, of course, is that maids are increasingly difficult to find and to retain, and during the 1974 recession, when many factory workers were laid off, several persons of middle and upper-middle class backgrounds remarked, with some relief, that perhaps now it would be easier to find maids.

3.   There are some women who believe that the physical demands of such work are harmful to girls still in their teens—specifically, that it interferes with their physical maturation.

4. As noted earlier, the Ch'inan factory feels itself responsible for seeing that each woman returns home, but each year there are always a handful who stay a few more days to see what jobs are available in the north before returning to farmwork at home. They are in a difficult position, however, inasmuch as their salary expectations tend to be unrealistically high; wages offered by knitting firms and garment factories match their earnings in the tea plant only after a period of training and practice, and their patience does not always last that long. Nonetheless, the Ch'inan workers frequently joke about the plight of men in the south who are unable to find wives now that women prefer to come north for work and seldom return home.

Chapter 6

1. One woman who had lived outside gave the following reasons for returning to the factory dormitories: "The landlord can be very annoying, always checking how much electricity and water you use. And if he happens to raise chickens and pigs in the house, the place isn't very pleasant to live in. And guys come around and bother you because they know you're just a group of girls living together."

2. A young women, an adopted daughter, whose family lived in an isolated village some distance from Sanhsia, was not allowed to work in factories because her mother was afraid that she would meet other men and subsequently refuse to marry her foster brother. She remained at home and worked at picking tea leaves. It turned out that she did marry another man, after twice refusing to marry her foster brother, and despite her mother's attempts to "push them together."

3. In *House of Lim* M. Wolf quotes a mother explaining why she would not allow her daughter to accept a higher paying job in a more distant factory: "'A-hua,' she said, 'earns NT$15 a day in Lim Chieng-cua's factory. That isn't too bad. If she went out of the village to work, she would have to have better clothes and take her lunch. All considered, she probably wouldn't make too much more. That is part of the reason I won't let her go outside to work'"(1968:61). The issue today is one of whether to allow one's daughter to move to a company dormitory, but the same sort of logic prevails.

Chapter 7

1. Newspaper articles from time to time issue warnings to young job-seekers to be on the alert against "employment agencies" or persons who entice them to do "immoral work," and they note that the ones who are taken in by deception tend to be young women out in society for the first time who need cash, and who are lured by promises of high pay and good fringe benefits (*Lien He Pao,* 7 December 1974).

2. Dormitory supervisors are seriously limited in their power to effect improvements. They themselves are not always trained in personnel relations and communication between them and the office staff tends to be one-sided, with the latter issuing directives. Dormitory residents customarily see their dormitory supervisors only if there is a specific matter that requires the latter's attention. "If we keep going to see her, she'll think us a nuisance." On their part, dorm-mothers find their hands full merely carrying out their routine duties, and from conversations with them it is clear that they find the performance of their task rendered more difficult by the heterogeneity of the workkers—in age, personality, background, and education. "Some only have an elementary school education and are very immature: no matter how many times you remind them they don't seem to be able to keep their rooms neat." Dormitory supervisors also complain that they are hampered in that they lack the sanctions that back up the authority, say, a schoolteacher has at his/her disposal.

3. Stability becomes important to many workers. Adapting to a new environment (say, another factory) means not only acclimating oneself to a new job, but to new people and a different living situation as well. On the other hand some workers appear not to finds such efforts anxiety-provoking and welcome changes a new job brings.

4. It also emerges from such conversations that privacy is not a high priority. When asked where they would go if they wanted to be alone, a number of informants repeated the comments of one worker: "I prefer to be with my friends; it isn't good to be by oneself. One benefit of having many people around is that if a person has a problem, there are others who can offer suggestions." E. Anderson, in "Some Chinese Methods of Dealing with Crowding," states that "There is little ideology of conspicuous consumption of space, or of being alone... People work together: there are always several people (adults and children) around a house; and going off 'just to be alone' is unheard of" (1972:144).

5. I did come across a few cases at Western Electronics where long-time dormitory residents had managed, by speaking to the supervisors, to secure a place for a sister or classmate in their own rooms. In a similar fashion an even smaller number of women, by appealing to their foremen, were able to have a newly-hired friend assigned to the same work area in the plant as themselves.

6. A widespread stereotype about aborigines held by other women depicts them as especially prone to learning bad ways.

7. This is an opinion held by the public as well. The immediate response of one college student (female), upon learning that I was carrying out research in a factory dormitory, was, "the lives of those women must be very disorderly!" When Western Electronics began a training program to increase the effectiveness of dormitory supervisors, two secretaries at Western Electronics expressed their skepticism concerning how knowledgeable dormitory supervisors really are about what goes on in the buildings: "things are just too complex in there. But then, if I had to live in a dormitory and could only go back and forth between the plant and the dormitory all the time, I might not be able to take it either. No wonder those girls behave the way they do."

Chapter 8

1. This chapter, in revised form, was presented at a Conference on Anthropology in Taiwan, held in Portsmouth, New Hampshire, 18–25 August 1976. The conference was sponsored by the Joint Committee on Contemporary China of the American Council of Learned Societies and the Social Science Research Council. This chapter appears in *The Anthropology of Taiwanese Society*, edited by Emily Martin Ahern & Hill Gates, as "Perceptions of Work Among Factory Women," Stanford University Press, Stanford, CA., 1981.

2. This is probably an understatement. To resign is an embarassing situation for a woman to go through; some worry about the inconvenience that may ensue, some are afraid that wages due them will not be given to them (apparently a practice some smaller firms have—to induce workers to stay), or that her foreman will "scold" her. My tabulation of the reasons women give for leaving is incomplete, but my impression is that only rarely are the true reasons offered. In part, this pattern has to do with a problem of face; women feel that if they give their real reasons, they may lose face. For example, if a person admits that the wages are too low, the implication is that she truly needs the money and places a lot of weight on what may be a small amount. On the other hand, if the company requires that they give a reason, women are willing to comply, usually citing school or family-related factors, reasons that are hard for a company to argue against. The point is to be able to depart with as little fuss as possible. One worker in a garment factory explained why women rarely refer to the company in a critical

way: "They want to leave behind a good impression in case their next job doesn't work out and they decide to return."

3. Table 23 presents separation figures for production workers at Western Electronics during three months in 1974. The first point to note is the high number grouped under "leave of absence." This term refers to workers absent from work for three consecutive days without informing the company as to the reason(s) for absence; most often, these are workers who leave the company without giving notice. Their actions indicate a desire to avoid an awkward and embarrassing encounter with a supervisor who must determine the reason(s) for a worker's departure. The company's practice of discharging workers after a three-day unexplained absence is intended to discourage them from going to other factories and "trying out" another job without having to sacrifice their position at Western Electronics.

    Another pattern that deserves some comment concerns wages. We know that a sizable proportion of workers would like to see an increase in wages. In view of this, the negligible number of those at Western Electronics (one person in three months) who name wage dissatisfaction as a reason for leaving can be explained by the fact that to cite this factor is tantamount to admitting to one's supervisor that one *needs* the money. To admit that even NT$100 or NT$200 more a month *would* matter cannot but bring embarrassment.

4. Towards the end of the year Western Electronics began a series of foreman training sessions, and in these meetings groups of foremen listed their most urgent problems in order of priority. I have information for only two such groups, and in Group A's list of eight needs, the eighth was "how to motivate and encourage assemblers." This was also number eight in Group B's list, followed by ventilation problems, equipment shortages, neat working environment, and safety.

5. One foreman in his twenties said, "Being young myself, it's easier to relate to the girls; if a foreman happens to be an older man and the girls don't listen to him, he might feel he has lost face." He also felt that knowing the name of each girl was important: "If I call a girl by her name, it makes her feel happier to know that I remember; I know I would feel that way."

6. I have heard only one worker (herself a Mainlander) make the claim that having a Mainlander for a foreman was a better arrangement.

7. Quality control women and testers are paid more than assemblers, and group-leaders of the former in turn receive higher wages than group-leaders of assemblers. Quality control workers are classified into two categories depending on whether one enters the companies through examinations or whether one is promoted to a quality control position from within. The former have slightly different uniforms and are better paid.

8. On one occasion I was speaking with an informant while she was working; shortly thereafter, her group-leader came over and said somewhat reluctantly that their foreman wanted to know what I was doing there (he being new and not having seen me there before, and I not being in uniform). My informant later indicated that her group-leader gave a somewhat different interpretation of the episode: "The fact that he sent over the group-leader already means that he was giving you 'face.' If he had come over himself, no girl would dare come back."

9. At Western Electronics approximately two hundred male workers were laid off and were given severance compensation. Two weeks later approximately three hundred women were laid off, also with compensation; in addition, third- and fourth-year working-students were permitted to take loans from the company so they could meet their living expenses while continuing school (since tuition fees were not refundable) and they were also permitted to remain in the dormitories even though they were no longer employed by the firm.

10. The monthly company magazine, however, is named *Family*.

Table 23. Separation Figures for Production Workers at
Western Electronics

	Female Assembler	Tester	Inspector	Group-leader	Male Assembler
March 1974					
Marriage	0	1	1	0	0
Sickness	7	0	0	0	2
Leave of absence	59	2	4	0	47
Military Duty	N/A	N/A	N/A	N/A	3
School	31	1	2	2	2
Not Interested in Work	0	0	0	0	0
Accepted Other Work	62	3	5	4	45
Family-Related Reasons	51	2	2	1	6
Wage Dissatisfaction	1	0	0	0	0
Work Dissatisfaction	60	3	4	3	17
Poor Attendance	0	0	0	0	0
Violation of Company Rules	1	0	0	0	2
Transportation Inconvenient	0	0	0	0	0
Moving	0	0	0	0	0
April 1974					
Marriage	1	0	0	2	0
Sickness	15	3	2	0	4
Leave of absence	102	1	5	2	90
Military Duty	N/A	N/A	N/A	N/A	2
School	32	2	1	1	13
Not Interested in Work	0	0	0	0	0
Accepted Other Work	57	3	2	1	59
Family-Related Reasons	76	5	3	2	5
Wage Dissatisfaction	0	0	0	0	0
Work Dissatisfaction	65	5	3	2	5
Poor Attendance	0	0	1	0	0
Violation of Company Rules	1	0	0	1	6
Transportation Inconvenient	1	0	0	0	1
Moving	3	1	0	0	0
July 1974					
Marriage	3	1	1	0	0
Sickness	14	0	1	1	0
Leave of absence	108	0	3	0	45
Military Duty	N/A	N/A	N/A	N/A	3
School	76	3	1	1	7
Not Interested in Work	0	0	0	0	0
Accepted Other Work	148	10	11	5	43
Family-Related Reasons	111	5	10	4	3
Wage Dissatisfaction	0	0	0	0	0
Work Dissatisfaction	59	1	1	1	2
Poor Attendance	0	0	0	0	0
Violation of Company Rules	2	1	0	0	1
Transportation Inconvenient	0	0	0	0	0
Moving	0	0	0	0	0

11. There are now some 635 unions in Taiwan (K.C. Liu 1974:29). The law does not require factories with less than fifty workers to organize their own unions. Since I was requested not to ask too many questions about union affairs, my notes on the union at Western Electronics are not as extensive as I would have liked them to be. The manufacturing managers are the union's standing directors, and sections in the factory elect representatives who meet once a year and who choose a board of directors. There are approximately one hundred union representatives, and they attend lower-level branch meetings as well. Membership for office workers is optional.

12. One worker in such an establishment in Ch'inan, for example, described the small factory as "being like a family." As for fringe benefits, "even in a factory a person doesn't get to enjoy that many benefits, and if we go on outings, our *lao-pan* [boss] pays for everything. And few people would think about medical insurance; generally if you're sick, it's just a matter of buying some medicine and getting some shots. If a person is seriously ill, our *lao-pan* has *kan-ching*, and he wouldn't let us down." But relations can be complex in even a small factory. Another woman from Sanhsia left one knitting business because her *lao-pan* repeatedly asked her to go out with him, and as another worker pointed out, there are disadvantages in a small factory as well: "In a large company, if you argue with someone it doesn't matter much, it won't be difficult for you to stay on because this sort of thing happens all the time; everyone is like that. But if a problem should come up in a small firm, it'd be hard to stay on; it'd be too awkward if you didn't get along with someone."

13. Robert Silin reaches a similar conclusion in his study of firms in Taiwan. He states that the relationship between working and administrative divisions is marked by distrust: there is the feeling among workers that staff use their positions irresponsibly and that their motives are questionable (1976:153–55).

14. Hence the notion that it is easier for women to find jobs than for men; since a man's job will be more permanent, he cannot settle for an unpleasant one, while it "matters less for women because it's temporary—women just come out for a few years to earn some money."

15. Arranging the data according to the following constraints—ascription/achievement, diffuse/specific relations, particularistic/universalistic, and affective/affectively-neutral (Dore 1973:270)—might seem the most obvious way of handling the data. But as Dore shows (1973:269–75) these are not always simple concepts, and his use of them is qualified with detailed references to his analysis of a Japanese factory. However, if I may be permitted an oversimplification, it would appear that the workers at Western Electronics find themselves in a position similar to that of the British workers Dore describes, and yet factory women in Taiwan also wish to enjoy some of the features characteristic of the Japanese factory. But given the temporary nature of their work, the Japanese system would make little sense.

Chapter 9

1. As noted in an earlier chapter some women at Western Electronics derive additional income from part-time jobs in fruit shops or noodle stalls; those who live at home also help other family members in assembling plastic flowers, repairing fish-nets, and the like.

2. At Western Electronics a new assembler's monthly base-wage in 1974 was NT$1,350, with an additional food allowance of NT$180 and a transportation allowance of NT$180. The monthly base-wage for an evening shift worker (who works one hour less) was NT$1,480. After thirty days there is an increase of NT$25, after ninety days—NT$50, after six months— NT$50, after one year—NT$100, and annual increments thereafter equal NT$100. In comparison, Wang and Apthorpe report that in a village in central Taiwan in 1971, wages for women hired as agricultural laborers was NT$50 a day during peak season and NT$40 a day during slack season (1974:66–67).

3. See M. Wolf (1972:223) on how credit clubs operate.

4. Occasionally the sense of obligation may be felt so keenly that some women resort to extremes to fulfill their "duty." The high incidence of thefts reported in dormitories may in part be attributed to new wants that women cannot attain without detracting from the sums sent home. The pressure to meet parental expectations some workers may feel is demonstrated by one case involving a theft of cash in a dormitory:

> "A," 17, had stolen NT$1,000 from "C," which she subsequently took to her mother when she went home for a visit. "B," a coworker, is a neighbor of "A's" and had learned of the large sum of money that "A" had brought home because "A's" mother had proudly shared this information with "B's" mother. "B," also a dormitory resident, knew of the theft, and when she returned to the dormitory she reported her suspicions to the supervisor. After first denying any part in the theft, "A" later admitted that she had taken the money, stating that she had done so only because she wanted to bring a large sum of money home when she returned south for a visit. (It turned out that "A" and "C" are friends, thus explaining how "A" came to know where "C" kept her money.)

5. William Kessen's observation, based on his visits to schools in the People's Republic of China, applies equally well to Taiwanese: "... the Chinese *attitude* toward the development of children contains the expectation that the developmental approach to desired behavior is inevitable, regular, and without need of instrumental manipulation" (1978:32, emphasis in original).

Chapter 10

1. As table 18 indicates, yet another way in which young men and women are brought together is through pen-pal correspondence. The convenience of an address away from home and being able to bypass the scrutiny of one's parents make pen-pals especially popular in dormitories, and letter-writing seems a major past-time. (I have encountered some women who simultaneously keep up a correspondence with three or four young men.) It is not surprising that the male recipients of these letters are almost always of a higher educational level than the woman who writes them. Sometimes, face-to-face meetings are arranged (with the women inevitably accompanied by her friends), and occasionally, the couple may go out a few times. Not all women, however, are in favor of making friends in this manner: "I think having pen-pals is too risky: you never know what kind of person you'll end up with."

2. Fertility attitudes and education are related in another way. In one study of consumption and its relation to fertility in Taiwan, the investigator found that the largest proportion of husbands, forty percent, singled out the education of their children as the most important purpose for saving (with thirteen percent citing emergencies or old age, eleven percent investing in business, and only seventeen mentioned consumption as a goal) (D. Freedman 1975:104). In addition most husbands were more aware of the economic costs that children entailed than of the possible financial benefits that might follow in the future; only twelve percent of the men named financial help from children as an advantage of a large family while sixty-five percent mentioned the expense of raising children as the main disadvantage (D. Freedman 1975:109).

3. In contrast, I might include the comments of two women at Western Electronics concerning bride-price and dowries that suggest that ideas may be changing. One said, "Girls are smarter now about how large a bride-price to ask for. If a woman demands a large one, she's only asking for trouble because after she's married, she'd only be in debt along with her husband's family and would suffer together." The other added: "Besides, that money still belongs to his side because it all goes back in the form of a dowry."

4. Parental objections to a particular match did not appear to be of much consequence. There were four instances where in spite of parental opposition the marriage took place, and as one parent said: "since there was no way to change their minds, there was nothing I could do." In these cases opposition was based on personal qualities of the men involved; one was thought too old, another was a Mainlander, and two were reputed to drink. Parents with a pregnant daughter, on the other hand, are not likely to raise arguments, although one Ch'inan woman was placed in a more difficult position. Because of strong parental opposition to the man involved, Liu was not married until she was in the fifth month of her pregnancy. The engagement (which took place one morning) and the wedding (which followed in the afternoon) were hastily arranged affairs with a minimum of the usual wedding paraphernalia and fanfare, with her father muttering about the shamefulness of it all.

Chapter 11

1. The clearest instance of a married woman achieving a good deal of economic influence as a result of her income—which was, in a real sense, an independent one—is a Liu woman who operates a one-woman barbershop in her home. Established originally because of financial need, Mrs. Liu's business in Ch'inan has developed to the point where she has acquired a young assistant. As for her husband's (a cab driver) complaints about housework that is neglected, festival foods that aren't prepared, and so on, Mrs. Liu insists that these remarks are made half-heartedly, for with the earnings they have been able to acquire better food and clothing and more household appliances. Since her business varies from day to day, her husband has no idea precisely how much she takes in. Referring to the time when she was not working, she said, "I was always the one to give in when we argued and the one to take the first step to make up. Now I talk back more or sometimes don't even listen to my husband."

2. For instance, a woman in Ch'inan watches her three grandchildren while their mother works in a factory. Her son had left her to live with another woman, and his mother is clearly on the side of her daughter-in-law: "My son acts as if he doesn't have a family of his own. He doesn't bring home one cent but squanders his money on gambling and his girlfriend. It's a good thing this daughter-in-law is filial, otherwise she would have left long ago and then where would her children go? And where would I get the money to support them?" The mother earns approximately NT$3,200 a month and gives NT$2,000 to her mother-in-law for the children's needs. There is another son, but he married uxorilocally and has gambling debts. The older woman said, "It's as if I didn't have any children at all. People should have an easier life when they are old, but first I had to raise my children, and now I have to raise my grandchildren."

3. According to the *China Yearbook* for 1976 there are two public and 322 private nursing centers that can take care of a total of 32,479 infants (Chen and Shih 1976:314); in 1975 there were 1,783,000 children under age five in Taiwan (Chen and Shih 1976:133).

4. Although the community Cohen studied is Hakka, he presents evidence from other areas of China to show that women's "private money" is a characteristic of Chinese complex families in general and not a pattern unique to the Hakka (1976:187–90).

5. This is not, however, necessarily the perspective that young women have. Their ideal is to marry a man or into a family whose economic position would not require them to continue working. Married women who work in factories do acknowledge that they have a greater say in economic matters at home, but they are generally situated in circumstances that make it necessary for them to work. In this context, then, greater influence at home comes at the fairly high price of eight or more hours a day in a factory and housework besides.

6. One might expect that education would be a determining variable ("those with higher-paying jobs would not be so willing to give it up and would hire a baby-sitter"), but this is not entirely

accurate. Considering that few factory women are able to progress beyond the high school level, their chances for obtaining truly desirable and well-paying jobs are not encouraging. But beyond this, so long as one important purpose of educating women is perceived as improving their nurturing role at home, mothering and wage-earning will be viewed as incompatible.

Chapter 12

1. A revised version of this chapter (entitled "Factory Work and Women in Taiwan: Changes in Self-Image and Status") first appeared in *Signs, Journal of Women in Culture and Society,* 1976, 2:35–58.

2. Solomon's respondents were middle- and upper-class males, but the features he finds in social relations overall apply in many respects to women as well, and we may expect that in areas such as obedience, its importance goes double for daughters.

3. One writer offers the following appraisal of social relations in Chinese society:

> With the conviction that to deal with strangers is to ask for trouble, the Chinese have little choice . . . but to develop "friendships" that will insure access to goods and services. Chinese *kuan-hsi* relationships begin not with a vague, undefined feeling of compatibility, but with purposeful estimates of each person's value to the other . . . Material benefits are expected in *kuan-hsi* agreements (quoted in Stover and Stover 1976:207).

According to such a description Chinese social behavior should lend itself particularly well to analysis based on an exchange model. Applying such an approach to relations in an African factory, Kapferer, for instance, suggests that:

> relations will develop between individuals when gains from the transaction of resources in the relationship are equal to or greater than the costs (1972:189), [and that the degree of commitment can be] measured according to the extent with which the possible gains from investing in an alternative set of relationships exceeds or is less than the costs of giving up the benefits from current investments [which may be time, energy, or material investments] as the individual perceives them (1972:103).

As Kapferer rightly points out, however, persons cannot always assess, with precision, gains against costs. This leads Kapferer to believe that individuals "would only contemplate a move if the gains from their perspective *clearly* outweighed the costs" (1972:103, emphasis in original). While factory women in Taiwan speak of impersonal and instrumental relations, I am hesitant to use terms such as "investment," "strategy," and "resources" to describe the motivations of female workers. There are women who consciously curry favor with their foreman in the hope of attaining a promotion, but these are a minority whose actions are criticized by their peers. If women have objectives, by and large, it is a wish that one's work goes smoothly, that one is not bothered by supervisors, and that no unpleasantness arises in relations with coworkers. Kapferer can legitimately speak of approval and support as resources, but factory women are generally not in a position where others seek *them* out for such rewards. It is true that a foreman requires the cooperation of his workers if his production quotas are to be filled, but compliance on the part of women cannot be withheld for long without jeopardizing their jobs.

The picture that Kapferer offers of individuals devising tactics and weighing the balance of investments and benefits seems more suited to the business managers Silin studied than to factory women. The latter possess neither the skills nor command the prestige that would allow them to mobilize themselves in order to stimulate their employers into a desired course of action. As Kapferer found in his study, most unskilled workers in the factory had little expectation of gaining many further benefits from continued work in the factory, and in contrast to skilled workers, unskilled workers tended to have few relationships at the work place (1972:116–17).

4. Under somewhat similar conditions elsewhere in China the importance of daughters also turned on their economic contribution to their families. In her analysis of female silk workers in one area of Kwangtung in the last century, Topley (1975) is careful to underline that an entire complex of conditions rather than wage-earning itself served as the impetus for the pattern of changes she sets forth: the refusal of certain young women to marry or to consummate their marriages. But one fact emerges clearly: mothers of silk workers did not always object to their daughters' decision not to marry (certainly an aberration given the Chinese family structure) and even encouraged celibacy in many cases because those daughters brought them additional income.

5. While older women state hypothetically that, if they were younger, they would gladly go to work in factories, they are not always so prepared to grant this "privilege" to their daughters-in-law (see chapter 11).

6. I should note here that women's ambivalence about the work role itself is quite independent of the question of their status in the family. In other words, it is quite possible that a woman might better her status in the family by working *and* still not enjoy working. Wage-earning has accorded women a greater degree of autonomy in personal matters, but not enough to warrant saying that they now have the right to enter into family decisions. Wage-earning has not conferred upon them the power to influence family matters, and at the same time they are situated at the lowest level in the factory.

Chapter 13

1. We need to remember, however, that women are not totally unrestricted in where they may seek jobs: some may not be allowed to live away from home; some must consider school schedules, and so on.

2. "Employers or workers shall not suspend business, close up a factory, call a strike, or start a work-slowdown on account of any labor-management dispute before such a dispute has been brought to the Labor Dispute Arbitration Board for Judgment" (Article 7, "Measures for Handling of Labor Disputes During the Period of National Mobilization for the Suppression of Communist Rebellion," *Labor Laws and Regulations of the Republic of China* 1965:56).

    "Where any party involved in a dispute does not submit to the award issued by the Labor Dispute Arbitration Board, the authority-in-charge may resort to compulsory execution, and where the case is serious, punishment may be inflicted in accordance with the Provisional Regulations for the Punishment of Persons Obstructing National Mobilization" (Article 8, "Measures for Handling of Labor Disputes During the Period of National Mobilization for the Suppression of Communist Rebellion," in *Labor Laws and Regulations of the Republic of China* 1965:57).

3. We might contrast this with the British situation described by Dore; contrasting the British system with the Japanese, Dore writes, "by not offering security of tenure in cozy niches in a particular organization [the British factory] teaches [workers] the only thing they have to rely on is individual capacities—that which can be sold on the market, or, if the market does not work to give them their due, the egalitarian solidarity of the union or class seeking to change the system. As such it fosters a spirit of independence and willingness to resist arbitrary authority" (1973:277).

4. One idea floated at Western Electronics but not adopted was the promise of a sum of money for a woman's dowry after she had worked at the company for a certain number of years.

5. Some workers are promoted on the basis of seniority alone, but at Western Electronics the highest position female workers can attain through seniority, without further formal technical training, is that of a quality-control worker. And even then, these women in quality-control are distinguished (by their uniforms and wages) from other quality-control workers who obtain their position by way of their diplomas.

6. It is estimated that between 1970 and 1980, 276,000 persons annually will enter the labor market; 90,000 of these will replace those who leave the labor force by reason of marriage, injury, and so on, leaving 194,000 (male and female) workers who will seek jobs (Cheng, Kuan and Tai 1972:321).

Chapter 14

1. Goode correctly calls attention to the influence or economic factors on women's attitudes toward work, and notes that where there is an assumption that, whatever job a woman takes, she is still responsible for household tasks, this will constitute a barrier to sexual equality (1971:30–32).

2. One question future research into the lives and attitudes of married women who had been factory workers will be whether they continue to define their role within the framework of the family economy; Scott and Tilly, for instance, found that married women seemed almost a backwater of pre-industrial values within the working-class family; long after their husbands and children adopted some individualistic values, these women, who had been employed in factories, continued in self-sacrificing, self-exploitative types of work (1975:54).

3. Anderson claims that the relationship between children and parents is almost always a short one because these families lacked a property base, and so children do not remain dependent until marriage or the death of a parent. We may note here that this does not apply to Taiwanese daughters since parents and the women themselves recognize that they will leave in any event; nonetheless, we still find loyalty on the part of women to their natal families.

Chapter 15

1. The following discussion is based on a book and a series of newspaper articles on women's roles in Taiwan; this does not purport to be representative of messages women receive from similar essays, magazine articles, and television programs. In addition, one ought to bear in mind that without specific questioning it is difficult to ascertain how much and which views women actually adopt from these articles, much less how these affect their behavior. These excerpts, then, should be taken as selections from comparable articles that reach a wide audience.

    The first, entitled "Man Should Be Grateful to Her" (H.C. Hung 1977c), discusses the modest expectations of most women: women cook and clean but as long as they are able to take care of their husbands and children, and have a clean house, then that's enough and women don't mind hard work. When a woman's husband receives a promotion and must relocate, it means that she must give up her friends and perhaps even give up her own happiness for her husband's love and happiness. But all this a woman does for the sake of a happy home, and yet, in many cases, men are not grateful to women. The author then goes on to say that in part women themselves are to blame: a woman tends to be lax after marriage, whereas she ought to show her appreciation to her husband for his hard work.

    The second article (H.C. Hung 1977d) also begins by listing inequities women must tolerate: friendships established before marriage are temporary and there is little freedom for a married woman to make friends; even though a woman might be self-supporting, ultimately her life is in the hands of the man, and women are therefore economically dependent persons; men back away from "intellectual" types of women and find women with "simpler minds" more attractive, and in marriage a woman is not the equal of her husband. The author claims that it is futile to talk about equality because the notion that women can be better off than men is an empty abstraction; rather, a woman can liberate herself by developing abilities that are economically useful, an independent spirit, and strive to create a happy marriage and family. Rather than allowing herself to be distressed by increasing age or a husband's mistress, the author exhorts her readers to develop their own interests, hobbies, and character.

A third article (H.C. Hung 1977e) defends women at home, claiming that the life they lead is no easier than that of a man who works outside. "We women slave at home; men slave outside to support the family. Both work hard; isn't this equality? What more can one say about sexual equality?" Since men devote all their energies to work, it follows that women should put their efforts into helping their husbands become successful. In the process of doing so a woman also works hard at home, and thus there is no reason why a woman should feel guilty about being supported. [A point that the author clearly misses here is that by being assigned to the role of consumer, the role of housewife is further devalued, for consuming is not as respected as producing (cf. Hammond and Jablow).] The writer assures her readers that working at home is easier than working in the outside world, and that homemaking is a choice made by women and not dictated by tradition. The author claims that there can be no better arrangement than this: women carry on the work at home while men struggle outside to provide security for their families. She concludes: "each works hard and each is to be admired; a couple who contributes to a harmonious family and society, therefore, are deserving of praise."

An essay entitled "A Talented Woman" (H.C. Hung 1977a) reiterates some of the points mentioned above, defining a talented woman as one who helps her husband develop his talents. As examples, the author suggests that a woman with an executive husband should not pester him with questions about his work but should make him as comfortable as possible; if her husband is an ordinary office employee she should express her contentment with their standard of living and be frugal, and the wife of a scholar or doctor ought to show how much she enjoys the life he has provided her. Confrontation is not advised; instead, the author states that "to support him means to have no opinions and only to agree; it doesn't matter whether he is right or wrong, succeeds or fails; you are always the first to support him, not the one to change him." Women are also encouraged to be patient and not to expect quick results; "an investment of two or three months' effort is small when you have a life of twenty or thirty years together."

A fifth article (H.D. Hung 1976b) declares that the conditions for a woman's happiness are simple: to have enough to eat, a considerate husband, and a harmonious family life. If in addition a woman has financial security, then she can truly be considered fortunate. But the author points out that these can all be easily taken away from a woman, if she should lose her husband or if he becomes involved with another woman. A woman must therefore be prepared to create her own happiness. [The steps a woman can take in this direction, however, are basically passive.] One example the author gives concerns how to deal with a husband who has taken a mistress; she advises playing "deaf and dumb," which will lead her husband to feel guilty, to treat his wife better, and after a time, the affair will lose interest for him and he will return to his wife.

Taiwan is not without its more feminist works (for example, Lu 1974), although it would be hard to arrive at an estimate of the number of women books of this type reach. Lu writes, for instance, that women no longer need regard marriage as a career; nowadays, if one is educated, one can be self-supporting, and so to marry should not mean that one has obtained a "life-long meal ticket" (1974:141). She stresses that women are now independent and autonomous persons, and they no longer need to go through men to be in touch with society. Another book (Ts'ai 1975) recommends steps that should be undertaken to improve women's position in society (1975:120). Some of these urge women to cultivate their special skills and an ability to maintain their independence, to perform well on the job, to be receptive to those women better educated than oneself and to help those less educated, to take part in women's organizations, and to be firm in the concept of sexual equality and to teach one's children the same.

As an example of the programs that might be implemented, Ts'ai notes that women have a natural ability and interest in managing household affairs. Since service occupations in restaurants and hotels in fact resemble housework, she pleads for better training for women in those fields (1975:52–54). What she fails to recognize, however, is that placing women in those sectors is based on and only reinforces the notion that their real place is in the home. Moreover, most of her recommendations are actions that fall on women as individuals and are not solutions conceived in broader societal terms with the major share of the responsibility taken up by the government. Without a more complete dissection of social, political and economic forces that relegate women only to certain positions, both Lu's and Ts'ai's suggestions seem a trifle too optimistic. Ts'ai does state that the government should set up nation-wide study groups on women's rights and virtues (1975:117), but these remedies and reforms are proposed without a further consideration of how women's place in the schools, in employment, in the government, and in the family are connected to the larger economic and political system.

2.   Where in the People's Republic of China hard work and diligence often mean manual labor, in Taiwan the equivalent is represented by academic achievement and being a good student (Martin 1975:245). Chinese in Taiwan, of course, are far from being alone in this line of thinking. Citing the "widespread and deeply ingrained prejudice" she found against women's, particularly married women's, participation in industry, Boserup writes, "as yet, the idea of women in the role of industrial worker is frowned upon by respectable women; since women have access, at best, only to unskilled and low-paid industrial jobs, industrial employment has no prestige value for women who aspire to a career, and earning capacity is not high enough to compensate for the social stigma attached to women's industrial work" (1970:212).

3.   Silin discovers, for instance, that managers of both large and small firms in Taiwan feel they operate at the will of the government, and he states that the government is deeply involved in all aspects of industry, and that the government actively controls the nature and tempo of economic activity (1976:16–18). With respect to the government's four-year plans for economic growth, Silin writes that "to be successful, these plans require coordinated action frequently achieved through direct suggestion to industry from top officials. Large firms receive unofficial and semi-official suggestions as to the direction of the expansion. In some instances, allegedly, particular products lines are specified" (1976:18).

Bibliography

Ahern, Emily M. 1973. The Cult of the Dead in a Chinese Village. Stanford, California: Stanford University Press.
_____. 1975. The Power and Pollution of Chinese Women. In Women in Chinese Society. M. Wolf and R. Witke, eds. Stanford, California: Stanford University Press.
Althusser, Louis. 1971. Ideology and the State. In Lenin and Philosophy and Other Essays. Louis Althusser, ed. New York: Monthly Review Press.
American Rural Small-Scale Industry Delegation. 1977. Rural Small-Scale Industry in the People's Republic of China. Berkeley: University of California Press.
Anderson, Adelaide M. 1928. Humanity and Labor in China. London: Student Christian Movement.
Anderson, Eugene N., Jr. 1972. Some Chinese Methods of Dealing with Crowding. In Urban Anthropology 1:141–50.
Anderson, Michael. 1971. Family Structure in Nineteenth Century Lancashire. Cambridge: Cambridge University Press.
Anonymous. 1927. Women's Work in Kwangtung Province. In Chinese Economic Journal, Vol. 1:564–78.
Ballon, Robert. 1969. Participative Employment. In The Japanese Employee. Robert Ballon, ed. Tokyo: Sophia University Press.
Barth, Fredrik. 1967. On the Study of Social Change. In American Anthropologist 69:661–69.
Bee, Robert L. 1974. Patterns and Processes, An Introduction to Anthropological Strategies for the Study of Sociocultural Change. New York: The Free Press.
Bendix, Reinhard. 1967. Tradition and Modernity Reconsidered. In Comparative Studies in Society and History 9:292–346.
Boserup, Ester. 1970. Women's Role in Economic Development. New York: St. Martin's Press.
_____. 1977. Preface, Special Issue: Women and National Development. In Signs, Journal of Women in Culture and Society 3:xi–xiv.
Bossen, Laurel. 1975. Women in Modernizing Societies. In American Ethnologist 2:587–601.
Buvinic, Mayra. 1976. A Critical Review of Some Research Concepts and Concerns. In Women and World Development. Irene Tinker, Michele Bo Bramsen, Mayra Buvinic, eds. New York: Praeger.
Chan, Anita. 1974. Rural Chinese Women and the Socialist Revolution: An Inquiry into the Economics of Sexism. In Journal of Contemporary Asia IV:197–208.
Chang, Chi-yun, editor-in-chief. 1967. National Atlas of China, Vol. 1, Taiwan. Yang-Ming Shan, Taiwan: The National War College.
Chen, Chen-tzu and Shih, Hwa-Chang, eds. 1976. China Yearbook 1976. Taipei: China Publishing Company.
Chen, Li-an. 1976. Education and Manpower Supply. Conference on Population and Economic Development in Taiwan, 29 December 1975 to 3 January 1976. Taipei: Institute of Economics, Academia Sinica.

Cheng, Tracy T.S., Kuan, William W.L., and Tai, Theodore T.O. 1972. The Evaluation and Prospect of Manpower Development Planning in Taiwan. *In* Sino-American Conference on Manpower in Taiwan. China Council on Sino-American Cooperation in the Humanities and Social Sciences, ed. Taipei: Academia Sinica.

Chesneaux, Jean. 1968. The Chinese Labor Movement 1919–1927. H.M. Wright, trans. Stanford, California: Stanford University Press.

China News (Taipei). 23 April, 3 May 1976.

China Post (Taipei). 17 April, 2 May, 12 May, 17 September, 1 October, 3 November 1974.

Ching, Chung-shou and Bagwell, May. 1931. Women in Industry in the Chapei, Hongkew, and Pootung Districts of Shanghai. Shanghai: Young Women's Christian Association of China.

Chow, Tse-tsung. 1967. The May Fourth Movement, Intellectual Revolution in Modern China. Stanford, California: Stanford University Press.

Chung Kuo Shih Pao [China Times] (Taipei). 17 April, 1 May, 10 July 1974.

Cohen, Benjamin I. 1975. Multinational Firms and Asian Exports. New Haven, Conn.: Yale University Press.

Cohen, Myron. 1970. Introduction. *In* Village Life in China. By Arthur H. Smith. Boston: Little Brown & Co.

———. 1976. House United, House Divided. New York: Columbia University Press.

Cole, Robert E. and Tominaga, Ken'ichi. 1976. Japan's Changing Occupational Structure and its Significance. *In* Japanese Industrialization. Hugh Patrick, ed.

Davidson, James W. 1903. The Island of Formosa. Shanghai: Kelly and Walsh, Ltd.

Davin, Delia. 1973. Women in the Liberated Areas. *In* Women and China, Studies in Social Change and Feminism. Marilyn B. Young, ed. Ann Arbor, Mich.: University of Michigan Press.

———. 1975. Women in the Countryside of China. *In* Women in Chinese Society. M. Wolf and R. Witke, eds. Stanford, Calif.: Stanford University Press.

———. 1976. Woman-Work, Women and the Party in Revolutionary China. Oxford, England: Clarendon Press.

Diamond, Norma. 1969. K'un Shen, A Taiwan Village. New York: Holt, Rinehart and Winston.

———. 1973. The Status of Women: One Step Forward, Two Steps Back. *In* Women and China, Studies in Social Change and Feminism. Marilyn B. Young, ed. Ann Arbor, Mich.: University of Michigan Press.

———. 1975. Women under Kuomintang Rule. *In* Modern China 1:3–45.

Directorate-General of Budget, Accounting, and Statistics, Executive Yuan 1974. Monthly Bulletin of Labor Statistics. No. 8. Republic of China. June.

Dixon, Ruth B. 1976. Measuring Equality Between the Sexes. *In* The Journal of Social Issues 32:19–32.

Dore, Ronald P. 1967. Introduction: Aspects of Social Change in Modern Japan. *In* Aspects of Social Change in Modern Japan. Ronald P. Dore, ed. Princeton, N.J.: Princeton University Press.

———. 1973. British Factory, Japanese Factory, The Origins of National Diversity in Industrial Relations. Berkeley, Calif.: University of California Press.

———. 1975. The Future of Formal Education in Developing Countries. *In* International Development Review XVII:7–11.

Dos Santos, Theotonio. 1973. The Structure of Dependence. *In* The Political Economy of Development and Underdevelopment. Charles K. Wilber, ed. New York: Random House.

Economic Planning Council, Executive Yuan. 1974a. Sixth Four-Year Plan for Economic Development of Taiwan, 1973–1976. Republic of China.

———. 1974b. Taiwan Statistical Data Book. Republic of China.

Elliott, Carolyn M. 1977. Theories of Development: An Assessment. *In* Signs, Journal of Women in Culture and Society 3:1–8.

Engels, Frederick. 1973. The Condition of The Working Class in England. W.H. Chaloner and W.D. Hendersons, eds. and trans. Oxford, England: Basil Blackwell.

England, Joe. 1971. Industrial Relations in Hong Kong. *In* Hong Kong, the Industrial Colony, A Political, Social and Economic Survey. Keith Hopkins, ed. Hong Kong: Oxford University Press.

England, Joe, and Rear, John. 1975. Chinese Labor under British Rule, A Critical Study of Labor Relations and Law in Hong Kong. Hong Kong: Oxford University Press.

Fang, Fu-an. 1930. Shanghai Labor. *In* Chinese Economic Journal VII: 853–85.

———. 1931. Chinese Labor, An Economic and Statistical Survey of the Labor Conditions and Labor Movements in China. Shanghai: Kelly and Walsh, Ltd.

Fei, Hsiao-tung. 1939. Peasant Life in China. London: George Routledge & Sons, Ltd.

Fei, John. 1972. General Discussion. *In* Sino-American Conference on Manpower in Taiwan. China Council on Sino-American Cooperation in the Humanities and Social Sciences, ed. Taipei: Academia Sinica.

Fong, Hsien-ding. 1932. Cotton Industry and Trade in China. Tientsin: Chihli Press.

Foster, John. 1974. Class Struggle and the Industrial Revolution, Early Industrial Capitalism in Three English Towns. New York: St. Martin's Press.

Freedman, Deborah S. 1975. Consumption of Modern Goods and Services and its Relations is Fertility: A Study in Taiwan. *In* The Journal of Development Studies 12:95–117.

Freedman, Maurice. 1970. Lineage Organization in Southeastern China. London: The Athlone Press.

———. 1971. Chinese Lineage and Society: Fukien and Kwangtung. London: The Athlone Press.

Friedl, Ernestine. 1967. The Position of Women: Appearance and Reality. *In* Anthropological Quarterly 40:97–108.

———. 1975. Women and Men, An Anthropologist's View. New York: Holt, Rinehart and Winston.

Galenson, W. 1972. Discussion on "Wage Structure and Wage Policy" by Chen Sun. *In* Sino-American Conference on Manpower in Taiwan. China Council on Sino-American Cooperation in the Humanities and Social Sciences, ed. Taipei: Academia Sinica.

Gamble, Sidney D. 1968. A North Chinese Rural Community. Stanford, Calif.: Stanford University Press.

Goode, William J. 1964. The Family. Englewood Cliffs, N.J.: Prentice-Hall, Inc.

———. 1970. World Revolution and Family Patterns. New York: The Free Press.

———. 1971. Civil and Social Rights of Women. *In* The Other Half: Roads to Women's Equality. Cynthia F. Epstein and William J. Goode, eds. Englewood Cliffs, N.J.: Prentice-Hall, Inc.

Gordon, Leonard, ed. 1970. Taiwan: Studies in Chinese Local History. New York: Columbia University Press.

Grichting, Wolfgang L. 1973. The Value System in Taiwan 1970. A Preliminary Report. Beckenried: Neue Zeitschrift für Missionswissenschaft, Switzerland.

Gusfield, Joseph R. 1967. Tradition and Modernity: Misplaced Polarities in the Study of Social Change. *In* American Journal of Sociology 72:351–62.

Hall, John W. 1975. Changing Conceptions of the Modernization of Japan. *In* Changing Japanese Attitudes toward Modernization. Marius Jansen, ed. Princeton, N.J.: Princeton University Press.

Hammond, Dorothy and Jablow, Alta. 1975. Women: Their Economic Role in Traditional Societies. Addison Wesley Module in Anthropology No. 35. Addison-Wesley Publishing Co.

Hareven, Tamara K. 1976. Modernization and Family History: Perspectives on Social Change. *In* Signs: Journal of Women in Culture and Society 2:190–206.

Ho, Franklin L. and Fong, Hsien-ding. 1929. The Extent and Effects of Industrialization in China. Shanghai: China Institute of Pacific Relations.

Ho, Samuel P.S. 1975. Industrialization in Taiwan: Recent Trends and Problems. *In* Pacific Affairs 48:27–41.

Hou, Chi-ming and Hsu, Yu-chu. 1976. The Supply of Labor in Taiwan: Unlimited or Limited? Conference on Population and Economic Development in Taiwan, 29 December 1975 to 3 January 1976. Taipei: The Institute of Economics, Academia Sinica.

Hsieh, Tien-chiao. 1972. Migrant Factory Workers' Social Adaptation of Kaohsiung City, Taiwan. Tainan, Taiwan: Tainan Theological College Research Centre.

Hsieng, En. 1977. Kua kuo kung ssu tsai T'ai-wan ti shih li ying hsiang [The Strength and Influence of Multinational Corporations in Taiwan]. *In* Ch'i-Shih Nian Tai No. 88:76–79, May.

Huang, Fu-san. 1977. Nu kung yu Tai-wan kung yeh hua [Women Workers and the Industrialization in Post-War Taiwan]. Taipei: Cowboy Publishing Co.

Hung, Hsiao-ch'iao. 1977a. I ko tien ts'ai [A Talented Women]. *In* Chung Kuo Shih Pao, 4 March 1977.

———. 1977b. Shui jang hsing fu i ch'i [Who Let Happiness Slip Away]. *In* Chung Kuo Shih Pao, 7 March 1977.

———. 1977c. Nan jen ying kai kan hsieh t'a [Men Should Be Grateful to Her]. *In* Chung Kuo Shih Pao, 8 March 1977.

———. 1977d. Shui jan wo men nu jen ku tu...ning wei nu jen [Even Though Women Are Lonely...We Still Prefer to Be Women]. *In* Chung Kuo Shih Pao, 16 March 1977.

———. 1977e. Wo men to hen hsin k'u [We All Work Hard]. *In* Chung Kuo Shih Pao 13 April 1977.

Industrial Development and Investment Center, Ministry of Economic Affairs. 1975. Taiwan Industrial Panorama. Vol. 8, No. 3. August.

Johnson, Elizabeth. 1975. Women and Childbearing in Kwan Mun Hau Village: A Study of Social Change. *In* Women in Chinese Society. M. Wolf and R. Witke, eds. Stanford, Calif.: Stanford University Press.

Johnson, Paula. 1976. Women and Power: Toward a Theory of Effectiveness. *In* Journal of Social Issues 32:99–110.

Johnston, R.F. 1910. Lion and Dragon in Northern China. New York: E.P. Dutton & Co.

Kapferer, Bruce. 1972. Strategy and Transaction in an African Factory. Manchester, England: Manchester University Press.

Kessen, William. 1978. The Chinese Paradox. *In* Yale Alumni Magazine and Journal XLI, No. 6, pp. 29–33, February.

King, Wayne. 1977. United States Textile Industry Beset by Imports and Labor Woes. *In* The New York Times, 15 May 1977.

Kobayashi, Shigeru. 1969. Motivational Management, Its Exploration in Sony. Mimeograph. Japan Management Center.

Kyong, Bae-tsung. 1929. Industrial Women in Wusih, A Study of Industrial Conditions. Shanghai: National Committee of the Young Women's Christian Association of China.

Lamson, H.D. 1930. The Standard of Living of Factory Workers, A Study of Incomes and Expenditures of 21 Working Families in Shanghai. *In* Chinese Economic Journal, VII:1240–56.

———. 1931. The Effect of Industrialization upon Village Livelihood. *In* Chinese Economic Journal IX:1025–82.

Lang, Olga. 1946. Chinese Family and Society. New Haven, Conn.: Yale University Press.

Leacock, Eleanor Burke, ed. 1975. Introduction. *In* The Origin of the Family, Private Property, and the State. By Frederick Engels. New York: International Publishers.

Levy, Marion J., Jr. 1968. The Family Revolution in Modern China. New York: Atheneum.

Liang, Kuo-shu. 1972. Trade and Employment in Taiwan. *In* Sino-American Conference on Manpower in Taiwan. China Council on Sino-American Cooperation in the Humanities and Social Sciences, ed. Taipei: Academia Sinica.

Lien He Pao [United Daily News] (Taipei). 3 May 1976.

Lieu, D.K. 1936. The Growth and Industrialization of Shanghai. Shanghai: China Institute of Pacific Relations.

_____. 1940. The Silk Industry of China. Shanghai: Kelly and Walsh, Ltd.

Liu, Hui-chen Wang. 1959. The Traditional Chinese Clan Rules. Locust Valley, N.J.: J.J. Augustin, Inc.

Liu, Keh-chung. 1974. The Present Situation of Labor Movement and Youth Workers in the Republic of China. *In* Third International Metalworkers' Federation Asian Youth and Women Symposium Report. Taipei.

Liu, Melinda. 1976. Taipei: Halt to Revival. *In* The Far Eastern Economic Review Vol. 94, no. 48, p. 60.

Liu, Paul K.C. 1976. The Relationship between Urbanization and Socio-Economic Development in Taiwan. Paper presented at the Conference on Population and Economic Development in Taiwan, 29 December 1975 to 3 January 1976. Taipei: Academia Sinica (The Institute of Economics).

Liu, Tchin-ching. 1969. The Process of Industrialization in Taiwan. *In* The Developing Economies VII:63–81.

Lu, Hsiu-lien. 1974. Hsin nu hsing chu i [New Feminism]. Taipei: Yu Shih Wen Hua Kung Ssu.

Marsh, Robert. 1968. The Taiwanese of Taipei; Some Major Aspects of Their Social Structure and Attitudes. *In* Journal of Asian Studies 27:571–84.

Martin, Roberta. 1975. The Socialization of Children in China and on Taiwan: An Analysis of Elementary School Textbooks. *In* China Quarterly 62:242–62.

Ministry of Interior and Council for International Economic Cooperation and Development. 1965. Labor Laws and Regulations of the Republic of China. Republic of China.

Mintz, Sidney. 1971. Men, Women, and Trade. *In* Comparative Studies in Society and History 13:247–69.

Moore, Wilbert E. 1965. The Impact of Industry. Englewood Cliffs, N.J.: Prentice-Hall Inc.

Mueller, Eva and Cohn, Richard. 1977. The Relation of Income to Fertility Decisions in Taiwan. *In* Economic Development and Cultural Change 25:325–47.

Murphy, Yolanda and Murphy, Robert F. 1974. Women of the Forest. New York: Columbia University Press.

Myrdal, Jan. 1966. Report from a Chinese Village. New York: The New American Library.

Negandhi, Anant R. 1971. Management Practices in Taiwan. *In* Michigan State University Business Topics. Autumn 1971:47–55. Graduate School of Business Administration.

Nelson, Cynthia. 1974. Public and Private Politics: Women in the Middle Eastern World. *In* American Ethnologist 1:551–63.

Paine, Robert. 1974. Second Thoughts about Barth's Models. Occasional Papers No. 32. Royal Anthropological Institute of Great Britain and Ireland.

Papanek, Hanna. 1976. Women in Cities: Problems and Perspectives. *In* Women and World Development. Irene Tinker, Michele Bo Bramsen, and Mayra Buvinic, eds. New York: Praeger.

Parish, William. 1975. Socialism and the Chinese Peasant Family. *In* Journal of Asian Studies XXXIV:613–30.

Patrick, Hugh. 1976. An Introductory Overview. *In* Japanese Industrialization and Its Social Consequences. Hugh Patrick, ed. Berkeley, Calif.: University of California Press.

Perlmutter, E. 1977. Curbs on Imports Urged at Apparel Union Rally. *In* The New York Times 14 April 1977.

Pruitt, Ida. 1967. A Daughter of Han, The Autobiography of a Chinese Working Woman. Stanford, Calif: Stanford University Press.

Ranis, Gustav. 1973. Industrial Sector Labor Absorption. *In* Economic Development and Cultural Change 21:387–408.

Rawski, Evelyn Sakakida. 1972. Agricultural Change and the Peasant Economy of South China. Cambridge, Mass.: Harvard University Press.

Republic of China. 1976a. Economic Growth with Stability. Advertisement. *In* The New York Times 25 January 1976.

———. 1976b. Free China Salutes the American Bicentennial. Advertisement. *In* The New York Times 4 July 1976.

Rogers, Susan C. 1975. Female Forms of Power and the Myth of Male Dominance: A Model of Female/Male Interaction in Peasant Society. *In* American Ethnologist 2:727–56.

Rosaldo, Michelle Z. 1974. Women, Culture, and Society: A Theoretical Overview. *In* Woman, Culture, and Society. M. Rosaldo and Lamphere, eds. Stanford, Calif.: Stanford University Press.

Safilios-Rothschild, Constantina. 1970. The Study of Family Power Structure: A Review 1960–1969. *In* Journal of Marriage and the Family 32:539–52.

Salaff, Janet. 1971. Social and Demographic Determinants of Marriage Age in Hong Kong. *In* The Changing Family, East and West. H. White, ed. Hong Kong: Baptist College.

———. 1975. The Status of Unmarried Hong Kong Women and the Social Factors Contributing to their Delayed Marriage. Ms.

Sanday, Peggy. 1973. Toward a Theory of the Status of Women. *In* American Anthropologist 75:1682–1700.

———. 1974. Female Status in the Public Domain. *In* Women, Culture, and Society. M. Rosaldo and Lamphere, eds. Stanford, Calif: Stanford University Press.

Saxonhouse, Gary. R. 1976. Country Girls and Communication Among Competitors in the Japanese Cotton-Spinning Industry. *In* Japanese Industrialization and Its Social Consequences. Hugh Patrick, ed. Berkeley, Calif.: University of California Press.

Schwartzbaum, Allan and Tsai, Chin-lan. n.d. The Relationship Between Residence, Work Attitudes, and Organizational Commitment in the Republic of China. Mimeograph.

Scott, Joan W. and Tilly, Louise A. 1975. Women's Work and the Family in Nineteenth Century Europe. *In* Comparative Studies in Society and History 17:36–64.

Shapiro, Donald. 1977. Isolated Taiwan Thrives on Trade. *In* The New York Times 26 January 1977.

Shih, Chien-sheng. 1972. High-Level Manpower and Higher Education in Taiwan. *In* Sino-American Conference on Manpower in Taiwan. China Council on SinoAmerican Cooperation in the Humanities and Social Sciences, ed. Taipei: Academia Sinica.

Shih, Kuo-heng. 1944. China Enters the Machine Age, A Study of Labor in Chinese War Industry. Ksiao-tung Fei and Francis L.K. Hsu, trans. and eds. Cambridge, Mass.: Harvard University Press.

Sidel, Ruth. 1974. Families of Fengsheng, Urban Life in China. Baltimore, Md.: Penguin Books.

Silin, Robert H. 1976. Leadership and Values, The Organization of Large-Scale Taiwanese Enterprises. Cambridge, Mass.: Harvard University Press.

Slotkin, James S. 1960. From Field to Factory, New Industrial Employees. Glencoe, Ill.: Free Press.

Smelser, Neil J. 1968. Sociological History: The Industrial Revolution and the British Working-Class Family. *In* Essays in Sociological Explanation. Neil J. Smelser, ed. Englewood Cliffs, N.J.: Prentice-Hall, Inc.

Smith, Anthony D. 1973. The Concept of Social Change, A Critique of the Functionalist Theory of Social Change. London: Routledge, Kegan & Paul.

Smith, Arthur H. 1970. Village Life in China. Boston: Little, Brown & Co.

Solomon, Richard H. 1971. Mao's Revolution and the Chinese Political Culture. Berkeley, Calif.: University of California Press.

Speare, Alden, Jr. 1974. Urbanization and Migration in Taiwan. *In* Economic Development and Cultural Change 22:302–19.

Speare, Alden, Jr., Speare, Mary C. and Lin, Hui-sheng. 1973. Urbanization, Non-Familial Work, Education, and Fertility in Taiwan. *In* Population Studies 27:323–34.

Stavis, Benedict. 1974. Rural Local Government and Agricultural Development in Taiwan. Ithaca, New York: Center for International Studies, Cornell University.

Stover, Leon E. and Stover, Takeko K. 1976. China: An Anthropological Perspective. Pacific Palisades, Calif.: Goodyear Publishing Co., Inc.

Sun, T.H. 1976. Prospects of Population Growth and its Socio-Economic Duplications in Taiwan. Conference on Population and Economic Development in Taiwan, 29 December 1975 to 3 January 1976. Taipei: Institute of Economics, Academia Sinica.

Taiwan Provincial Labor Force Survey and Research Institute. 1973a. Establishment Survey on Employment, Hours, Earnings, and Labor Turnover in Secondary Industries in Taiwan Area. Republic of China.

———. 1973b. Quarterly Report on the Labor Force Survey in Taiwan. Republic of China.

———. 1973c. Report on the Female Labor Force Survey in Taiwan. Republic of China.

T'ao, Ling and Johnson, Lydia. 1928. A Study of Women and Girls in Tientsin Industries. *In* Chinese Economic Journal 2:519–28.

Thompson, Edward P. 1963. The Making of the English Working Class. London: Victor Gollancz Ltd.

T'ien, Ju'k'ang. 1944. Female Labor in a Cotton Mill. *In* China Enters the Machine Age A Study of Labor in Chinese War Industry. By Kuo-heng Shih. Hsiao tung Fei and Francis L.K. Hsu, trans. and eds. Cambridge, Mass.: Harvard University Press.

Tinker, Irene. 1976. The Adverse Impact of Development on Women. *In* Women and World Development. Irene Tinker, Michele Bo Bramsen, and Mayra Buvinic, eds. New York: Praeger.

Topley, Marjorie. 1975. Marriage Resistance in Rural Kwangtung. *In* Women in Chinese Society. M. Wolf and R. Witke, eds. Stanford, Calif.: Stanford University Press.

Ts'ai, Che-ch'en. 1975. Fu nu yu she hui [Women and Society]. Taipei: The Mei Hsin Press Co.

Tsui, Tsu-kan, Loh, Kwang, and Chang, Maria M.Y. 1972. Women Workers in Taiwan. *In* Sino-American Conference on Manpower in Taiwan. China Council on Sino-American Cooperation in The Humanities and Social Sciences, ed. Taipei: Academia Sinica.

Tumin, Melvin M. 1960. Competing Status Systems. *In* Labor Commitment and Social Change in Developing Areas. Wilbert E. Moore and Arnold S. Feldman, eds. New York: Social Science Research Council.

United Nations Commission on the Status of Women. 1970. Participation of Women in the Economic and Social Development of Their Countries. New York: United Nations.

Wan, Henry Y., Jr. 1972. An Economic Analysis of the Technical and Vocational Education in Taiwan. *In* Sino-American Conference on Manpower in Taiwan. China Council on Sino-American Cooperation in the Humanities and Social Science, ed. Taipei: Academia Sinica.

Wang, Sung-hsing and Apthorpe, Raymond. 1974. Rice Farming in Taiwan, Three Village Studies. Taipei: Institute Ethnology, Academia Sinica.

Wieman, Earl. 1974. Taiwan's Electronic Industry: Reaching for Maturity in Troubled Times. *In* Echo (Taipei) 4:4–6, 54–56.

Wilson, Richard W. 1970. Learning to be Chinese: The Political Socialization of Children in Taiwan. Cambridge, Mass.: The M.I.T. Press.

Wolf, Arthur P. 1975. The Women of Hai-shen: A Demographic Portrait. *In* Women in Chinese Society. M. Wolf and R. Witke, eds. Stanford, Calif.: Stanford University Press.

Wolf, Margery. 1968. The House of Lim. New York: Appleton-Century-Crofts.

———. 1972. Women and The Family in Rural Taiwan. Stanford, Calif.: Stanford University Press.

———. 1974. Chinese Women: Old Skills in a New Context. *In* Women, Culture, and Society. M. Rosaldo and Lamphere, eds. Stanford, Calif.: Stanford University Press.

———. 1975. Women and Suicide in China. *In* Women in Chinese Society. M. Wolf and R. Witke, eds. Stanford, Calif.: Stanford University Press.

Wong, Aline K. 1973. Rising Social Status and Economic Participation of Women in Hong Kong, Review of a Decade. *In* Southeast Asian Journal of Social Science 1:11–27.

Wu, Rong-I. 1976. Urbanization and Industrialization in Taiwan: A Study on the Specific Pattern of Labor Utilization. Conference on Population and Economic Development in Taiwan, 29 December 1975 to 3 January 1976. Taipei: Institute of Economics, Academia Sinica.

Yang, Ching-Ch'u. 1976. Chia kung chu kou chu ti nu erh chuan [Women in the Export Processing Zones]. *In* Hai Nei Wai, No. 2:64–66.

Yang, C.K. 1969. The Chinese Family in the Communist Revolution. Cambridge, Mass.: The M.I.T. Press.

Ying, Diane. 1977. In Taiwan, A Will to Compete. *In* The New York Times, 30 January 1977.

Zaretsky, Eli. 1973. Capitalism, the Family, and Personal Life. *In* Socialist Revolution. Part I— 3(1):69–125, Part II—3(2):19–70.

Zenith Taiwan News (Taoyuan, Taiwan). Vol. 3, No. 2, 20 December 1973. Vol. 3, No. 3, 5 January 1973.

Index

Author Index

Subject Index

q